Service Encounters in Tourism, Events and Hospitality

ASPECTS OF TOURISM

Series Editors: **Chris Cooper**, *Leeds Beckett University, UK*,
C. Michael Hall, *University of Canterbury, New Zealand* and
Dallen J. Timothy, *Arizona State University, USA*

Aspects of Tourism is an innovative, multifaceted series, which comprises authoritative reference handbooks on global tourism regions, research volumes, texts and monographs. It is designed to provide readers with the latest thinking on tourism worldwide and in so doing will push back the frontiers of tourism knowledge. The series also introduces a new generation of international tourism authors writing on leading edge topics.

The volumes are authoritative, readable and user-friendly, providing accessible sources for further research. Books in the series are commissioned to probe the relationship between tourism and cognate subject areas such as strategy, development, retailing, sport and environmental studies. The publisher and series editors welcome proposals from writers with projects on the above topics.

All books in this series are externally peer-reviewed.

Full details of all the books in this series and of all our other publications can be found on http://www.channelviewpublications.com, or by writing to Channel View Publications, St Nicholas House, 31-34 High Street, Bristol BS1 2AW, UK.

ASPECTS OF TOURISM: 87

Service Encounters in Tourism, Events and Hospitality

Staff Perspectives

Miriam Firth

CHANNEL VIEW PUBLICATIONS
Bristol • Blue Ridge Summit

DOI https://doi.org/10.21832/FIRTH7277
Library of Congress Cataloging in Publication Data
A catalog record for this book is available from the Library of Congress.
Names: Firth, Miriam, author.
Title: Service Encounters in Tourism, Events and Hospitality: Staff
  Perspectives/Miriam Firth.
Description: Bristol, UK; Blue Ridge Summit, PA: Channel View
  Publications, 2020. | Series: Aspects of Tourism: 87 | Includes
  bibliographical references and index. | Summary: 'This book offers
  insights into the demands made on staff in service encounters in
  tourism, events and hospitality roles. It hinges upon storied incidents
  offered by workers about which the reader can reflect and apply
  theoretical knowledge. Each chapter includes learning objectives,
  questions and summaries' – Provided by publisher.
Identifiers: LCCN 2019029543 (print) | LCCN 2019029544 (ebook) | ISBN
  9781845417260 (paperback) | ISBN 9781845417277 (hardback) | ISBN
  9781845417284 (pdf) | ISBN 9781845417291 (epub) | ISBN 9781845417307
  (kindle edition) Subjects: LCSH: Tourism – Customer services. | Special events
  industry – Customer services. | Hospitality industry – Customer services.
  | Customer relations.
Classification: LCC G155.A1 F557 2020 (print) | LCC G155.A1 (ebook) | DDC
  338.4/791--dc23 LC record available at https://lccn.loc.gov/2019029543
LC ebook record available at https://lccn.loc.gov/2019029544

British Library Cataloguing in Publication Data
A catalogue entry for this book is available from the British Library.

ISBN-13: 978-1-84541-727-7 (hbk)
ISBN-13: 978-1-84541-726-0 (pbk)

Channel View Publications
UK: St Nicholas House, 31-34 High Street, Bristol, BS1 2AW, UK.
USA: NBN, Blue Ridge Summit, PA, USA.
Website: www.channelviewpublications.com
Twitter: Channel_View
Facebook: https://www.facebook.com/channelviewpublications
Blog: www.channelviewpublications.wordpress.com

The policy of Multilingual Matters/Channel View Publications is to use papers
that are natural, renewable and recyclable products, made from wood grown in
sustainable forests. In the manufacturing process of our books, and to further
support our policy, preference is given to printers that have FSC and PEFC Chain of
Custody certification. The FSC and/or PEFC logos will appear on those books where
full certification has been granted to the printer concerned.

Typeset by Riverside Publishing Solutions
Printed and bound in the UK by Short Run Press Ltd.
Printed and bound in the US by NBN.

Contents

Tables and Figures

Tables

Figures

Table 0.1 Table of incidents and participants

Chapter	Title	Participant names and business	Page
2	Local pronunciation of dishes	Jessica – Hotel	44
	Confronting colleagues	Martha – Hotel	45
3	Non-verbal communication (2 incidents)	Tom – Pub Sophie – Hotel	58
	Working with different vocal accents	Lucy – Restaurant	59
	The phonetic alphabet	Martha – Hotel	61
	Dealing with rude customers (2 incidents)	Martha – Hotel Beth – Travel company	62
4	Comforting guests	Sophie – Hotel	77
	Scripted service and emotions	Lucy – Restaurant	78
5	Uniform as a character	Emma – Youth Hostel	90
	Suited and booted (3 incidents)	Phil – Event booking agency Katy – Travel agent Taylor – Group travel company	90
	Sexualised labour	Sophie – Hotel	92
6	Misunderstanding language	Mary – Youth hostel	107
	Educating customers on cultural difference	Sophie – Hotel	107
	Tipping cultures	Lucy – Restaurant	108
7	Supporting colleagues in Co-creation	Holly – Event venue agency	121
	Customer querying prices	Martha – Hotel	122
	Being the middle person	Martha – Hotel	124
8	Holiday request	Jessica – Hotel	138
	Sensitive issues in work	Jessica – Hotel	139
	Customer health and safety	Tom – Pub	141
	Cleaning up after customers	Tom – Pub	142
9	Making fun of customers	Lucy – Restaurant	156

Acknowledgements

This book has been written with the support of a number of people. First, I would like to offer heartfelt thanks to all the participants who offered storied incidents from their work experience. These incidents enable the reflection of theory and contextualisation of staff perspectives in working situations. Without these, this book would not be possible. The dedication of these workers, their enthusiasm for caring for customers in service encounters, and their passion for maintaining excellent service and experiences was inspiring.

Thanks also go to a family and friends: Pauline Firth, Dave Firth, Emma Livesey, Catherine Powell, Thorsten Jansen, Phil Tragen and Tom Charles. These people have all supported and inspired me to write this text to further enhance critical perspectives in tourism, events and hospitality.

Colleagues Tom Baum, John Swarbrooke, Susan Horner, Conrad Lashley, Richard Fay, Liz Smith, Steve Courtney, Su Corcoran, Helen Gunter, Steve Jones and Neil Robinson are thanked for their advice and support offered during the completion of the study and writing of this book.

Editors Sarah Williams, Flo McClelland, Chris Cooper, Michael Hall and Dallen Timothy are thanked for their time in reviewing and supporting the book through to publication.

Finally, acknowledgement is given to all staff working in tourism, events and hospitality contexts. Research and publication on staff voice in these contexts is still relatively limited and it is hoped that this book will inspire others to consider their views and perspectives in the literature that is dominated by management and the consumer. Instead of looking to manage, motivate and train staff, let us praise, inspire and support their professional development to aid their creation of new and exciting customer experiences that every person can enjoy in the delivery of services.

Foreword

It is not often that I get really excited when I read a new book in the field of tourism, events and hospitality, but Miriam Firth's fabulous exploration of the service encounter from an employee perspective in this volume brought a smile to my face. I have been researching and teaching in this area for over 35 years and this is a genuinely original combination of practical, and theoretical and critical thinking, which is a 'must-read' for anyone involved in frontline service work and its management.

There has long been a real need in the tourism, events and hospitality workplace literature for works that are both practical in their application and critical in their analysis. This book sets a template in its focus on the service encounter. It is hoped that this can guide future contributions in allied areas relating to this diverse, complex and paradoxical sector. Tourism, events and hospitality, especially the latter, have long been awash with practical, 'how-to' texts that address workplace outcomes, whether operational, supervisory or managerial. Such texts tend to be prescriptive and offer clear 'best solutions' that are designed to enable students, teachers, industry employees and their supervisors to do their job better against clear and uncritical performance criteria. 'How to' manuals and texts may have value in helping students prepare for a role in tourism, events and hospitality organisations; however, they tend to offer a 'one best way' to do things. In my experience, they do not equip students and employees for inherent and accelerating change and uncertainty in the workplace, indeed confronting the challenging paradoxes in tourism, events and hospitality employment that authors such as Richard Robinson, David Solnet, Shelagh Mooney and myself have sought to highlight. Miriam's narrative in this book about service encounters in tourism, events and hospitality, focusing on the employee perspective, represents a context where the ability to handle paradox and contradiction and make sensible judgements in relation to them is a skill that is in perpetual demand. You cannot train people to understand and apply the consequences of cultural diversity to the service encounter in a mechanistic, 'one size fits all' way; you can only help them to be sensitive to the service needs of each individual and apply 'real-time' decision making to the specific context with which they are confronted.

To achieve this wider, more flexible objective, students and employees need to be able to apply critical analysis to situations, but also to the context in which they arise. Service encounters in the tourism, events and hospitality workplace take place in the context of a complex intersection of culture, which is where the focus of this book lies, but also of social class, gender, ethnicity, sexuality and disability as they apply to both customers and frontline service workers. Understanding such complexity is challenging. This book is well equipped to enable learners (whether students, employees or their managers) to adopt a critical lens and apply it to real-life encounters with their customers in tourism, events and hospitality. Miriam combines practical thinking with reference to some complex and challenging theoretical sources and, it is hoped, learners will see the value of theory in informing action as a result of this, something with which students in tourism, events and hospitality do not always engage.

Discussion about the service encounter has largely been the preserve of the emergent services marketing community from the 1980s onwards, in the hands of authors such as Mary Jo Bitner, and this has resulted in a lopsided narrative where the prime consideration was ensuring customer satisfaction as an outcome. Miriam is one of the few writers to provide balance and to look at the other side of the encounter, at the experience and expectations of those involved in service delivery. As she rightly says, 'there is an overreliance in service quality theory when considering service encounters' and the consequence is that so much valuable theory and thinking, representing factors that influence the employee perspective, are generally ignored. This book redresses this imbalance in a readable and enjoyable way. After all, understanding the contribution that frontline staff make to the success or otherwise of the service encounter is critical and the case studies in this book bring the employee perspective to light.

Professor Tom Baum
Strathclyde Business School, Glasgow
July 2019

Preface

Before reading the key chapters of this text, it is important to understand two perspectives that frame the positions taken:

(1) Culture is individually felt and constructed based on experience.
(2) Staff ability to negotiate customer demands and maintain high service quality is due to individual experience and development of interpersonal competence within the practice of service encounters.

These two points are important when considering the position from which theory and critical reflections are offered in this book. These will be discussed below to offer clarification on why they are important to understanding service encounters.

Position 1 Relating to Culture

Starting with culture, this is based on my own history and experience. At the age of 11, I went on an International Summer Camp from Sheffield, UK to Tokyo, Japan, and lived with 60 other children from 12 countries without my parents for a month. This was with a charity called Children's International Summer Villages (CISV). Between the ages of 11 and 18, I went on numerous summer camps and lived with people from all over the world to learn about their culture, language, traditions and heritage. CISV was set up with the purpose of ensuring children learn that national culture does not dictate a person's actions or behaviour (a prime motivator for the world wars of the 20th century) and that all people could be viewed as equal (once language barriers are navigated). As a result of this experience, my own view of culture is that it is not defined by nationality nor constructed via citizenship. Instead, culture is individual to each person and evident in their actions, behaviour and thought. In this way, my position on culture is small (Holliday, 2011) and ethnorelative (Bennett, 1986).

This position is of note here, as I identify all participants used in this book with English pseudonyms and do not address their nationality in the discussion of their data. Of the 12 participants in this publication, only three are English nationals. One of these has lived in the UK their whole life. Indigenous and non-Western perspectives are also not explicit in this volume. Tourism, events and hospitality contexts are not bound by their geographical location as they are international experiences being created by staff who all have individual and complex cultures. This clarifies that although the participants may appear English, the data represent detail from a range of nationalities and from staff who can be seen as transnational. From my perspective, their nationality is not important for understanding culture, as this can be seen as individual and emergent rather than predefined owing to their location of birth. I explore this position within a range of chapters.

The main critique I have of current literature from tourism, events and hospitality contexts on culture is that authors do not accurately identify large culture (Holliday, 2011) and yet specify that this is the cause of problems in service encounters. Examples of this are inferring culture via the location of travel origin (see Strauss & Mang, 1999) or student status (see Barron & Dasli, 2010). The majority of research referring to culture in Tourism, Events and Hospitality is also founded upon Hofstede's (2006) definitions of culture. Hofstede's cultural dimension survey did not ascertain the culture (nationality) of each individual either and inferred this based upon the location of their working environment. Contemporary mobility of people working in tourism, events and hospitality is extensive (Duncan *et al.*, 2013) and this book contends that if we are accepting that service encounters include transnational flows of customers, we also need to accept there are transnational flows of individuals with small cultures (Holliday, 2011) creating the experiences.

Position 2 Relating to Experience Needed to Develop Competence in Service Encounters

In order to satisfy customers, you need to know what they are expecting (Parasuraman *et al.*, 1991) and ensure their perceptions of the service matches these expectations. Discussion in this book spans knowledge on service quality for tourism, events and hospitality from its origins in services marketing to co-creation and co-production. Service quality is integral to discussion on service encounters as this is the yardstick from which customers gauge their experiences and management maintain a competitive advantage.

Historically, service quality literature has offered models on, and recommendations for, policies supporting service encounter delivery to management and is largely based on customer opinion. This book offers the often ignored and yet vital perspective in these contexts: the staff's perspective. From these perspectives, and through discussion in this book, it will become apparent that delivery of service quality is only possible because of the exceptional skills of staff. These skills are not replicated from training and explicit knowledge on what specific customers require, but based on interpersonal competence and experience of serving transnational flows of people. It is the implicit knowledge staff develop through experience in which service quality is possible in service encounters. This is evident in the narrated incidents and in the theory discussed in this book. This position has largely been ignored in research as colleagues have been trying to maintain the professionalisation of these positions, while searching for frameworks and models to direct management towards. Once you assume the position that staff will offer good service subsequent to experience and interpersonal skill development, reflected upon and challenged through customer demand and query, it will be possible to support and develop these workforces. This position is acknowledged in other vocational professions such as medicine and teaching as work-based experience is used to develop competence for employment. In the UK, technical, work-based education for tourism, events and hospitality (such as working kitchens or placements) have largely been closed owing to funding issues in further and higher education. Although these were important for technical skills in creating products for service encounters, they were also vital for testing competence in dealing with customers in receipt of the products and experiences. This book offers material that can be used by students, management and educators in order to appraise and reflect on responses in service encounters, in order to understand individual reactions and perspectives on customer demands.

Introduction

This book offers readers an insight into the demands made on staff within service encounters in tourism, events and hospitality roles. Using data from research completed in these industries, it hinges upon storied incidents offered by workers from which the reader can reflect and apply theoretical knowledge. A key distinction between this text and others is that this text focuses on staff perspectives and considers staff perceptions of service encounters and service delivery, rather than customer or management perspectives. It is hoped that this will enable students, lecturers, management and customers to gain a clearer insight into the demands made of staff, but also the perspectives from which the demands are seen.

This introduction will outline the structure of the book, vocational education and training, businesses associated with tourism events and hospitality, and the methodology employed to gain staff perspectives on service encounters.

Type of Publication

An important feature of this volume is that it focuses on staff perspectives and perceptions of service encounters and delivery, rather than on customer or management perspectives. As a research book, it offers a discussion of key theory linked to service delivery, with each theory followed by staff narratives (stories) on their perspectives from working contexts. By considering the theory, applying this understanding of staff perspectives offered, and then reflecting on positions and reactions possible in these encounters, this book will aid understanding and reflection of how to complete service encounters in tourism, events and hospitality management.

In terms of contributing to current knowledge, three main elements are offered in this publication:

(1) A contribution to knowledge regarding service encounters.
(2) Learning tools for students in tourism, events and hospitality management looking to reflect on their ability to manage demands made within service encounters.
(3) An alternative methodology for understanding staff perspectives.

As a research book, it is limited to the participant accounts and literature available at the time of writing. However, as the contribution to knowledge, the structure of the chapters and methodology behind the study is seen as innovative, this book presents an exciting addition to the associated fields of the study discussed. These fields include human resource management, services marketing, vocational education and training, and employability. The book is published based on a particular study and using the resources currently available. As such, it is not an exhaustive account of the positions in these fields of study; rather, it should be used as a critical tool to reflect on how staff could (or should) react in service encounters.

Chapter Structure

To aid chapter navigation, please observe that all chapters in this book follow a specific structure to enable understanding and knowledge development in service encounters in tourism, events and hospitality.

Learning objectives

Each chapter opens with a set of learning objectives identifying the potential learning gains from completing the chapter. Critical incidents offered in each chapter enable readers to situate and reflect on the theoretical discussion in order to understand working contexts in which the theory can be perceived. In this way, the learning objectives can be tested through the completion of key questions on the critical incidents, or through discussion of questions from each annotated bibliography list at the end of each chapter.

Theoretical review

After a brief introduction to each chapter, discussion and analysis of the secondary literature are presented. This includes definitions of the key terms, critical analysis of positions from esteemed authors in the respective field and critical commentary on issues perceived in the current knowledge found. It is noted that this review is limited in terms of the language of sources used (English) and the time frame in which this text is published. However, as the topic areas relate to longstanding areas of interest in tourism, events and hospitality, it is acknowledged that the authors and theories discussed here are both pertinent and longstanding.

Critical incidents with key questions

Critical incidents are then quoted from workers in the industry. These stories were elicited from workers as participants in a doctoral study completed in 2013 (the method is outlined in the this chapter).

These incidents (or stories) enable readers to apply theory in a working context and understand potential issues that staff and management may have in performing the theory discussed. Each critical incident is complemented with a list of questions. These questions challenge the reader to consider how the theory is manifested in working conditions. It is suggested that readers use the stories to reflect on how they would react in similar situations and discuss alternative approaches to respond to the demands seen.

Summaries

The chapters each conclude with a summary of its contents based upon the learning objectives set. These enable the reader to consider the information presented in the chapters, as well as reflect on their positions through understanding the narrated incidents from staff.

Annotated bibliography

At the end of each chapter, there is an annotated bibliography offering a review of key sources referenced in the chapter. Sources here are offered in date order. This annotation enables readers to understand the context, methodology and perspective from which key references were written. A question is offered for each source discussed here. This relates to content, and in some cases, figures or frameworks from the source, to enable readers to consider their own critical observations on key theory linked to service encounters in tourism, events and hospitality. Students, tutors and lecturers can use this to aid wider reading and support further learning.

Reference list

As this book is written by one author and based on a single study, the references from citations noted are offered in a single list at the end of the book.

Background: Education and Businesses Associated with Tourism, Events and Hospitality

Although this text uses tourism, events and hospitality as the focus for service encounters, these encounters are also seen in a number of other vocational industries. Vocational work is supported by vocational education and training in a range of education and training establishments. As such, this book can also be applied in wider vocational training sessions. Vocational education is the 'social development of labour' (Clarke & Winch, 2007: 1). It is referred to as vocational education and training (VET) and, ultimately, prepares a person for work. This differs from liberal or civic education, as it requires students to develop specific skills and competencies for specific employment. This book focuses on supporting students in higher education; traditionally, universities have sought to educate on liberal matters to improve the thinking and understanding that a person has in relation to matters in the world (knowledge and thought rather than skills linked to practical employment skills). The increasing impetus on employability in universities in recent years (see Dearing Report, 1997; Leitch, 2006; TEF, 2011) seems to have stemmed from the increase in vocational and technical courses taught at universities. By including vocational and liberal courses in universities, VET has become more visible in UK higher education. But what does this mean for tourism, events and hospitality management VET in universities?

> It is important to have an essence of hospitality in a school. Without it how do students become socialised into the hospitality environment/ way of thinking? With it you have the noise, the smells, the deliveries, the refuse, the issues, the customers, the problems. It's something that you don't normally get in a business school. It makes us different to other departments. (Case 2, Participant 4) (Alexander *et al.*, 2009: 62)

This quotation from Alexander *et al.* (2009) exemplifies the difficulties faced when educating and learning VET for tourism, events and hospitality management students. VET requires work-specific training within working environments in order to develop and assess employment skills fully. When the UK government began reducing funding to universities, hospitality course facilities such as kitchens and restaurants were also forced to close (Alexander *et al.*, 2009). Without the ability to practise these skills in university modules, it is evident that there could be a shortfall when students graduate to industry roles:

> university graduates may be deficient in the ability to reflect on, and ameliorate industry and management practices. (Morrison & O'Mahony, 2003: 39)

This book seeks to support this potential gap by offering storied incidents from workers within the industry so as to enable the reader to reflect on key cases based in working environments. Similar to the continued professional development stages of reflective practice, this book is structured to enable the reader to understand the theory supporting a working situation, consider how a member of staff reacted, reflect on how they might naturally respond and then outline other ways to respond.

In terms of the types of businesses within which the storied incidents can be applied and considered, please see Table 0.2. Table 0.2 clarifies the range of businesses (and contexts for employed staff) that can utilise this

Table 0.2 Tourism, events and hospitality businesses

Hotels	Hospitality services
Tourist services	Youth/backpacker hostels
Restaurants	Membership clubs
Events	Holiday centres
Pubs and nightclubs	Travel services
Gambling	Self-catering accommodation
Food and service management	Visitor attractions

Source: Based on People 1st (2011).

book to reflect on and apply theoretical knowledge for service encounters. As tourism, events and hospitality businesses often overlap and produce similar leisure experiences (Torkildsen, 2005) the service encounters discussed in this book are seen as linked to all three sectors. For example, a hotel worker (hospitality) may serve a leisure guest (tourist) while creating a leisure experience (event). As such, although tourism, events and hospitality are key terms framing this book, they are treated as the same, or overlapping, within the service encounters discussed.

Researchers, students and workers can use this book when considering any of the businesses noted in Table 0.2, regardless of qualification title or role title, which may be specifically aligned to tourism, events or hospitality.

The Study

The study completed was informed by an interpretivist epistemology. It is important to acknowledge this, as it is how I aligned myself to the research (Cohen *et al.*, 2009) and outlines the objective and subjective approaches taken (Scott & Usher, 2002). Using an interpretivist epistemology, I was interested in the human interactions present in usual daily routines (Egbert & Sanden, 2013) between staff in tourism, events and hospitality. Thick data and description are yielded from this position and it is usually from a situation known or usual to the researcher (Geertz, 1973). The staff perspective is something I have already experienced and I was interested in understanding current graduate staff perspectives on service encounters without my position being present in the creation of new data.

If you review my PhD publication, you will also note that it is focused on leisure students. The alteration of this to tourism, events and hospitality staff in this book is not due to a perceived change in scope, but due to my observation that students of leisure will become workers in tourism, events and hospitality and that the participants in the study studied one course (on tourism, events of hospitality) and then worked in another sector within these three. This interlinked and overlapping position is supported by Laing (2018) and Baum *et al.* (2016) who noted that literature supporting staff in these industries is published in narrow fields of study, rather than cross-disciplinary. In reality, these sectors and fields of study often represent the same working environment.

From analysing secondary published data on service encounters, and service quality which informs standards of the encounter, it was clear the staff perspective was missing (see Chapter 1). As such, my study investigated service encounters from the staff perspective using a theoretical framework of usual skills and knowledge required, but not outlined as a specific framework for service encounters. This book offers the theoretical framework in the chapters presented and includes soft skills (Chapter 3), emotional (Chapter 4), aesthetic and sexualised labour (Chapter 5), intercultural sensitivity (Chapter 6), co-production and co-creation (Chapter 7), legal frameworks (Chapter 8) in employment and humour (Chapter 9) in service encounters. In the final chapter (Chapter 10), a new model of service encounters is offered in a combination of this theoretical framework and data analysed from participants in the study.

While reading the sources for these terms, I used Wallace and Wray's (2011) critical synopsis questions to ensure that my reading, understanding and use of the literature were valid. I then analysed these data using thematic analysis and constant comparison (Bell, 2009). The study, therefore, offered an emergent theoretical framework. The framework is emergent because it was created by secondary text analysis. My study has aligned key theory with a new framework in order to assess the skills and knowledge used, and needed, by graduates working in tourism, events and hospitality service encounters.

To ensure that all research gathered was valid and reliable, I chose a narrative research approach to gather the data so that my own knowledge and bias were managed effectively. Narrative research was an appropriate method to utilise, as participants were required to offer information through the recollection of their own stories rather than questions from my research and experience (Connelly & Clandinin, 1990). Using participant stories as research can enable researchers to understand 'human interaction in relationships' (Clandinin, 2007: 427). Furthermore, research authors on intercultural service encounters (ICSEs), as noted in Chapter 1, also used this method (Warden *et al.*, 2003); therefore, it fits within the known discourses in customer service encounters around which the study is framed. Interestingly, though, ICSE authors only use narrative research with customer research participants and not staff research participants.

To gain a sample of participants who were working graduates to offer data on service encounters, I used purposive sampling (Cohen *et al.*, 2009). Purposive sampling is when a researcher hand-picks participants based on judgements made on the 'particular characteristics being sought' (Cohen *et al.*, 2009: 115). The specific characteristics needed of participants in this study are noted as follows:

- Graduates or students from tourism, events or hospitality UK higher education courses.
- Working in Manchester.
- Employed in a leisure-based company and role.

The three characteristics noted above identify that the study needed to choose purposefully participants with these traits in order to gain data that would yield results with which to explore staff perspectives of service encounters. Obtaining these participants was completed using the following steps:

(1) Contact graduates via LinkedIn.
(2) Ask for their assistance with the study.
(3) Agree to a meeting.
(4) Meet and discuss the study (including the information and consent forms).

Using LinkedIn to approach participants is a relatively under-used, but beneficial sampling method:

> Researchers may also consider other avenues to recruit online participants. One potentially fruitful, but largely untapped source for such participants is LinkedIn. Using LinkedIn, researchers could identify and contact working professionals based on the identifying information in their profiles. (Knemeyer & Naylor, 2011: 298)

Contacting known graduates on LinkedIn enabled me to see their current role and the leisure business in which they are located. This meant that I could ensure that I contacted only the graduates who met the participant criteria, thus supporting the purposive sampling method.

When meeting and briefing potential participants, I considered a number of ethical issues related to the study based upon the criteria for my studies (Table 0.3).

The considerations made in terms of the briefing and informed consent sheet were important in maintaining the safety and integrity of myself and the participants.

Informed consent is where research participants confirm their participation, but that they do so in the knowledge that they have the freedom and ability to choose to participate (Cohen *et al.*, 2009). As the study looked into the demands felt by graduates in customer service encounters, it was identified that participation could lead to emotional stress. Emotional stress could occur because of the emotionally charged incidents that participants may wish to offer. As such, it was necessary to

Table 0.3 Briefing and informed consent of participants

Area of documentation	Considerations for the study
Autonomy – The participant must be free to take part in the research without coercion or penalty, and must be free to withdraw at any time without giving a reason and without a threat of any adverse effect.	Inform participants verbally that they can rescind their participation at any time, even after signing the consent form.
Beneficence – The research must be worthwhile in itself and have beneficial effects that outweigh any risks; it follows that the methodology must be sound so that positive results are yielded.	The methodology must fit the study and the processes involved must enable a viable and reliable study.
Non-maleficence – Any possible harm must be avoided or mitigated by robust precautions.	Risk assessments are needed when considering the location of the briefing and data collection.
Confidentiality – The right of the participant and his/her personal data remaining unknown to all but the research team must be respected (unless the participant agrees otherwise).	All participant names will be removed from all publications of their data.
Integrity – The researcher must be open about any gains, financial or otherwise, that he or she makes from the research, acknowledge the relevant contribution of third parties, and ensure that research outcomes are disseminated appropriately.	The consent sheet will identify the publications possible as a result of participant data.

Source: University of Manchester (2014).

inform participants of this during the briefing, as well as plan for additional support if they needed it afterwards.

Thus far, I have identified that primary data were gathered from research participants using a purposive sampling strategy; they were contacted via LinkedIn, briefed and needed to consent to participation before gathering data. Data gathered for my study used critical incident narrations, stimulated recall interviews and semi-structured interviews. These are each discussed in brief, but for visual clarification, Figure 0.1 below shows all stages of data collection completed.

As Figure 0.1 illustrates, there were a number of stages planned for gathering primary data for my study. These stages were staggered for each participant, to ensure that the concepts and theories can emerge from the data obtained. Specifically, Participant 1 started their participation and once they had finished, Participant 2 then started. This cyclical and staggered approach ensured that I gained focused discussion from each participant in the stimulated recall and interview, as well as enabling new questions and probing with each new participant.

The study gathered participant stories of critical incidents that they had experienced in working contexts. The reason for using the critical incident technique is that it is widely used in other customer service encounter research Bitner *et al.* (1990), Grove and Fisk (1997), Nyquist *et al.* (1985), Nyquist and Booms (1987), Lin and Fu (2017) and Warden *et al.* (2003) all used the critical incident technique to elicit customer stories of service encounters. Bitner *et al.*'s (1990) paper on customer service encounters is seen from the customer's point of view and states that staff must ensure

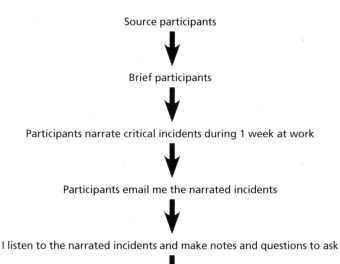

Source participants

Brief participants

Participants narrate critical incidents during 1 week at work

Participants email me the narrated incidents

I listen to the narrated incidents and make notes and questions to ask

Participants and I meet for a stimulated recall interview to probe and question the data gained

Figure 0.1 Stages of primary data collection

that their service is deemed satisfactory. This research reviewed 700 incidents of customer service to understand what customers perceive to be good or successful service in a range of leisure businesses.

> The CIT (critical incident technique) can identify what employees need to know by making clear what general information customers consider important in different encounters. It is crucial that employees not only be taught scripts, but also be given appropriate knowledge. Training programs should be designed to develop a broad repertoire of responses (range of knowledge) and to allow for practice in selecting from the repertoire. (Bitner *et al.*, 1990: 82)

In the conclusions to Bitner *et al.*'s (1990) paper, they assert that their study can aid successful customer service encounters by giving staff the skills and knowledge needed to appease customers. Contrary to Bitner *et al.*'s (1990) study, the one informing this book sought to understand staff (graduate) perceptions of customer service encounters. As intercultural service encounter research also used this method, it was deemed an appropriate method through which to gather graduate perceptions of customer demands made in industry (McCollough *et al.*, 2000; Strauss & Mang 1999; Warden *et al.* 2003).

Critical incidents are seen as a form of narrative research, as they offer stories from research participants. Flanagan (1954) documented the use of the critical incident technique in research to observe and collect data on human behaviour. He noted that participants were asked to think of a situation in a specific context and relay their thoughts and emotions relating to it. Fifty years on from Flanagan's work, Butterfield *et al.* (2005) reviewed the developments of the term since his original paper. Although recent authors have adapted the term and applied it in other contexts, I have used Flanagan's stages for gathering critical incidents. First, I noted the aims of the data: what are the demands felt by graduates? What skills and knowledge are seen in the encounters? This enabled me to frame participant briefing so that I could request incidents that would answer these questions. Next came collecting the data. During the course of one week at work, participants were allowed to use either their personal phone or a Dictaphone provided by me to record their incidents. Participants would not be asked to record a set length, time or number of incidents and I kept this open. This decision was made because I was curious as to how many and what types of incidents they would produce. If they could not produce many and they were short and simplistic incidents, then it would be evident that customer demands, skills and knowledge were not seen as important to participants. Equally, if they declined to participate after the briefing, it would be clear that either they were too busy or could not provide me with the incidents requested. Each participant completed these narrations over one week and I organised them consecutively with the other participants. This enabled me to analyse and complete the next step with each participant separately, ensuring that my attention and reflection were on one participant independently and not on all of them at once. The incidents were either emailed directly to me or brought into the university on a USB stick.

After collecting all incidents from each participant, the next stage was to complete a stimulated recall (Lyle, 2003). This is a form of narrative interview, as it is based upon narrated incidents. A stimulated recall incorporates the narrated incident recordings into the interview to allow the participant and researcher to reflect and make comments on the recorded incident. Prior to the stimulated recall with each participant, I listened to each incident twice and made notes on the location, participant and my reflections on the incident. This enabled me to reflect on my own understanding of their stories before completing the stimulated recall. The premise of a stimulated recall is to stimulate further comments on, and insight into, an event that has happened (Lyle, 2003).

The incidents transcribed in chapters in this book enable the reader to reflect on these incidents from their own position and therefore extends the methodology used in the study as a teaching and learning tool for anyone interested in completing service encounters in the industry. The incidents are direct transcriptions from the narrated incidents offered by some of the participants from the study. I have removed areas where participants paused or thought out loud to enable these to be read clearly and seamlessly.

Stimulated recalls allow the researcher to check their own understanding of an incident to ensure that they have fully understood the problems and emotions felt by the participant in relation to the incident. As such, checking and probing the data was completed both by me and each research participant.

A summary of all primary data collection is noted in Table 0.4 for clarification:

Table 0.4 Data collected and methods of recording and storing

Method of data collection	Obtained and stored
Critical incidents	Participants record audio narratives on either their personal devices or a Dictaphone provided by me.
	Recordings are handed in with the Dictaphone or emailed directly.
	Once received, all recordings will be stored on an encrypted device.
Stimulated recall	Recorded on a Dictaphone by me and uploaded to a safe and encrypted device.

As Table 0.4 confirms, all data are produced in audio format and presented on a Dictaphone or via email by all participants. By staggering the collection of critical incidents and then listening to these in the stimulated recall with each participant, I was able to probe and understand fully the meaning and issues felt by participants in each one. Writing notes when listening to the submitted audio incidents enabled me to clarify the logical chain of events in each incident as described by the participant, and raise any queries that I had without the participant being present. I also identified how each incident linked to my own experience in industry so that I could clearly perceive my own lens and potential bias. By making notes and raising questions for each incident, I also had a clear plan of what to probe participants about during the stimulated recall.

In terms of analysis conventions available, Miles and Huberman (1994) identified 12 tactics possible in dealing with transcribed qualitative data. For this study, I completed a thematic analysis of all gathered data. Thematic analysis is where a researcher identifies patterns arising from a transcription or matches current themes identified in the literature. An important component of thematic analysis is to evidence the processes undertaken to obtain the themes in order for successful auditing of the research (King & Horrocks, 2010). As noted earlier, the theories used to analyse the data were identified through a theoretical framework of the skills and knowledge needed for service encounters. These themes are represented in the chapters offered in this book.

The study was born from my experience in lecturing on tourism, events and hospitality students in UK higher education institution. As it is based on my own experience, it is important that I reflect upon my own position as a researcher:

Objectivity is a false claim by researchers. (Cohen *et al.*, 2009: 36)

This quotation from Cohen *et al.* (2009) confirms why my own reflexivity and subjectivity needed to be addressed. Trying to be impartial or unbiased in writing up the results of the study would be dishonest, as the premise was born from my own professional practice and I am therefore professionally motivated. Furthermore, in using narrative research with participants who know me (due to our connection on LinkedIn or a previous teaching relationship), I am also emotionally connected with the data offered by people with whom I already had a professional relationship.

Reflexivity brings into the process a more personal dimension. (Bold, 2011: 3)

Bold's (2011) text on narrative research confirms that researcher reflexivity is important as it aids identification of the human elements of the data offered. Reflexivity is also important in narrative research as:

the researcher will be both a member of the group and yet studying the group. (Cohen *et al.*, 2009: 178)

Therefore, as I am inextricably linked with the participants, my own reflexivity regarding the research presented in this book is vital to ensure that my own opinions and responses are clear.

Briggs *et al.* (2012) suggest another way to be a reflexive researcher is to critically reflect on my own race, class, gender, education and background. Although they talk about this tool as being important in feminist research by women, it is poignant to my study as I have also studied and worked in the same positions as my participants:

Researchers are in the world and of the world. They bring their own biographies to the research situation and participants behave in particular ways to their presence. (Cohen *et al.*, 2009: 171)

Biggs *et al.*'s (2012) suggestion is confirmed with Cohen *et al.*'s (2009) quotation above, and it is clear that education research requires researchers to accept and identify their own position and history in order to fully reflect on their position in the research. The preface to this book outlines my position explicitly to ensure it is clear for readers using this book.

A final point of note regarding reflexivity in this study is in sexual dichotomism (Cohen *et al.*, 2009: 35). As noted in Chapter 5, sexualised labour is present in service encounters. Thus far, the literature has seen this from female employees' perspectives in that attractive female workers are desirable to provide services in leisure experiences. As a female and as a member of staff who has also been asked to wear a uniform that enhanced my own aesthetics, I was mindful of my own position if participants narrated incidents of a sexual or aesthetic nature.

Finally, to consider the ethics and limitations of the study:

> The inherent ethics of narrative research lies in the resolute honesty of the researcher's reflexivity, which states clearly the biases, aims, and positioning of the knower and the circumstances under which the knowledge was created, with the researcher taking full responsibility for what is written. (Clandinin, 2007: 549)

The quotation above was important in the study, because I was gaining narrative data from a context that I was acutely aware of. It was vital that I adhered to researcher ethics to ensure that the study and contents of this book are honest and clear accounts of how the research was undertaken.

In order to complete the study, I was required to apply for, and obtain, ethical approval. Through consideration of ethical compliance and data management, the study followed a number of stages and strategies to maintain the validity, trustworthiness, reliability and accuracy of the data gathered. After gaining consent from each participant to meet and discuss the research, a briefing and informed consent sheet were created to use at the meeting. Each participant was asked for a date and location convenient for them to meet me for the research briefing. Some participants wanted to meet near work and others wanted to meet near their home. This required me to use situated judgement (BERA, 2004), as it was important that participants felt safe and comfortable in discussing the research, and yet, at the same time, I had to assess the risks in meeting them in a range of locations (ESRC, 2012). The participants chose a range of public service businesses in which to complete the briefing, including Starbucks, Caffè Nero, Biko's Cafe, Café Rouge, Beach Road Cafe, and the Spread Eagle pub. When meeting a potential participant in a strange location, I assessed the risks by completing a site visit prior to the meeting. This ensured that I knew where I was going and that the business was a safe location.

An informal tone and relationship were important in this briefing so that the participant could trust and feel at ease with me. If they agreed to participate, there was potential for narrating incidents which were emotionally charged; therefore, I needed them to trust and feel comfortable with me quickly while maintaining professional integrity (BSA, 2002). The briefing sheet used at these meetings explained the process and participant requirements within the research. This was read through with each participant, allowing them time and consideration to ask questions about their role. There were an additional four participants who attended a briefing meeting, but these four decided not to complete the research. This identifies that participants knew that they could opt out after completing informed consent and used this right to withdraw where necessary. I also confirmed at the briefing that they would be anonymised in a future publication of their data (confirmed in the new names given to participants in this book).

A key ethical consideration when obtaining critical incidents was the potential for incidents to arouse emotional discomfort in each participant. To mitigate this potential for discomfort, I implemented nine strategies. An example from these is the inclusion of a risk assessment to identify potential emotionally charged encounters and discussions. In this risk assessment, I identify the contingencies put in place to lessen the risk or severity of the potential risk to participants completing the narrated incidents. The consent sheet also clarified possible emotional risks to each participant. In this way, they were aware of this possibility before narrating the data. My own reflective notes and researcher diary were used when listening to each incident so that I was aware of potential emotionally charged incidents before the stimulated recall.

Finally, the limitations of the study and the data offered in this book are noted below:

(1) Participants were linked to me via LinkedIn and some were taught by me previously. This means my own professional practice and positions were known by participants. This was managed by asking participants to create the data in working environments where I was not present.
(2) Participants were working in Manchester, UK, thus offering a geographical limit to the service encounters discussed.
(3) Data were gathered in 2013 and so is situated in a specific time within industry practice.
(4) The literature discussed in the chapters is limited to ones available at the time of publication.

Through discussion of the study completed the positions, methods, ethics and limitations have been presented. Being reflective and open about my own positions is crucial in understanding links drawn between the theoretical framework and incidents narrated by staff in tourism, events and hospitality.

Participants Presented in this Book

Data from 12 participants are presented on staff perspectives on service encounters in this book. Their pseudonyms, working location and roles are clarified in Table 0.5.

Six of the 12 participants noted above completed the PhD study, but six were students completing a unit on employability during the 2017/18 academic year. After completing the study, I used the methodology from

Table 0.5 Participant names, businesses and roles used in the incidents

Name given	Business	Independent or national company?	Role
Tom	Irish pub	National	Assistant manager
Sophie	5* Hotel	International	Waitress and bar staff
Lucy	Restaurant	National chain	Door host
Martha	4* Hotel	International	Finance assistant
Beth	Travel Company	Independent	Social media assistant
Emma	Hostel	National	Reception and housekeeping assistant
Phil	Event booking agency	Independent	Customer service agent
Katy	Travel agent	National	Customer service agent
Taylor	Group travel company	Independent	Customer service agent
Jessica	3* Hotel and serviced apartments	National	Food and beverage server
Mary	Hostel	National	Reception and housekeeping assistant
Holly	Event venue agency	Independent	Event sales assistant

the study in my teaching practice to ask students to reflect on their own perceptions of service encounters through diarising service encounter incidents. These additional six participants have also confirmed consent for their stories to be used.

The names given to each participant in Table 0.5 and throughout this book are pseudonyms. Where manager, colleague or supplier names are offered in incidents, these are also amended to maintain their anonymity. This is to ensure both the anonymity of the staff, but also the protection of the company in which they worked and reported incidents.

As Table 0.5 notes, participants were working in a range of national and independent businesses. Even though they were working in Manchester, some of these were managed by international staff training schemes. As such, their ability to manage service encounters was not only due to the location of their work, but the training enforced by the company they worked for. Further, as the encounters were completed with transnational tourists and customers, the incident's geographical location can be seen as a space of dislocation (MacLeod, 2006).

Audience

This book presents staff perspectives on service encounters in tourism, events and hospitality. As such, students on any course, module or unit noting these three sectors will benefit from the contents. As workers in businesses associated with these sectors often create leisure experiences and might be located within recreation contexts, the following list outlines all programmes of study that might choose to use key chapters or incidents to aid student reflection on service encounters:

- Tourism management.
- Hospitality management.
- Events management.
- Services marketing.
- Business management.
- Human resource management.
- Services management.
- Sports management.
- Arts management.
- Culinary arts management.
- Hotel and restaurant management.
- Tour guide management.
- Leisure management.
- Recreation management.
- Outdoor activity management.
- Theatre and stage management.

Chapters included in this book link to psychology, sociology and anthropology disciplines of study. As such, the book can also be used to consider the human elements of service encounters and how people prepare, react and manage these situations in working environments.

Note

(1) Chapter 1 does not offer incidents, as this presents definitions on key terms for the text and all subsequent incidents in proceeding chapters are seen as customer service encounters.

1 What are Customer Service Encounters?

Chapter Learning Objectives

(1) To identify definitions of customer service encounters and intercultural service encounters.
(2) To understand customer perceptions of customer/intercultural service encounters.
(3) To evaluate how staff use their skills to perform and create personalised service.
(4) To critically assess positions taken on culture, the individual and 'other' in customer service encounters.

Introduction

As noted in the guidance for using this book, this chapter will present analysis of secondary published literature on customer service encounters without critical incidents. This is because service encounters are the focus of the book and the following chapters present incidents alongside key theory supporting delivery of these. This chapter will identify definitions of customer service encounters and intercultural service encounters, each followed with an evaluation and critical assessment of the positions taken on culture, the individual and 'other' within service encounters.

Customer Service Encounters

Customer service encounters is the founding term from which service encounters is taken. This section will briefly outline definitions, fields of associated study and issues seen in research published on this term. This book presents staff perspectives on service encounters, which are multidimensional for staff, but in the current literature they are often termed customer service encounters.

Solomon *et al.* (1985) are seen as the seminal authors in customer service encounters and they saw customer service encounters as being important due to:

> the increased recognition of the importance of the person-to-person encounter between buyer and seller – client and provider – to the overall success of the marketing effort. (Solomon *et al.*, 1985: 99)

This quotation identifies that the term 'customer service encounters' was instituted by recognising face-to-face interactions between a buyer and a seller. The term derives from business scholars who saw problems in service encounters in a range of industries such as banking, dentistry, tourism, events and hospitality, and retail. The focal relationship in customer service encounters is the binary aspect of people selling services and other people buying services. There was a perceived difficulty seen in the service encounter context, wherein the service is intangible and based upon behaviour and action, rather than products. The difficulty regarding intangible services is that the customer perceives the service as a subjective experience rather than a quantifiable product. For example, if you purchase a washing machine and it does not clean your clothes, you can inform the manufacturer, who can get you a new one. Services use intangible skills such as communication, which is interpreted and offered differently. If a customer perceives that communication with a member of staff is not working, they still have to try to communicate with that person and define the nature of the issue until their query is resolved. Furthermore, the perceived satisfaction of this service is determined by one person and thus with a single set of subjective associations with the service.

Solomon *et al.* (1985) also accepted that these encounters rely on intangible services, and noted that service industry management prioritise this owing to their services being between customers and staff:

> it is primarily in the service sector that the dyadic encounter has generated a great deal of managerial concern. (Solomon *et al.*, 1985: 100)

Tourism, events and hospitality businesses operate entirely in the service sector, as they offer experiences and provide accommodation and consumable goods to customers. Therefore, Solomon *et al.*'s (1985) research, although not based in tourism, events and hospitality contexts, is a beneficial definition to start with when considering service encounters within these businesses. It is accepted that tourism, events and hospitality businesses serve food and beverages, which are physical products, but these are consumed rather than taken away and used repeatedly. The following review of customer service encounter literature will identify how this term is perceived in different locales. This broad scope is important because it enables an overview of the term and elicits key issues present as a result of the research and within the research itself.

From these early definitions of customer service encounters the term maintained pace within services marketing fields of study. Fisk *et al.* (1993) identified that satisfied customers are created through the management of internal and external marketing. Internal marketing (upselling) is created by staff who are 'satisfied employees' (Fisk *et al.*, 1993: 82) and external marketing is managed via customer relations and marketing of core business services. Within the services marketing literature, the satisfaction of staff is linked to training, retention and the satisfaction of employees as a human resources function. This book considers employee satisfaction as their ability to manage effectively service encounters, a position relatively under-represented in this field.

The majority of texts on service encounters use a service quality (Parasuraman *et al.*, 1991) paradigm to assess the success from a customer position:

> managing service delivery to satisfy customers. (Walker, 1995: 5)

Walker (1995) acknowledges that the encounters are to deliver a service, but that the key focus of evaluation on this is from customers receiving the products or experiences. He clarifies three supporting elements for successful service encounters:

(1) The atmosphere within the business (décor and lighting).
(2) Interactions with customers before and after the encounter (services marketing).
(3) Adequate service does not lead to satisfaction (customers need to perceive improved or superior service).

None of these elements outline the work that the management or staff complete when creating and producing the service. Coye (2004) later confirmed that management requires acknowledgement of customer satisfaction via meeting the expectations and perceptions of the service from the customers in the encounter.

There are only a handful of academic articles that consider staff perspectives of service encounters and these tend to inform management on how to train, educate and ensure staff perform to the correct service quality standards. Lin and Fu (2017) most recently address the performance elements required in creating the front and back of house stages for service encounters in restaurants. Even though they acknowledge back of house contexts, such as kitchens, they still omit consideration of staff perspectives. Mattila and Enz s (2002: 273) article (discussed further in Chapter 4) outlines how staff need to 'accurately predict customers' service quality expectations' via interpretation of facial expression and emotions presented within a service encounter. These two articles are interesting, as the first one confirms the presence of performed roles in a service encounter, and yet the latter suggests staff should interpret emotions in a service encounter to predict service satisfaction (which, if performed, would not be real nor true).

Customer service encounters are presented as dyadic situations whereby customer satisfaction is required and service failure is avoided. Originating from services marketing, the term was originally produced for any retail or service context. The term is consistently considered from customer positions and recommendations are made to the management of businesses creating these.

Intangibility, Individualism and Ignorance in Customer Service Encounters

Perceived issues within customer service encounter literature will now be discussed. These issues include, but are not limited to, the intangibility of the service, individualism and ignorance. The literature on customer service encounters is discussed from all foci and locale to enable a thorough discussion of current knowledge.

In terms of issues identified in customer service encounter research, it is evident that intangible services and consumable products present a problematic context. However, I would also suggest that the focus and lens through which research has been completed are also problematic. Papers from Bitner *et al.* (1990), Nickson *et al.* (2007), Reimann *et al.* (2008), Ryoo (2005), Solomon *et al.* (1985), Sparks and Callan (1992), Surprenant *et al.* (1987) and Weiermair (2000) focus on the customers' perception of these encounters, and not the staff's. As the definition offered by Solomon *et al.* (1985) suggests that the priority is in maintaining customer satisfaction, the primary focus on customers' perceptions in the encounter is valid. However, their definition also states that the encounter involves a 'person-to-person' interaction. By acknowledging two people within a customer service encounter and then only focusing research on customer perspectives in the encounter, it can be suggested that the origin and following research are deficient through not fully analysing both parties involved in the context. This book will rectify this in part by only focusing on the staff present. Similar to previous research that only considered customer positions, it is also accepted that this book is limited in only offering the staff perspectives in the encounters without customer, colleague or management positions being explored in the contexts.

As noted, the research on customer service encounters fails to explore the staff perceptions in these situations. This does not mean that the staff are ignored entirely, but they are seen as the agents of change who are malleable within the encounter. The majority of current research investigates encounters from a customer's perspective and then offers recommendations to tourism, events and hospitality management as to how they can improve the services offered. There are only two papers found which refer specifically to staff in the customer service encounter literature (Bowen, 2016; Yang et al., 2015). Within these there are persistent recommendations as to how staff should act. These are seen as recommendations stipulating that staff have to *give* a good service:

> the capacity to use his or her (staff) skills and resources to perform customer service to a satisfactory level. (Yang et al., 2015: 829)

Yang et al.'s (2015) paper sought to understand the variability in both customers and staff within the customer service encounter, but again failed to analyse fully the perspective of the staff when they needed to 'perform' for customers. A literature review offered by Bowen (2016) confirmed that service research still focuses on customer satisfaction and that staff are seen as innovators of service quality, differentiators of service quality and enablers of service quality for customers. What is interesting about these two papers is that the recommendations identify the importance of staff in encounters, but then state that they should offer excellent service and perform to a high standard without acknowledgement or investigation of staff opinions or defining clearly what is 'excellent' or 'high'. This finding of the lack of research in this area encouraged me to develop this text and offer clarification on a staff perspective regarding customer service encounters.

It is also clear from the published literature that personalised service is needed in a customer service encounter. A personalised service will satisfy and delight guests and is seen as a superior service. To offer examples of a personalised service, we can consider an encounter in which a customer in a Starbucks café orders a latte. Staff can personalise this service by asking if the customer wants additional ingredients or products to be added to the order, by acknowledging them as a regular customer or by developing a successful customer relationship with an informal conversation about appropriate topics. These examples are all possible service standards that can be achieved through training of scripted service to staff. However, Surprenant *et al.* (1987) identified a further problem in this:

> There appears to be consensus among service providers that personal service is something their customers want, but little consensus about just what personal service means. In many cases it seems to mean a smile, eye contact, and a friendly greeting. In other cases it means offering to customize the basic service to suit the customer's needs or tastes. It may mean spending time with the customer, or it may mean offering advice, making small talk, or taking a personal interest in the customer. (Surprenant *et al.*, 1987: 86)

The quotation above confirms that a personalised service is difficult to manage and create. For example, going back to the Starbucks situation noted above, the customer could equally be annoyed by any attempt at small talk with staff or at having to decide options for their coffee if they wanted to order a simple hot beverage. Owing to a limited number of new publications and definitions on service encounters, there is an issue here in applying an old definition of customer service encounters to a new hospitality experience and process: it is not directly comparable.

Surprenant *et al.* (1987) identified that facial expression, and non-verbal and verbal communication are all required in these encounters. These skills are difficult to regulate or control within the context, as customers in tourism events and hospitality do not simply want a product but want to be 'served' by 'personal' and 'friendly' staff (Surprenant *et al.*, 1987). (The need for facial expression and appearance of staff in the encounter is explored in Chapters 4 and 5 on emotional and aesthetic labour theory.) It is evident that early research on customer service encounters identified that personalisation is important to customers, but that this was seen as problematic owing to each customer's perception of what they wanted or expected as personalised service. For example, if you have a customer who is rushing to get to work, they may not have time for a conversation with staff. In this example, staff conversation may not be perceived as personalised service, but as potentially dissatisfactory service.

In summary of the definition and issues identified in customer service encounter theory, it is evident from the theory discussed and analysed in the chapter that it originates from marketing research completed in the USA in the 1980s. Solomon *et al.*'s (1985) definition of customer service encounters and research into this context have been because of management interest in how they can fully satisfy their customers. Publications on this term stem from academic awareness of problems associated with offering an intangible service. Since then, research into customer service encounters has fragmented into a range of other theoretical areas, including communication theory (Sparks & Callan, 1992), non-verbal communication in the encounter (Sundaram & Webster, 2000), staff human resource management [see emotional labour (Hochschild, 2012) and aesthetic labour (Witz *et al.*, 2003) for examples] and service marketing (Wu & Liang, 2009). Although the body of literature on customer service encounters has fragmented, it is evident that it is still seen by other academics as an important research context in which customer satisfaction is achieved and maintained.

This book does not question the premise that all tourism, events and hospitality businesses need to succeed via satisfied customers. It acknowledges this construct in customer service encounters and identifies why more analysis and understanding of staff perspectives on these are imperative to fully understand the issues present. Current literature on customer service encounters could be viewed as ignorant as it fails to acknowledge the opinions or feelings of the staff and it only seeks to ensure that the staff are *given* the right skills and knowledge for dealing with customers. None of the papers analysed whether the staff possess these skills and knowledge or whether they are *happy* or *able* to offer them in the customer service encounter. Therefore, this book is based on an agreed construct and definition of customer service encounters but seeks to discuss the concept and issues from a service provider's perspective. This means that the definition is altered within this book due to the emerging knowledge gained from staff stories and incidents from tourism, events and hospitality contexts.

Customer-to-Customer Perspectives

Although the majority of literature published on customer service encounters considers customer perspectives regarding the service from staff and management, there is a body of knowledge considering the customer-to-customer positions also. This is interesting, as it is often seen in tourism, events and hospitality contexts as being a barrier to successful customer satisfaction. For example, customers on a tour will naturally talk to other tourists or diners during the experience. If these customers upset other customers, the service encounter will be negatively affected. This position is further clarified in Chapter 7 on co-creation and co-production and Chapter 9 on the use of humour in service encounters. Here, a brief overview of the customer-to-customer dynamics in service encounters is offered to clarify recommendations noted to management.

Grove and Fisk (1997) evaluated tourist experiences based on the customer-to-customer interactions. They identified that customers might raise complaints owing to misconceptions about the service outlined by other guests. This links to the subjectivity of service quality in that expectations and perceptions of service are individual to each customer.

If another customer voices a problem within the encounter, other customers are alerted to consider this position also. Further, the actions and behaviour of other customers may negatively affect the experience:

> bumping, shoving, and cutting in line. (Grove & Fisk, 1997: 77)

Within queuing for tourist experiences, the behaviour and actions of other customers may be attributed to poor management of the leisure experience. In this way, customer service encounters need to attend to all customer behaviour and ensure all customers are safe and able to complete the experience to the standard planned by the business.

Wu (2007) later considered tourist reactions within the customer-to-customer interactions in service encounters and recommended new business marketing strategies to support potential negative effects. Specifically, they noted:

> It would be best to avoid attracting incompatible customers together in the first place. (Wu, 2007: 1526)

This statement suggests that tourism businesses should look to market to specific consumer groups in order to mitigate issues in customer-to-customer interaction within service encounters. The specific elements of customer compatibility are not defined in this publication, but are presumed to reside within the customers' interests, hobbies and usual leisure activities. This is presumed, but it is also noted that compatibility is usually linked to love, sex and personal relationships. Wu's (2007) article is not based on dating or sex tourism and so customer likes and dislikes are noted and linked to the tourist experience. Customers' recommendations are seen as problematic as tourists are able to access destination and leisure experience information from a number of sources and so are not limited to business marketing alone. TripAdvisor, for example, is not set to show tourism experiences relevant only to a person's leisure history and hobbies. You can search for all businesses and experiences. Furthermore, other customers who know more about a tourist experience, such as the heritage or history of an area, for example, may be seen as an asset within the customer-to-customer interactions. Therefore, targeting specific compatible customer groups to complete a tourist experience based on their compatibility with other customers is rejected.

Finally, Moore *et al.*'s (2005) research within hair salons (a similar vocational business) noted that staff should not interrupt customer-to-customer interactions as these are a core component of the expected service:

> inform service contact staff about the importance of CCI (customer-to-customer interaction) and staff should be trained as to when they should intervene in customer interactions. (Moore *et al.*, 2005: 488)

This suggestion is also offered as a concluding recommendation from their research and identifies that part of the service is for customers to meet, talk to and develop relationships with other customers. The social element within this context has parity with tourism, events and hospitality as a number of these businesses offer leisure experiences. Being able to accurately predict when to interrupt customer-to-customer interactions is therefore noted as an asset that staff need to develop. Politeness and turn-taking are accepted as part of this ability and it is therefore discussed in Chapter 3 within soft skills for service encounters.

Through discussion of the customer-to-customer elements in service encounters, it is evident that management is recommended to train staff to manage customer-to-customer dynamics. This presents an additional layer of responsibility for staff completing customer service encounters.

Intercultural Service Encounters

After the development of customer service encounter theory, researchers then defined the term intercultural service encounters. This is an important term to consider as it relates to the development and expansion of tourism, events and hospitality businesses and thus the expansion of the varied types of guests and staff completing the encounters. Discussion of this related term will offer more evidence from research within tourism, events and hospitality contexts and identify further positions present in the face-to-face encounters completed by staff.

Intercultural service encounters are perceived as a service encounter wherein the customer and staff are from different cultures (Strauss & Mang, 1999). Again, it is noted that the definition and use of this term were researched from an analysis of service marketing and that the focus of intercultural service encounters is placed upon customer satisfaction. Culture in intercultural service encounters is defined using Hofstede's texts on cultural difference in business management.[1] From a review of Hofstede's (2006) definition and classification of culture, it is clear that culture is based on nationality or citizenship. Strauss and Mang's (1999) paper identified that customers perceive culture shocks within tourism airline service encounters and that this can lead to customer dissatisfaction. Although this seminal paper focused purely on cultural differences, other authors (as discussed later in this chapter) have considered individual identity, body language and self-reflection as important in an intercultural service encounter.

When Culture is Defined, Ignored and Inferred Incorrectly

The first issue that I want to raise in consideration of intercultural service encounter research is that basing these on a Hofstedian definition of culture is inappropriate for tourism, events and hospitality industries. Hofstede's seminal research on culture was between 1967 and 1973, and used surveys of IBM staff to consider cross-cultural communication in business. This definition is used consistently in research on culture (Taras *et al.*, 2009). As staff in IBM are not all required to complete face-to-face encounters, nor provide tourism, events and hospitality experiences, this definition should be rejected in consideration of tourism, events and hospitality contexts.

Hofstede's definition of culture states that each individual has certain personality and communication traits owing to the environmental grouping in which they grew up and/or live: 'Culture is always a collective phenomenon' (Hofstede *et al.*, 2010: 5). By defining culture as a large national group to which each person belongs, his research sought to find differences and similarities between staff working in different countries.

> In research on cultural differences, nationality – the passport one holds – should therefore be used with care. Yet it is often the only feasible criterion for classification. Rightly or wrongly, collective properties are ascribed to the citizens of certain countries: people refer to 'typically American', 'typically German' and 'typically Japanese' behaviour. (Hofstede *et al.*, 2010: 21)

This excerpt identifies how Hofstede uses a person's nationality as the foundation for cultural differences. Interestingly, he notes that differences in nationality should be used with 'care', but then goes on to state that it is a common way in which people talk and, therefore, it is acceptable to group according to nationality. Using nationality as a way in which to group people's culture is problematic, as it can lead to racist statements. What is interesting in Hofstede's work is that even by defining culture as nationality, he fails to ascertain the nationality of his participants and simply infers their nationality based on the country in which they are working. Hofstede's survey did not ascertain the nationality of each participant. This happens with stark regularity within the literature on intercultural service encounters. Therefore, by basing intercultural service encounters upon a definition of culture which does not fully elicit research participants' nationality, the basis and definition of culture are unclear.

Intercultural service encounters are also seen as ethnocentric (Bennett, 1986) and do not allow for ethnorelative development analysis in the encounter. Ethnocentrism is seen as viewing the world according to set cultural norms, whereas ethnorelativism is where a person can identify a range of accepted behaviour from different cultures present (Bennett, 1986). Ethnocentrism and ethnorelativism are discussed in Chapter 6 on intercultural sensitivity. Intercultural service encounters are ethnocentric because they use the Hofstedian definition of culture, which only identifies nationality in the definition. Ignoring ethnorelative development and individual behaviour in an intercultural service encounter will only serve to highlight differences between customers and staff and may lead to staff feeling uncomfortable and unable to adapt to the demands required by guests. To analyse the intercultural service encounter literature further, seven articles will now be addressed. Strauss and Mang's (1999) article started the academic debate on intercultural service encounters, so this paper will be considered first, followed by publications by Warden *et al.* (2003), Barker and Härtel (2004), Sharma *et al.* (2009, 2012) Tam *et al.* (2014) and Kenesie and Stier (2017).

Strauss and Mang's (1999) journal article was based on research completed in Tokyo, Frankfurt and Atlanta airport service encounters. They interviewed 220 passengers who were travelling and asked them to narrate critical incidents from their service experiences within the airport. Here the definition of culture is also taken from a Hofstedian approach and sees people as having specific and discrete cultures based on their ethnic origin. They use the critical incident technique (CIT) within interviews to ask customer participants about satisfying or dissatisfying encounters within a service business. This paper raises a number of concerns. First, passenger culture is based on the origin and destination of their journey and the authors do not ascertain the precise nationality of each participant. For example, the hypotheses are looking for specific problems between German and US people, as Germany and USA are where participants are travelling to and from. Nowhere in the paper does it acknowledge or identify the specific nationality of the customers or the staff. In this way, they are applying a Hofstedian frame of culture to a location and transportation method rather than to the people themselves. As Hofstede also did this in his original publications on cultural dimensions there are two layers of ambiguity in culture: IBM staff being seen as a culture owing to the location or their work, and Strauss and Mang basing a culture on the location or transportation method. Strauss and Mang (1999) conclude that in order to satisfy guests, management needs to understand that their customers attribute service failure to cultural distance. This is evidently incorrect. Without acknowledging the customers' or staff's nationality or background experiences with airlines their conclusions are incomplete. Moreover, participants who travel and who may be of multiple nationalities or descent are also more likely to be familiar with or expect differences within an intercultural service encounter. By using a rigid definition of culture and yet failing to mention or ascertain the culture of both the server and the guest, Strauss and Mang's (1999) conclusions can be seen as incomplete. Their use of the terms 'foreign customer' and 'domestic service' (Strauss & Mang, 1999: 331) is also misplaced, as the encounters are completed within an airport which is built to cater to multicultural customers in a fundamentally global context.

Warden *et al.*'s (2003) research focuses on service failures between local and non-local people. They use Strauss and Mang's (1999) zone of tolerance to consider customer problems within a restaurant intercultural service encounter. Based on an online survey in Taiwan, the authors again fail to identify the nationality of the servers or guests. Instead, they consider that all customers are travellers (foreign and not Taiwanese) because eating is 'equally required of all travellers' (Warden *et al.*, 2010: 437). It is an accepted fact that eating is required of every human; therefore, suggesting that all customers in this research location are foreign is incorrect. This research is also based on Hofstede's cultural distance dimension and compares USA to Taiwanese cultural differences. Warden *et al.* (2003: 447) conclude:

> An American who subjectively decides a restaurant service encounter is a failure, when he or she is served food not cooked to order, will have the same culturally learned reaction when visiting a restaurant in the USA or in China.

Even though the basis of this paper is ethnocentric, this conclusion identifies that service failure is not purely limited to cultural distance, and that service failure can be the same regardless of the service environment and the culture of the person serving them. I would advocate this and repeat that, regardless of the geographical location, members of staff and customers can be from anywhere in the world and that the difference is individual.

Barker and Härtel's (2004) study in Australia specifically targeted customers who looked foreign according to the usual appearance of Australian nationals.

> Limited prior contact presupposes limited psychological interaction, which in turn elevates the role of observable cues to ascribed stereotypes. (Barker & Härtel, 2004: 4)

Their paper suggests that if a server and guest are from different cultures, they will not share the same expectations and perceptions of service and therefore the service failure will be a result of cultural differences. This research specifies race rather than nationality within the intercultural service encounter and the authors suggest that if staff have not had contact with customers from other races, they will experience service failures. Again, it is not clarified if the customers are Australian and the authors used customers who look Australian according to 'ascribed stereotypes'. Furthermore, I would argue that there is an individual element missing here. Even if staff have never served someone from, for example, Japan or Africa, they will still understand that the customer requires something and can begin communication. The research considered the tone of voice and body language as part of this cultural difference exhibited by customers, but they ultimately chose participants who had 'non-Anglo-Celtic/Saxon appearance' (Barker & Härtel, 2004: 7). Here again, neither the race nor the nationality of the member of staff is specifically identified. This research, therefore, focuses on aesthetic differences between people and yet does not recognise that these people could already be familiar to customers due to repeat custom or the customer's prior experiences. I would argue that their participant sampling method is also flawed, as they do not elaborate on how this is judged from the outset. Focusing on cultural diversity and racism within a service encounter, they recommend that human resource practices need changing in order for staff to improve service for the multinational customers present. As one of the three locations of participants from the study was a tourism, events and hospitality business it can be noted these recommendations are suggested for these industries. Even with this (perceived) flawed recommendation, they are unable to offer specific measures or procedures for this change in training practice for an intercultural service encounter. I would argue that customers and staff all look different in an intercultural service encounter, as they are strangers to one another. If staff are trained to accept general differences in every customer, then the service will be flexible and adaptable enough to meet all demands from all customers.

Publications from Sharma and colleagues are the only available sources of research noting staff perspectives on intercultural service encounters. This is an improvement upon earlier research, as it enables an analysis of both parties within the encounter and also acknowledges that both people (customer and staff) may have different cultures from the location in which they are meeting. Three publications from their research are now discussed (2009, 2012 and 2014) to outline recommendations and issues seen in their concluding discussions:

> an Intercultural Service Encounter gives an opportunity to the new immigrants to learn about their host culture in order to adapt and integrate better (Sharma et al., 2009: 228)

Again, an intercultural service encounter is seen through an ethnocentric lens: if the server is not from the local culture, the business can offer them a place in which to integrate and adapt. I have two problems with this quotation. First, the business and staff will not necessarily conform to the usual elements of the host culture (staff may not even be from that area) and secondly, I find this quotation patronising to the individual concerned, as they may not need to adapt or integrate. Furthermore, it may not be possible, appropriate or suitable for a person to adapt or integrate into the local culture. These points noted, the article improves on Warden et al. (2003) and Strauss and Mang (1999) by considering the multinational context of tourism, events and hospitality rather than the nationality of the location in which the encounter is completed. Sharma *et al.* (2009) found that perceived cultural distance is the main factor contributing to a service failure in an intercultural service encounter. A perceived cultural distance is how the customer or server perceives the cultural difference between themselves and the other person in the encounter. It is not clear if this factor is to be perceived by the customer or server, but they assert that each customer will prefer to be served by an employee of the same race as themselves owing to 'greater trust and familiarity' (Sharma *et al.*, 2009: 229). Again, this is inappropriate to suggest for every customer in every situation. The purpose of tourism, events and hospitality experiences for some customers is to be served by staff who are different from themselves, as there is a learning element to the encounter. In their concluding discussion, Sharma *et al.* (2009) suggest that managers of tourism, events and hospitality businesses should not allow any service failure to occur owing to intercultural problems and that these should be pre-empted by management. They do not clarify how this could be completed.

Both Sharma *et al.* (2012) and Tam *et al.* (2014) use photos of local and foreign staff in their data gathering to understand staff and customer perspectives of intercultural service encounters. They presented photos of East Asian, Chinese and Western people to customers and staff in order to ask how they would react and complete a service encounter with the person depicted. Again, they fail to acknowledge the specific nationality of the staff and customer. Sharma *et al.* (2012) state that they gained local Chinese customers and Hong Kong employees. The customers could have been born elsewhere and had more service encounter experiences elsewhere, and the employees could have been from anywhere in the world. Using race in this article, the method employed would not only ask for an incorrect link to their race and the race of others, but would support ethnorelativism (Bennett, 1986) and produce racist judgements of others. In acceptance of the difficulty of judging culture via race, they conclude:

> employees are also only human after all and they all have similar feelings and failings. (Sharma *et al.*, 2012: 526)

This quotation implies a patronising position towards staff serving these customers. It is not simply that staff may incorrectly judge the culture of the customer, but that they do not need to do this if using a small culture position (see Chapter 6 for a full discussion). What is interesting is the authors then conclude that management should support staff to ignore potential intercultural elements and offer all customers the same service standards. Tam *et al.*'s (2014) paper also supports the experience of different cultures as being core to the management of intercultural service encounters. They note that customers with experiences of intercultural encounters are more adept at managing the potential shocks when liaising with someone who is considered different to them. However, this can be applied more widely: any person with experiences of tourism, events and hospitality encounters will have completed intercultural service encounters, as all staff and customers have unique cultures through their nationality, parental influence, and life, work and leisure experiences. Therefore, it can be argued that intercultural service encounters are not simply due to the perceived different race of the other person, but that every experience within tourism, events and hospitality utilises intercultural interactions and are all locations of interculturality.

Kenesie and Stier (2017) also considered staff positions towards intercultural service encounters and they interviewed hotel receptionists to identify these perspectives. Hofstede's definition of culture was utilised again here as it was seen as 'largely consistent' (Kenesie & Stier, 2017: 308). Being consistently used in other research on culture does not mean this definition is appropriate for hospitality locations. As noted earlier, this definition is seen as deficient owing to the lack of nationality ascertained by his participants. Support for this position is confirmed by Taras *et al.* (2009: 4):

a single model cannot comprise all aspects of such a highly complex, multidimensional and multi-layered phenomenon as culture.

Taras *et al.*'s (2009) paper confirms that from the analysis of 121 models on culture, Hofstede's cultural dimensions are ever-present, but are not always appropriate within all contexts. Taras *et al.* (2009: 4) clarify that the Earth can be perceived as a 'global village' and that we can no longer infer culture from nationality, race nor language. This is a position accepted in this book, as tourism, events and hospitality encounters require people from transnational backgrounds and experiences. In Kenesie and Stier's (2017) paper, they recommend that staff can be supported in delivering intercultural service encounters through management providing training on 'the culture' (Kenesie & Stier, 2017: 316) as much as possible. *The* culture implies a singular culture to be trained and educated upon whereas the authors note that staff need to serve a range of customers with different cultures. The conclusions support the position offered in this book, in that both work and personal experiences will lead to the staff's ability to deliver effective intercultural service encounters.

The intercultural service encounter articles critiqued in this section have identified that customers are the focus, that local and foreign elements of the encounter can cause service failure, and that a geographical location can be used to identify a person's nationality and culture. My critique of these points not only identifies my own position on cultural differences, but also clarifies the lack of attention devoted to how staff in encounters are meant to cope with the various demands placed upon them. An excerpt from Lashley and Morrison (2007) clarifies an example of the type of demand present:

> People just come down and say 'I've had a long day, I'm very stressed out, do you know where I can get a blow job...' (Lashley & Morrison, 2007: 266)

This quotation does not suggest that this request is acceptable or unacceptable, but requesting information about a private, sexual service in a hotel could be a distressing request for a member of staff. This example serves to identify that staff in the encounter are not only seen as providers of services to satisfy guests, but also seen as non-judgemental assistance for any and all customer demands. Thus, they need to be fully trained in responding to a variety of demands and customers so that they, too, can be confident in the satisfactory performance of their roles.

From a review of these articles, it is clear that intercultural service encounters were defined through cultural differences and a perceived distance between the server and customer within tourism, events and hospitality businesses. Like customer service encounter theory, this term came about from focusing on service quality and satisfaction for the customer. Intercultural service encounters are only deemed important because of the possibility of a service failure for the customer. Whether based on Hofstede's cultural dimensions, race, ethnicity or nationality, an intercultural service encounter has been defined from an ethnocentric and grouping version of culture. Therefore, the research to date does not fully consider intercultural service encounters from the staff's point of view, whether the staff are prepared for the intercultural service encounter and what types of difficulties staff perceive in the encounter.

Theories Linking to Service Encounters for Tourism, Events and Hospitality Management

From the discussion of customer service encounters and intercultural service encounters in this chapter, Figure 1.1 is presented to identify the key components needed to deliver these in tourism, events and hospitality.

Figure 1.1 was created after a consideration of the literature on customer service encounters and intercultural service encounters. These all link to key theories for service management in tourism, events and hospitality management and are used as the focus for Chapters 3–7. Chapters 2 and 8–10 are emergent components identified through completing the study (see the Introduction for full details of the study).

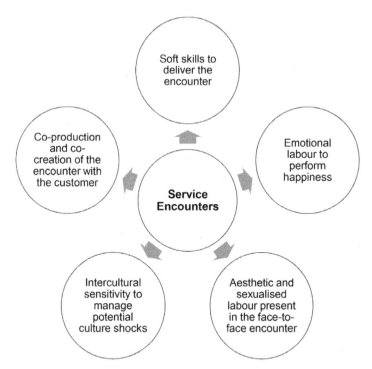

Figure 1.1 Staff components to deliver service encounters in tourism, events and hospitality

Summary

(1) To identify definitions of customer service encounters and intercultural service encounters,
(2) customer service encounters are defined as the delivery of a service person-to-person. Originating in services marketing, this term has had significant attention and has been researched since the 1980s. Focused on improving services for customers, this term is seen as devoid of staff perspectives in order to fully consider the duality of the encounter. Intercultural service encounters are defined as a service encounter with two people of different cultures. Culture is defined through the nationality of a person. To understand customer perceptions of customer/intercultural service encounters,

customers are noted as wanting personalised service whereby staff offer unique experiences. Service with a smile, being friendly and knowing their requirements are presented as assets leading to high quality service. Management of customer-to-customer dynamics are required in order to ensure tourist experiences are conducted appropriately without reducing customer perceptions of the service quality and leisure experience.

Culture shocks emerge when customers perceive a different culture in the staff serving them and this is seen to lead to perceptions of poor service.

(3) To evaluate how staff use their skills to perform and create personalised service,

they are required to learn how to perform and give personalised service based upon understanding customer expectations. Using their skills, staff are noted as being required to give personalised service without consideration of the demands being made and contexts of the service encounter.

(4) To critically assess positions taken on culture, individual and 'other' in customer service encounters.

Within the literature discussed in service encounters, culture is taken from a Hofstedian definition. This is presented in this chapter as being deficient due to intercultural service encounters not fully establishing the nationality of customer and staff within the encounters. Regardless of the nationality of a customer or staff member, their unique individual experiences will also affect the encounter. Without a body of knowledge on staff perspectives in service encounters, current publications show a gap in considering the 'other' within the service encounter: the staff.

Note

(1) Strauss and Mang (1999) refer to Hofstede's (1985) and (1990) publications on culture in international business.

Annotated bibliography

Solomon, M.R., Surprenant, C and Czepiel, J. (1985) A role theory perspective on dyadic interactions: The service encounter. *Journal of Marketing* 49 (1), 99–111.

Authors based at New York University in the USA wrote this perspective piece based upon marketing and retail management theory. Role theory is outlined in discussion and there is no primary research conducted or presented. They suggest that understanding consumer behaviour is not simply about links between a customer and a business, but within the specific service encounters where customers meet the service provider. Service encounters are seen as a social exchange between two people. The individual employee is not acknowledged, however. Definitions of role theory and service with a script are beneficial to service encounter studies as these enable clarification of the dyadic nature of the encounter. Use this article to understand the history and founding principles on customer service encounters. It is also particularly interesting in terms of event memories and customer psychology and motivations in encounters (noting an artificial intelligence approach to going to the dentist!).

Question: Table 5 on page 78 considered satisfactory and dissatisfactory employee actions. Are these actions scripted? Why do you think the employees acted in these ways?

Bitner, J., Booms, B.H. and Tetreault, M.S. (1990) Service encounter: Diagnosing favorable and unfavorable incidents. *American Marketing Association* 54 (1), 71–84.

Also published in the American Marketing Association (like Solomon *et al.*, 1985 above); however, this article improves on the latter as the authors are based in schools of hospitality, present primary research on service encounters and these are all located in hospitality contexts. Seven hundred critical incidents were elicited from customers of airlines, hotels and restaurants over a period of 3 weeks. These were collected by 75 students and interviews were conducted to collect the data from frequent customers (who were specifically not students). Founded in service quality theory, the interviews ascertained satisfactory or dissatisfactory incidents from these customers. Data were analysed by three researchers who identified 12 categories in which to place the incidents. Conclusions clarify that their research supports new reasons for customer dissatisfaction and acknowledges that management and employee voices are missing here. Critical incident technique is praised for its ability to showcase customer perceptions through storied accounts; however, there is no clarification on when the incidents occurred. If participants were re-telling incidents from their past, there is a potential for the stories to be inaccurate. This is a weakness in the research which is not fully acknowledged. Service encounter demands are clearly classified in Figure 1.1 and could be used for further analysis with customer queries and staff responses.

Strauss, B. and Mang, P. (1999) Culture shocks in inter-cultural service encounters. *Journal of Services Marketing* 13 (4/5), 329–346.

Researchers from Germany again use the critical incident technique to elicit stories of customer satisfaction in restaurants. Founded in service quality literature, these authors seek to ascertain if culture poses an additional dimension to perceptions of service quality. Culture is based on definitions from Hofstede, Hall and Riddle, but this is limited. Cultural distance is noted, but cultural similarity and language are not. The USA, Japan and Germany are used as three countries of focus for the research. There are a number of issues with the methodology used here include only using male participants and that they are in business or first-class seats only. The primary concern with this study is that they presuppose the incident completed in international airports are usual cultural encounters. So encounters in a Japanese airport involves a Japanese server and foreign customer. Nowhere is this queried or acknowledged that an airport is, by its very nature, an international context and that staff working there will not necessarily be from the local area. It is also presumed that the participants travelling to Japan, the USA or Germany are from that culture. Again, this is not clarified in the article. Although there are some methodological issues noted here, this article does raise important consideration of how a service encounter may create a shock to the customer when meeting someone with a different background to theirs. What is not acknowledged is that the staff will consistently face these and deal with these and so perhaps be in more need of support here.

Question: Can you list the differences you might expect in an intercultural (different) and intracultural (same) service encounter? Write a list for each and compare these.

Weiermair, K. (2000) Tourists' perceptions towards and satisfaction with service quality in the cross-cultural service encounter: Implications for hospitality and tourism management. *Managing Service Quality* 10 (6), 397–409.

Austrian author, Weiermair, is professor of the Institute of Tourism and Service Economics. His article focuses on whether cultural norms need further review in the value chain for tourists. Rather than focusing on primary research on specific encounters, this article benefits from its larger, strategic approach to considering potential issues in cross-cultural customer encounters. Similarly to Strauss and Mang (1999), this paper looks to assess the intercultural aspects of service encounters and how this may affect customer satisfaction. Hofstede again is acknowledged as a founding author in cultural difference and its use is deemed appropriate due to previous studies in tourism management using the same definition. Cultural distance and proximity are again noted as fixed and unchanging. The tourist's prior experiences are not fully addressed and it is again presumed that tourists have difficulties or problems in cultures unlike their own. The issues considering global and local tourism management decisions are an interesting set of questions to consider in tourism studies.

Question: On page 400, the authors offer a figure on areas of cultural interference. What are your perceived cultural filters when visiting a new place?

Barker, S. and Härtel, C.E.J. (2004) Intercultural service encounters: An exploratory study of customer experiences. *Cross Cultural Management: An International Journal* 11 (1), 3–14.

Written by colleagues in the Deakin Business School, Victoria, Australia, this article offers primary research on service encounters in an airport, finance business and retail store in Brisbane City. Instead of critical incidents, these authors interviewed every fourth non-Anglo Celtic/Saxon appearing customer and asked them if they felt they had been treated differently as a customer owing to their race. Like Strauss and Mang's article, the authors did not ascertain whether the staff serving these customers were of a different race. By identifying the customers' race simply by review of their appearance and implying this is different to the server, there are obvious ethical issues with this research. The encounters are deemed intercultural without clarification of the nationalities of the people completing them either. The conclusions offer appropriate considerations for business management in that diversity training for staff will not stop staff judging or stereotyping customers, but simply draw their attention to law supporting protection of certain traits.

Question: Could the elements identified in table 1, on page 7 be due to reasons other than race? Why else would staff behave like this towards customers?

2 Staff-to-Staff Support for Service Encounters

Chapter Learning Objectives

(1) To outline the importance of staff-to-staff work in support of customer service encounters.

(2) To distinguish three types of staff-to-staff work required to support customer service encounters and how staff perceptions of these are crucial for customer satisfaction.

(3) To evaluate the different types of staff-to-staff work needed in customer service encounters.

Introduction

This chapter offers an alternative model of customer service encounters: staff-to-staff perspectives of service encounters in tourism, events and hospitality. The focus is on the staff-to-staff tenets of this context

rather than a customer-to-staff. Previous research in customer service encounters (discussed in Chapter 1) focuses on management-to-staff, customer-to-staff and customer-to-management relations. The staff-to-staff collaboration in the service encounter is relatively underdeveloped but seen as of vital importance. Historically, research on staff in tourism, events and hospitality focuses on their motivation, training and skilling. This chapter offers a new focus: staff perceptions on completing service encounters with colleagues and management included, or as a component part, of the service. Discussion centres on the incidents offered by staff working in tourism, events and hospitality roles. An alternative model of customer service encounters is outlined, and incidents are then offered for critique and reflection.

Staff-to-Staff in the Encounter

The customer service encounter literature noted in Chapter 1 identified that it requires 'person-to-person' interaction with customers (Solomon *et al.*, 1985: 99). A key finding from the study is that the encounters also require staff-to-staff interaction. This book contributes to knowledge on customer service encounters as it acknowledges colleagues, management and suppliers as components of these encounters also. These other people are seen as part of customer service encounter theory, as participants in the study had to satisfy and create experiences for them, much like their customers:

> One of the clients in particular was a woman who wanted a conference for next week, so I had a very, very short lead time and she couldn't decide what she wanted. She kept ringing up and making changes and when I received the brief from my client yesterday, she had just added a lot more changes to the whole booking as well as added a load of bedrooms on, which proved to be a bit of a problem because in Bristol at the moment, which is where she wanted the conference, there is graduation going on. So they don't actually have enough space for everyone.

> We managed to find a few hotels that actually could accommodate what she was looking for, and then she decided in the afternoon she wanted to change it again. Obviously my colleague was in her training session, so I have to solve it. (Holly)

The example above serves as one example of many gained from the study to portray how staff in tourism, events and hospitality roles have to satisfy a range of people in work as well as their customers. The key element of Holly's incident above is that she was not working alone but within a team. Her colleague, who usually deals with this client, was in a training course. Holly, therefore, had to work with this customer in her absence and utilise colleagues in other venues (suppliers) to find and source an appropriate venue. Although, and perhaps on first read, this incident may seem like it is focused on how the customer changed their requirements and how Holly completed these tasks for them, Holly noted in the stimulated recall how this was difficult due to it not being her usual customer and how she had to appease a range of venues to confirm a solution to the customer's requests. This incident evidenced how a range of people were needed in the service encounter and that suppliers and colleagues were not simply part of a long process, but immediately contributing and impacting the service offered.

Data from the study support current knowledge on the intangible nature and problems associated with person-to-person service (Bitner *et al.*, 1990; Nickson *et al.*, 2007; Reimann *et al.*, 2008; Ryoo, 2005; Sparks & Callan, 1992; Sparks & Greene, 1992; Solomon *et al.*, 1985; Surprenant *et al.*, 1987; Weiermair, 2000), but the analysis of data from the study also suggests a gap in acknowledgement of other people concerned with customer service encounters. Co-production (Binkhorst, 2005; Binkhorst & Dekker, 2009; Rihova *et al.*, 2015) and co-creation (Chathoth *et al.*, 2013; Lovelock & Young, 1979) are also present between these people and a variety of interpersonal skills (Sparks & Callan, 1992) are used to deal with these people in maintaining and achieving service quality (Parasuraman *et al.*, 1991). Co-creation and co-production are discussed in Chapter 7 and interpersonal skills in Chapter 3 within soft skills.

Evidently, results from these data support aspects of current theory. However, it is clear from the analysis of all the data from this study that the previous focus between customer and staff in customer service encounters does not do justice to the plethora of elements present (notably the other people). This section will identify how this key finding from the study adds an additional dimension to current customer service encounter theory, how it can be incorporated into new models of service delivery and how it can be incorporated into training for tourism, events and hospitality staff.

This additional dimension is present in incidents from all participants. Examples are listed below for clarification:

- Sophie had consistent support from management and colleagues when serving guests.
- Lucy supported her colleagues via translating customer requests.
- Holly completed a colleague's work while she was in training using external suppliers and other internal colleagues.
- Martha trained colleagues on financial processes to aid customer billing.
- Jessica trained new supervisors to support their roles.
- Tom worked in different departments to support his colleagues.

These examples support the co-production (Binkhorst, 2005; Binkhorst & Dekker, 2009; Rihova *et al.*, 2015) and co-creation

(Chathoth *et al.*, 2013; Lovelock & Young, 1979) literature discussed in Chapter 7 on how staff produce service in collaboration with others, but specifically identifies how team working skills and interdepartmental knowledge assisted participants in completing the service encounters (confirming the reports of People 1st, 2011, 2013).

Thus, three additional types of support are presented and require inclusion in future consideration of customer service encounters:

(1) Staff-to-colleague support.
(2) Staff-to-management support.
(3) Staff-to-supplier support.

What follows is the identification of how these dimensions were present in the study and how they could be incorporated into new models of service delivery.

Three Staff-to-Staff Elements of Service Encounters

Three types of face-to-face interactions were noted above and include colleagues, management and suppliers. This section will discuss each of these in consideration of the data from the study.

Starting with staff-to-colleague support, Lucy's role as door host was specifically to support colleagues in completing service encounters. She greeted and seated all customers arriving at the restaurant and introduced them to their servers who would take their orders and serve their food. In this role, she began the service for all customers and handed them over to colleagues noting any key requirements of service requested by the customer. She not only acted as the foundation of the service but was seen as part of a chain of service within a larger team. Lucy went further in this role and also identified how she would also 'step in' and assist colleagues when they were seen to be struggling in service encounters. The opening to the incident in Chapter 9 from Lucy entitled 'Making fun of customers' outlines this in full. Here, Lucy perceives her colleagues having difficulties talking to a customer owing to a difference in accent. Lucy chooses to approach the encounter and support her colleague's understanding of customer requirements.

Martha also stepped in to help colleagues when she saw a customer with young children struggling to enter their hotel room:

> As I was walking through the first floor corridor to get to reception, I walked past a guest who was struggling to access their bedroom. It seemed like the keycard wouldn't let in through the door. Then, this guest in particular, she had two small children with her. She had an awful lot of luggage. She looked like she was having a bit of a hard time. One of the children was crying, and I thought, 'Oh gosh.' (Martha)

Martha's role was as a financial assistant in an international hotel chain. On a usual day, she was located in an office, back of house. This incident evidenced how she naturally looked to support customers throughout the hotel, regardless of her current tasks. Instead of walking past this guest, she consciously decided to ask the customer how she could help. Subsequent to approaching the customer, Martha then went to reception to get a new keycard and went to the bar to and asked the bar manager to 'give me some activities that we give out to children, colouring books and things, to take up with me because I thought, "That'll keep them occupied while Mum unpacks."' Here, Martha not only completed an effective service encounter with the customer, but used her knowledge of the venue to liaise with other staff in the customer's absence to ensure the customer could gain entry to her accommodation and settle with her children as easily as possible. Martha could have informed the customer to go to the other staff and ask for assistance, but by using her initiative and compassion, she worked as part of an effective team to relieve the perceived stress of the guest.

Staff-to-staff support in service encounters supports the literature on co-construction (Binkhorst, 2005; Binkhorst & Dekker, 2009; Rihova *et al.*, 2015) and co-creation (Chathoth *et al.*, 2013; Lovelock & Young, 1979), but contributes further insight into how team-working knowledge and skills affect staff ability to produce these experiences. If Lucy and Martha did not know about their colleagues' roles within the service encounters, they would not have known how to 'step in' and provide support. These two examples from the data gained in the study show how staff are not simply aware of customer requirements, but also aware of how to complete encounters with colleagues as well. This additional dimension to customer service encounters brings about a wider range of skills and knowledge needed. Cross-department knowledge and team-working skills should therefore also be noted in service models for customer service encounters and not simply skills needed from employers (as noted in People 1st, 2011, 2013).

The second area seen in addition to current theory is that of staff-to-management support. Jessica was most notable here as she was asked to train colleagues in support of a new supervisor starting in the hotel:

> I'm training people behind the bar. Why do I need to work, train, think about my customers, think about room services, and train in the same time? Is that really my job? (Jessica)

Jessica worked as a temporary employee on a zero-hours contract (see Chapter 8 for clarification), as a food and beverage worker in a national hotel. Jessica was asked to help a new supervisor by training colleagues working behind the bar while they attended management training. As such, she was acting as a manager on behalf of an absent manager. Although she was happy to support her colleagues behind the bar, she felt she was training her manager also: 'I was training him.' Jessica was, therefore, acting as colleague and manager in support of management duties supporting service encounters. Further, Jessica was also trusted by her colleagues and asked to approach and liaise with management on their behalf:

> I said to him that we all need to do a job that is not in our responsibility, but what is important is that person is not getting paid in the first place. (Jessica)

This quotation is from Jessica's comments about an incident where she asked the management for information on her colleague's wages. Her colleague had not been paid and was not confident to raise this query directly. As Jessica had liaised with management on their behalf, she was asked why she was doing this. As you can note from her discussion of this, she felt her role was to support all colleagues, regardless of written responsibilities in her job description.

Both of these examples from Jessica evidence how staff are not simply a component of a hierarchy in a tourism, events or hospitality business, but also work across management levels in order to support customer service and maintain business operations. If staff are required to train and support management, they need recognition of this and skills to negotiate complex hierarchical roles, which may need to be flexible according to skills and abilities of new recruits into the business. As a long-standing member of staff, Jessica was also treated as a supervisor by her peers and completed management roles to support colleagues and management.

Finally, staff-to-supplier support was evident in the participant data. Holly liaised with venue management on a daily basis. This was a component of service encounters, as Holly had to ascertain supplier costs and contractual details from venues, and inform customers of feasible booking options:

> after persuading venues to keep holding on to the rooms for longer than they actually would have done for us, and actually one of the venues actually went above their regional manager to their director to try and secure this busy booking. (Holly)

Here, Holly acknowledges her ability to convince suppliers to hold venue space for her customers and how they also liaise with senior management to acquiesce to Holly's customer requirements. As an events sales assistant within an event venues business, Holly constantly liaises between customers and venue suppliers. However, within her incidents, it was evident that liaising required constant service to suppliers as well as customers. She was part of a supply chain that required her to have overall knowledge and control of the event contract and logistics.

Martha was also seen completing staff-to-supplier support for service encounters, as she had to liaise with external suppliers to the hotel, most notably tourism agents:

> So we would either speak to the client directly, or the agent would book on behalf of the client and we would have all of the contact with the agent and then the agent would have contact with the client. (Martha)

Unlike Holly, who worked separately to the venue, Martha worked as a finance officer at an international hotel. In this role, she not only liaised with suppliers to the hotel (e.g. laundry providers), but also agents for customers. Tourism agents booking for large groups of hotel guests were her usual staff-to-supplier support work. As such, Martha would need to liaise with the agent up until the customer arrived, and then directly with the customer after departure to settle their invoice.

These examples showed how customer service encounters utilise a much wider network of face-to-face interactions than current literature portrays. As service relies on products being consumed, it stands to reason that some staff will also work with suppliers to book and create a service for their customers.

To clarify these points, a model has been created to identify traditional, colleague, management and supplier service encounters (Figure 2.1). The model in Figure 2.1 incorporates the traditional customer-to-staff and customer-to-customer interplay within the service encounter literature and it is acknowledged that this was present in incidents from participants. However, this book improves this dyadic approach by adding colleague, management and supplier encounters.

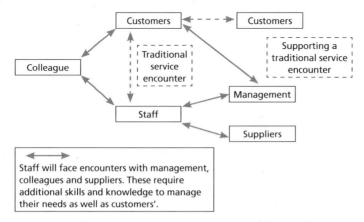

Figure 2.1 A model of service encounters incorporating staff-to-staff support required

This adds to the model of service delivery as it clarifies the others involved in creating and producing customer service in tourism, events and hospitality settings.

Within the staff-to-staff work completed in the incidents offered for the study, the following additions were acknowledged by staff:

(1) Cross-department knowledge is needed to support colleagues.
(2) Team working requires an appreciation of all business logistics and operations.
(3) Staff may act as manager and trainer across usual organisational hierarchies.
(4) Staff not only support management by completing successful service encounters with customers, but support colleagues by addressing colleague concerns to management.
(5) Persuasion, negotiation and liaising are required with suppliers in order to create and support service encounters.

Critical Incidents with Key Questions

From the discussion of the staff-to-staff work in service encounters, two full incidents from participants are now offered. These are offered to clarify the position in which staff perceived service encounters with colleagues, management and suppliers. Questions after each incident are offered to enable the reader to reflect on how they would react in a similar situation.

Local pronunciation of dishes (staff-to-management)

And, this situation happened the same day as well. In the late evening Robert (the manager) came to me and asked about what the soup of the day is. I said, 'Tomato and basil.' And he said that I need to say, 'Tomato.' Using the Mancunian accent because we are in Manchester and I said, 'Robert, you know what? I mean, I am a foreigner in UK and I understand, but I think my English is good enough.' Not to pronounce in a certain accent or something like that; and he said, 'No, we all need to speak in a Mancunian accent right now because he likes that.' And I said, 'If you're going to make me do that then I'm going to leave,' and he just laughed.

Then he asked me to repeat tomato again, and again, and again until he's got the point that I'm not going to change, so he said, 'Okay, fine then.' And he left, and I explained my situation, that I've been to university for three years and thought he'd know that. But I think my English is good enough and it's not written anywhere that you need to speak with a certain accent or with a certain dialect. So, I just told him that it's not going to happen.

Maybe he just trying to take the piss or something, but it just wasn't right to say; and made me really mad and it was really hard to open up to say anything to him in that moment; because he was just pissing me off. (Jessica)

Questions to consider from this incident:

(1) Jessica seems to have understood her manager's comments as being negative. How else could you have interpreted this encounter? What do you think the manager's intentions were?
(2) How do you think this management interaction with Jessica affected her mood and ability to complete service encounters?
(3) If Jessica pronounced tomato like a local Mancunian, how do you think other, non-UK national, customers would interpret this?
(4) How could Jessica have responded differently to this management request?

Confronting colleagues (staff-to-staff)

Today's been quite a stressful day, really. I've had a ... Not a confrontation, but I've had an interaction with a colleague of mine who is actually a really close colleague, she's probably one of my good friends within the hotel. But today I experienced a kind of communication which I really wasn't very comfortable with. I'm quite a ... I don't know how to say it. I'm quite a positive person. I don't like to get too stressed and I'm not very confrontational. As part of my job it's important for me to kind of ... In finance you've got to make sure that everything's ticking the right way. If things aren't controlled and if things aren't reporting to the right areas then your revenues are completely wrong and effectively then all of your balance sheets, your profits and losses counts, are wrong and then the accounts are void. And if we were ever audited, which we are audited quite often, then we would be in quite serious trouble.

So although I'm not very confrontational and I don't really like to cause confrontation, as part of my job it is important to constantly monitor the ways that things are reporting and if anybody's reporting anything the wrong way or doing something in the wrong process that they should be doing I have to tell them that, and find a balance of telling them that it's a bit wrong and showing them the right way to do it.

The communication that I had today with my colleague was: it started out something very simple. I received a purchase order from a client and I was phoning her to ask her if it belonged to one of her bookings so that I could forward it on to her so that she could make sure that she had all the details. It then turns out that the way that we had the room set up, the bedroom set up, in terms of invoicing it had been done the completely wrong way. And this colleague, she usually only deals with group bookings of 10 or more so she would never have to ... She would always invoice it onto a separate ... It's called a payment master so it's kind of like a separate bill, whereas all of our individual reservations they just get invoiced straight away to a different part of our system. So if it's groups of 10 or more it goes to a different part to if it's an individual reservation.

This booking in particular was for just one reservation but it was being invoiced in the way that we would do it for a group booking, and that was incorrect and it can cause quite a lot of problems. The booking is going to be in-house for 12 weeks and it meant the way that we were doing it we'd have revenue reporting for the month in a completely incorrect manner. So it was quite important for me just to question the way that she'd done it and to say, 'You don't need to do it this way. There's another way to do it, I can show you.' But she was getting really defensive and telling me that, 'It's going to be like this, you're going to have to speak to my manager if you're not happy with it.'

Then what I was trying to say to her was, 'Well, actually, there's another way to do it, which is the way that we do it for all of our other bookings', and that we can do that for this one. Anyway, she was being quite offensive and not letting me finish speaking and just saying, 'Well, how was I supposed to know that way? I would never know that way.' Just being quite negative and defensive. We weren't having a conversation, we were just having a discussion and it was just getting a little bit uncomfortable. To be honest, it kind of put me in a bad mood because I thought, 'Well, there's no need to be like that, you know. We're all just trying to do our job. I'm just trying to help you do it the right way.'

Anyway, she said she was busy and she needed to go because she had a conference call. And that was that, so we left it. But I went into my manager and I just said, 'You know, I'm really not happy with the way that was handled.' I said, 'I understand that people don't like being wrong.' I can quite openly admit when I'm wrong and I will just apologise and say, 'You know, I'm sorry, I've done it wrong.' But this one particular colleague, I know that from previous experiences she doesn't like to do that. So it was important for me to take that with a pinch of salt and to take that on board that I know that she doesn't like to be wrong.

In a way, the most important way to get out of this situation is that it's important that the job gets done the correct way, all of the way that the bedroom was done was being corrected. Sorry about that, I just had to go and answer a phone call. Yeah, I'm just coming back to where I was. The most important thing at the end of the day in these kind of situations is that the job gets done the correct way, is that you don't take these situations to heart and that you can move on from them. Don't let them stress you out, but at the same time don't just give in. It's still important that when these situations arise to still confront them, because at the end of the day everybody's got a job to do and we are only all doing our jobs.

About an hour later I did have a phone call from the colleague just saying, 'Oh, sorry about before. I was just in a rush and ...' So it was fine, she'd obviously had a bit of time to think and thought, 'Ooh, maybe I didn't handle that so greatly', and gave me a call back just to say 'no hard feelings' kind of thing, which I was completely happy with. The last thing that you want is to be causing confrontations with colleagues, especially ones that you are friends with outside of work as well. But sometimes it is just about getting the balance right of standing your ground and doing what you need to do, but at the same time not being argumentative about it as well, and remaining professional and calm at the same time, which I know can sometimes be easier said than done. But I think in this situation it worked out fine in the end. (Martha)

Questions to consider from this incident:

(1) What was Martha's intention in offering her colleague information on a different way to process the information on the system? How was this misunderstood?
(2) If you develop friendships in work, how would you deal with these friends when problems arise in their work?
(3) If tourism, events and hospitality roles naturally create inter-team friendships, how can management support these in professional contexts?

Summary

(1) To outline the importance of staff-to-staff work in support of customer service encounters,

staff in tourism, events and hospitality do not work individually, but in teams. As such, the binary element, of staff and customer, within service encounters is expanded upon in this chapter to appraise the colleagues, management and suppliers present in the delivery of the service. These will either be present in an ongoing process or immediate in the creation of a leisure or business experience.

(2) To distinguish three types of staff-to-staff work required to support customer service encounters and how staff perceptions of these are crucial for customer satisfaction,

Staff-to-staff, staff-to-management and staff-to-supplier support work for service encounters was presented. These were all evident from staff perspectives in tourism, events and hospitality and evidenced a wider number of people present in creating the encounters. Knowledge of internal and external operating procedures, customer requirements linked to suppliers, and skills in negotiation and persuasion were used within these.

(3) To evaluate the different types of staff-to-staff work needed in customer service encounters.

This chapter is based on Chapter 1's review of customer service encounter theory. The discussion offered here moves current knowledge forwards by presenting a model of customer service encounters with the addition of colleagues, management and suppliers. These are all seen as supporting components in the delivery of effective service encounters by staff. Within tourism, events and hospitality management, no service encounter is simply between two people creating one service. Colleagues and management are ever-present in service delivery and this chapter has highlighted how they can support or negatively affect staff. Acknowledging the other people present in the service encounter will enable staff to seek and offer support in their encounters with customers. Another key aspect to acknowledging managers and suppliers is how they are also seen by staff as creating separate service encounters to the customers. Staff need to understand management and supplier needs and react professionally to encounters and demands made by these people. Supporting and working with colleagues is intricately linked in delivery of service encounters in tourism, events and hospitality. Team working is not simply a consideration, but an obligation to deliver the service.

Annotated bibliography

Nyquist, J. et al. (1985) Identifying communication difficulties in the service encounters: A critical incidents approach. In J. Czepiel, M. Solomon C. Surprenant(eds) *The Service Encounter* (pp. 195–212). MA: Lexington Books.

This book chapter from the first and only edition of *The Service Encounter* offers research completed in restaurants, hotels and airlines. One hundred and thirty-one interviews were completed with staff working in these locations to ascertain communication issues present when staff deal with their customers. The chapter focuses on how most service companies prescribe operational duties well, but when it comes to customer service, there is simply a line in the employee handbook indicating how staff need to offer excellent service. Based upon the premise that all customer service encounters support marketing efforts, this chapter analyses 131 interviews with staff to identify what demands are made of customers to help identify to management the types of demands their staff need to manage. Interestingly, the main type of demand made by customers is a product or service that is not offered by the hotel. The discussion and conclusions offered in this chapter address management concerns in service encounters, rather than how the staff should manage their understanding and expectations of service encounters.

Question: On page 202, consider the three difficult interactions in group 2. How can these be managed so that they do not occur?

Sparks, B. and Callan, V.J. (1992) Communication convergence and the service encounter: The value of. *International Journal of Hospitality Management* 11 (3), 213–224.

Both authors are from Queensland, Australia, but write from differeing institutions (Sparks from Griffith University and Callan from the University of Queensland). Their desk-based research in this article focuses on communication standards required in hospitality contexts when serving intangible products (service in the service encounter). Communication accommodation theory (CAT) is analysed in relation to service quality features (RATER) to consider how verbal, non-verbal and vocal elements of speech need to be appropriate to all guests. Culture shocks are also noted as important for tourists in hospitality contexts and that these can make customers feel anxious, surprised and confused. Without stereotyping or suggesting a difference between the staff and customer in large cultures (Holliday, 1999) this paper has some salient points on how staff in hospitality should use communication procedures to offer effective service to all customers. In-house training, as well as effective recruitment, are identified as important components of maintaining a workforce who can deliver satisfactory service encounters.

Question: The authors refer to staff using 'foreigner talk' (page 221) in service encounters with foreigners. What do you think this talk involves and how does it manifest in verbal, non-verbal and vocal communication offered?

Nickson, D., Warhurst, C. and Dutton, E. (2007) The importance of attitude and appearance in the service encounter in retail and hospitality. *Managing Service Quality* 15 (2), 195–208.

Based at the University of Strathclyde, Glasgow, UK, these authors offer discussion and analysis of a survey distributed to management in retail and hospitality businesses in Glasgow. The focus of the survey is on understanding what management look for in new applicants and how they train new entrants to serve customers intangible products in a service encounter. Like other references noted, Parasuraman *et al*.'s (1985) service quality model is used here to identify previous theories on customer perceptions of service encounters. Focus in this article is on how the employee's appearance communicates politeness and professionalism to customers. These authors are passionate about the aesthetics of employees and how this requires management in order to communicate effectively with customers. However, they do not consider the employee's perspective on being required to wear uniforms and how these costumes could also affect their individual and natural responses in service encounters. I agree that new entrants need to be made aware of the potential uniform and presentation skills required, but again these are individual and objective to each entrant.

Question: Think about the uniform of a person serving drinks at a national music festival and a person serving drinks at a bar in a luxury hotel. Both of these are hospitality services at an event delivered to a range of tourists. What would customers expect staff to wear and how would this be interpreted if it were different to the expected?

3 Soft Skills in Service Encounters

Chapter Learning Objectives

(1) To present issues in the professionalisation of staff working, and academics publishing research, in tourism events and hospitality.
(2) To recognise definitions of, and key authors on, soft skills.
(3) To formulate an awareness of issues presented for soft skills development for staff in tourism, events and hospitality.
(4) To examine communication forms used in customer service encounters in working contexts.

Introduction

This chapter focuses on soft skills and identifies how these are used within service encounters. To begin, an overview of the professionalisation of the sectors and staff issues within tourism, events and hospitality is offered. This will outline the working context in which staff complete working duties. Following this, current knowledge on soft skills for tourism, events and hospitality is offered to clarify the core

skills associated with soft skills for service encounters. After this discussion, communication methods are presented and discussed to evidence how these skills are paramount for service encounters. Storied incidents are then detailed to enable the reader to consider soft skills and communication in practice. Four topics within communication are addressed through these stories: non-verbal communication; working with different vocal accents; benefits of the phonetic alphabet; and dealing with rude customers. These four areas are illustrative of the types of skills and knowledge used when producing soft skills in service encounters.

Employment and Research Professionalised

Before the discussion on soft skills, it is necessary to outline two key background issues: the employment for staff and research within tourism, events and hospitality. The professionalisation of work and research in these sectors is seen as an important context in which to discuss these skills as they have had an impact on the way in which skills are viewed in industry and academia. Soft skills for these sectors are accepted in this book as unique owing to the intangible and personalised nature of service encounters; however, they are not always perceived highly-valued skills across industry and academia.

At present, there is no mandatory post-graduate study required to work within tourism, events, and hospitality businesses. Employers in these sectors have also noted that their staff require level 4 (first year of degree) qualifications in order to gain and complete a role successfully (People 1st, 2011). This low level of qualification is due to a perceived lack of professionalisation within these industries and the associated low skills needed to complete employment roles (Burns, 1997). Henry (1993) suggested that professionalising employment within businesses providing leisure experiences was emergent in the UK in the 1980s and was due to city councils creating departments who had a responsibility in developing leisure services. Prior to this, workers in leisure sectors (such as those working in tourism, events and hospitality) were seen as being semi-professional (Henry, 1993). This perceived emergence of leisure as a profession was noted in conjunction with the emergence of tourism, events and hospitality (Lashley & Morrison, 2007). Publications on the emergence of the professionalisation of tourism, events and hospitality roles suggest that work was not seen as a core, nor highly skilled profession before the 1980s in the UK (Burns, 1997; Baum, 1996, 2006). This emergence of professionalism in tourism, events and hospitality was linked to the shift in Western economies from product manufacturing to services.

Laing (2018) and Baum *et al.* (2016) outlined the need for events (Laing) and hospitality (Baum *et al.*) management research to be included with tourism research. This is due to a perception within the academic literature that tourism studies are higher ranking than events and hospitality. This is interesting, as it is apparent that all three disciplines refer to the same workers, service environments and operations. The segmentation is due to research publication titles specifying a link to one or two, but not all three sectors (unless education or training are noted). In order to support future appreciation of research for festivals and tourism, Laing (2018) suggests academics avoid the 'narrow' labels within disciplines and sectors, and instead seek to complete research using wider positions. This book, although using tourism, events and hospitality in the title, does this by acknowledging the overlapping definitions of these sectors. The service encounters are not delineated according to the sector, but grouped according to the forms of experience, activity and skills presented.

Mooney and Ryan (2009), Robinson *et al.* (2014) and Solnet *et al.* (2015) all present issues in human resource management for tourism, events and hospitality. These include gender imbalance, increase in technology use leading to less staff and a lack of strategic human resource management. These issues are presented here in order to suggest that staff ability to utilise skills is not simply due to them being trained, but by being offered good working conditions and clear benefits and rewards within the company (Robinson & Barron, 2007). The initiative, motivation and self-esteem of these staff will contribute towards their stickability within the company.

The professionalisation of employment and research in tourism, events and hospitality have been discussed here to provide a backdrop to the skills issues and debates present. If employers and researchers used staff perspectives on these, instead of management and customer ones, they would find passionate, enthusiastic and driven people who want to complete a rewarding and satisfying job to the best of their ability.

The Ever-Present Skills Debate

Soft skills have received much academic attention in the last 20 years as it is seen as a vital component for offering good customer service, and thus, customer satisfaction. The need for higher-skilled staff and the evident skills shortages in the tourism, events and hospitality industries are also an identified and well-researched area among tourism, events and hospitality-focused academics (Baum, 2007, 2008; Burns, 1997; Lashley, 2009; Westwood, 2002).

The UK sector skills council for tourism, events and hospitality (People 1st, 2011, 2013) frequently publish data on the lack of soft skills in current applicants which industry roles require. These missing soft skills are seen as endemic in tourism, events and hospitality industries and are often seen as contrary to the general capabilities of a nation:

Given that nations are capable of producing Prime Ministers, Senior Military Officers, Lawyers, and Doctors, the difficulties found in producing a skilled pastry chef or an effective hotel manager is little short of astounding. (Burns, 1997: 244)

This quotation from Burns (1997) underlines the difficulty that tourism, events and hospitality business managers have in finding staff with the necessary skills. Here, Burns (1997) suggests that the lack of skilled applicants for kitchens is 'little short of astounding', suggesting that the skilling shortages are shocking to him. If the UK is able to produce staff for roles requiring more skills and knowledge, it seems odd to Burns (1997) that the soft skills are lacking for tourism, events and hospitality roles. This shortage could be due to the roles being seen as transient ones.

Within published academic literature on tourism, events and hospitality, interpersonal and soft skills are used in tandem and refer to similar skilling requirements for these staff. In tourism, events and hospitality research, Nickson *et al.* (2011) use soft skills to refer to interpersonal and intrapersonal skills; Bailly and Léné (2012) and Nickson *et al.* (2005) use soft skills to infer social and interpersonal skills; and Baum's research (Baum, 1996, 2006, 2007, 2008; Baum & Nickson, 1998) focuses on soft skills as interpersonal skills. To exemplify this, Table 3.1 considers just two papers from Sparks and Callan (1992) and Burns (1997). The types of behaviour and skills are listed in Table 3.1 to identify the similarities between these two terms.

Table 3.1 clarifies how tourism, events and hospitality skilling authors focus on the same types of staff behaviour when researching interpersonal or soft skills. Since these early articles, and as noted above, research has primarily focused on soft skills as the term with which to explain the types of skills needed in tourism, events and hospitality education and training. Furthermore, subsequent UK government reports (Dearing Report, 1997; Leitch, 2006;) on skilling in the UK also refer to soft skills rather than interpersonal skills. Thus, this text uses 'soft skills' as the term with which to infer both soft and interpersonal skilling.

Table 3.1 Interpersonal and soft skill staff attributes

Sparks and Callan (1992) – interpersonal skills	Burns (1997) – soft skills
Verbal and non-verbal communication	Verbal and non-verbal communication
Eye contact	Emotional behaviour
Attitude	Attitude
Behaviour	Empathy
Perceptions of people	
Motivation	
Social competence	

Source: based on Burns (1997) and Sparks and Callan (1992)

In terms of the context in which the current literature positions the use of these soft skills, it appears that they are needed in customer service encounters to deliver effective customer service and produce what Burns (1997: 240) calls the production of 'unreality'. Soft skills are needed when communicating and interacting with customers in an industry to create, perform and deliver tourism, events and hospitality experiences. Burns (1997) calls a customer service encounter in tourism, events and hospitality 'unreality' because customers are receiving an intangible service, part of which is intangible and unquantifiable, from graduates/staff. This ephemeral characteristic is perceived and experienced differently by each guest.

Textbooks for hospitality training often segment customers in tourism, events and hospitality according to their reason for visiting (e.g. tourism, events and hospitality versus business guest) (Chon & Maier, 2009; Hassanien, 2010; Smith & Warburton, 2012). This segmentation is to ensure that the business understands guests' needs and satisfies them through service. Thus, staff are not simply using their soft skills to replicate the same form of interaction, but creating varied 'unreal' experiences for different groups of guests with the aim of satisfying each one individually. Lashley's (2000) book on hospitality retail management problematises customer segmentation; however, by noting that the standard hospitality customer groups are no longer simple, stratified groups, in that:

> the same hospitality retail customers may visit different types of premises for different reasons and different times of the week. (Lashley, 2000: 287)

Therefore, customer groups do not demand the same services, products or experiences in every encounter and they may require these in a range of tourism, events and hospitality businesses throughout the week. This discussion has shown that the context of these soft skills is that of an 'unreal' space and that the skills are demanded by a range of customers who arrive with a variety of requirements and preconceptions. This context suggests that soft skills are neither general nor robotic, but need to be adaptable, flexible and reflexive for each service encounter. Staff members also need an ability to assess and analyse consistently what skills and knowledge are needed (as stated in the customer service encounter review in Chapter 1).

Soft Skills and Baum

To examine the soft skilling literature and issues within this research further, Professor Tom Baum's work will now be reviewed. Baum's work focuses on tourism, events and hospitality education and employee training both in the UK and internationally. His research spans the last

35 years on soft skilling and has followed the progress of issues and debates in this field. The discussion here will focus upon the general perceptions and importance of soft skills in tourism, events and hospitality, the viewpoint from which these skills are analysed and, finally, industry problems in maintaining a workforce with adequate soft skills.

Issues identified by Baum include how hospitality roles were deemed to be low- or semi-skilled, which was seen as an incorrect assumption of the skills used (Baum, 1996). Tourism, events and hospitality work being deemed as low or unskilled was noted as being an inappropriate portrayal of these roles owing to the inherent international dimension of the industry and multiple soft skills needed (Baum, 1996). This historical denigrating perception of tourism, events and hospitality work is also highlighted by People 1st (2011), which suggests that this perception is still felt throughout the sectors and, therefore, can lead to recruitment problems. Perceiving skills for tourism, events and hospitality work to be low or unskilled means that there has been a consistent 'myth that undermines their (staff) contribution' (Lucas, 2004: 31). Undermining the work and employee contribution to service owing to a poor perception of soft skills is an issue in the literature, as it suggests that the work is easy and menial. Baum's argument in 1996 was that this inadequate perception of soft skills needed addressing to support managers and staff in tourism, events and hospitality businesses. Later, research by Bailly and Léné (2012: 87) noted that, actually, most employers still do not 'fully understand' how these skills are demanded. The study completed sought to ascertain this by examining graduate workers' perceptions of soft skills in customer service encounters.

The next issue to be noted from Baum's work on soft skilling is the perspective from which these soft skills are analysed. Tourism, events and hospitality workers interact and serve guests who derive from a range of backgrounds and requirements. This means that the soft skills used are complex (Baum, 2002a). Baum and Nickson (1998) identify the weakness in this position is that soft skills research only focuses on service quality from the customers' perspective, when it should consider both employer and staff perspectives. Tourism, events and hospitality industry employers are consistently reporting a lack of soft skills (People 1st) in their applicants and by judging these skills in relation to customer service quality, current research appears not to engage fully with the variety of perspectives available. Hassanien (2010: 95) offered a partial response to this by noting that staff should be treated as 'internal customers' and served by their managers, but there is no clear definition or account of the service encounters and customer demands that require these skills. This book seeks to understand these from graduate perspectives in order to understand this problem from their perspective.

Baum's early work clearly sought to dispel the belief that tourism, events and hospitality skills are low or unskilled, and identified this through an examination of customer service encounters with international guests. This initial research on skilling for tourism, events and hospitality was in response to the negative connotations given to tourism, events and hospitality workers' skills, and identifies that there is a historical issue surrounding the importance of soft skilling and the perspective from which it is interrogated.

From Baum's research on soft skills, it is apparent that they are vitally important in tourism, events and hospitality businesses. Baum's research spans the developments in soft skills research in the tourism, events and hospitality industry and education, and identifies how diversification in labour markets, international travel and education have all affected the way in which soft skills are now prioritised. This is a shift from the 1980s and 1990s, when technical skills were prioritised by educators and industry, until now, when soft skills are seen as a priority. The poor perception of these skills has meant that there has been a negative perception of the skills needed to work in tourism, events and hospitality. Despite this perception, it is evident that soft skills are needed in staff working in the industry. By researching soft skills from a customer perspective in relation to service quality, the current literature does not fully address how staff perceive these skills. It is clear that industry cannot sustain training for soft skills on the job; therefore, it is imperative that students in tourism, events and hospitality look to develop these skills and address this deficit noted in the industry. Chapters 4 and 5 consider emotional, aesthetic and sexualised labour theory requires staff to create and perform specific behaviour, attitudes and communication in service encounters.

Communication in Service Encounters

To explore soft skills in practice, this section will now discuss communication. As every service encounter requires interaction between two or more people, communication is vital for the success of the encounter. A variety of stories will be presented after this discussion, in order to view these skills from staff perspectives.

Communication is accepted as a soft skill used to express yourself and respond to others (Chan, 2011; Jackson, 2010, 2012; Yorke, 2006). The context and individuals with whom you communicate will alter your approach and forms of communication offered. In order to discuss forms of communication, soft skills, verbal and non-verbal communication will be identified. Communication is not simply a rigid response, but a variety of methods to convey meaning appropriately and professionally. Therefore, barriers to effective communication are also important to consider staff perspectives within service encounters.

As customer service encounters are linked to an intercultural delivery of services (see Chapter 1), the definition of communication presented here is from an intercultural position. There are a range of definitions and models on communication and it is accepted that this is inconclusive regarding all positions related to this topic. Clyne (1994: 3) suggested that communication has three approaches:

(1) Contrastive Approach – native language across cultures
(2) Interlanguage Approach – non-native speakers in a second language
(3) Interactive Inter-cultural Approach – communication between two people of differing cultural and linguistic backgrounds using a lingua franca or one of the interlocutor's languages. (Clyne, 1994: 3)

Native speakers across cultures are evident when British and US speakers of English communicate. Non-native speakers could include a person who can use a language owing to parental influence in teaching it to their child in a different country. They are non-natives of the country of their parent, but they may still be able to communicate in this second language with other natives. The interactive intercultural approach, for example, would be a French or German national choosing to communicate in Italian (if this is seen as the common lingua franca for them). How you convey politeness, manners and agreement within this communication and native language compared with others could be a potential barrier to effective communication.

Communicating agreement in a verbal language is clear in all native tongues (if you understand their language). However, when communicating a non-verbal agreement there are intercultural differences noted within the contrastive approach. Nodding your head up and down is a way of an understanding agreement in the USA, most of Europe and India, for example. Conversely, in countries such as Lebanon, Syria, Turkey and Egypt, people nod their heads up and down to convey 'no'. In India, they also offer a head bobble in agreement to communication. These are examples of where non-verbal communication in different native languages could cause miscommunication. If someone is trying to speak English and does not know the word for yes, they may use non-verbal gestures to convey this.

Verbal and non-verbal differences in communication are clear when considering an intercultural lens; however, interpretation of this will depend on your previous experiences of language. If you have completed service encounters with customers from a range of native languages, you may already be aware of the subtle differences. Further, Williamson and Chen (2018: 7) noted that when English is not a native language for customers or staff, staff may choose to use this in order to 'minimise guest embarrassment'. Therefore, language choice is not only something required to complete effective communication, but also seen as a soothing or comforting tool to aid tourist entry into a leisure experience.

Communication is not only linked to language development (native and non-native language), but also links to awareness of politeness,

Table 3.2 Personal and professional telephone conversation

Personal	Professional
1. Answer when available.	1. Answer within three rings.
2. Welcoming the caller by name and ascertaining the reason for the call.	3. Noting your name on answer followed by asking how you can assist them.
4. Using colloquial and informal language.	5. Using professional terms and formal language.
6. Talking at length about personal or private issues.	7. Keeping the discussion to a minimum and ensuring you clarify how you will assist.
8. Ending with a personal clarification of your feeling of satisfaction with the discussion.	9. Ending professionally by thanking them for their time.

Source: Firth (2019)

attitudes and manners. Different contexts will require you to communicate using different professional scripts and schemas. Service encounter incidents from participants in the study not only noted differences in these scripts, but different processes used to complete the communication. To evidence this, telephone conversation etiquette is noted in Table 3.2.

By aligning personal and professional telephone call schema it is clear how differences in communication are not simply verbal or non-verbal, but are context and person-specific also. If you applied the usual methods of a personal telephone call to a professional one you might find the other person is confused and unsure why you are acting 'familiar' with them. However, personalisation is also accepted as a required component of service encounters. As such, it is noted that selecting and using appropriate communication is a complex soft skill.

Through a brief overview of communication as a soft skill, it is clear that staff need to understand the potential forms of communication that may be presented in service encounters. If there is no lingua franca between the two people in the encounter, non-verbal gestures may ensue and these need to be interpreted and presented clearly. Politeness and manners are present in all communication points, but because of the personalisation needed in service encounters, it is accepted that some communication points may fluctuate between formal and informal content. Use the following four incidents to consider how communication was used in a service encounter and how one might act and react in a similar position.

Critical Incidents with Key Questions

Non-verbal communication

German customer came to bar, ordered two Guinness, was using mainly sign language, and pointing. Didn't speak much English. Ordered crisps. When asked what flavour said, 'Not much English', so I brought a selection of three different types over to him and tried to communicate as best we could. All resolved fine. (Tom)

Today I get assigned to the bar section. I saw a guy raise his hand with me, so I decided to walk to him and ask what he needs. He asked for a cup of tap water, but said it as 'I need a water', so I assumed he wanted a bottle of water.

When I brought a bottle of water to him, he told me he asked for a cup of tap water, and not a bottle of water. Then he even asked whether I understand English. So I told him that when he said water, without mention of tap water I assumed he would like to have a bottle of water. Because if he needed a cup of tap water, why not just tell me that he needed a cup of tap water.

The customer talked to the manager, and the manager comforted the customer with not charging for the bottle of water. The manager told me that it's not my fault, some customers deliver their message in different way, so it's fine for me to have made this mistake. I should just bear in mind for the next time. (Sophie)

Questions to consider from these incidents:

(1) Neither customers in these incidents specifically state which product they required. What was needed to better understand their needs?
(2) Could Sophie have asked more questions to clarify the order? Why do you think she did not clarify the type of water requested?
(3) Do you have examples of when a customer speaks to a manager about your service? How does this make you feel?
(4) If Tom's customer did not like the crisps taken, what action would the customer have taken to change these?
(5) How would you manage a customer who did not speak the same language as you? Use role play to complete a service encounter where a customer requests something without full language ability.

Working with different vocal accents

Today there was an Irish mother and her son. The Irish lady was in her late 50s and her son was in his 30s somewhere and they happened to meet two of our most Spanish members of staff at the front door. Rachel (manager), who's a manager and Chloe (staff), who's new to learning English and is being trained at the moment sort of. She's been there about a week now.

Basically, there was a big, massive breakdown in communication. The Spanish girls couldn't understand Irish accents, and the Irish mother and son couldn't understand the Spanish girls at all, really. I stepped in and played translator.

My observation of this was firstly, that the Irish mom and son were getting more and more frustrated as they were having to repeat themselves. Getting annoyed. Generally my observation of people in the Hospitality industry, not being understood, they seem against to take ... Like I said in my first observation, they seem to take offence ... People take offence to things like this. It seems like they can't understand why people can't understand them when they are, in fact, speaking English. But then, I don't think people from Northern Ireland are aware of how difficult it is to understand them if you've never come across their accent before, or if English is your second language.

They seemed to all be getting quite frustrated with each other and there was loads of miscommunication, but the bigger observation was that by the time they had been seated and made placed an order ... Chloe had asked if they wanted crushed or sliced garlic, because she didn't really understand that there was just already pre-made garlic mayo and when they finally got the bottom of what they wanted to order, I overheard Chloe that in Spain you converse a lot more with people in the hospitality industry. You have a big chat. You really get to the nitty gritty of what people want, what they'd prefer, and you tend to make things more for the individual customers. Whereas in England, Rachel's observation was that you should rather just keep it simple. If they order something that's on the menu, just serve it as it is. English people prefer to just not go through the hassle of having to answer loads of different questions and it just makes life easier for everyone and that was her cultural observation.

For me, I'm not too sure I agree with that, because I think everybody likes to be given options and as long as you know where to stop, not to ask too many questions, I think it's just ... It's something you should be able to tell judging by the reactions of the person you're speaking to. It was interesting to see that that was what the Spanish staff had sort of come to the conclusion that that was ... That you're better off just keeping it simple and keeping it brief when it comes to serving English people. (Lucy)

Questions to consider from this incident:

(1) How did Lucy know that her colleagues needed assistance?
(2) Why did the staff member offer different types of garlic mayonnaise? Was this correct?
(3) What nationality did the manager think the customers were? What does Lucy note they are? How could this difference in perception be seen as potentially problematic?

(4) Have you viewed customer encounters completed by others and thought 'I would have dealt with that person differently'? If so, what was is about the service which you would have changed?

The phonetic alphabet

The experience that I want to talk about today is something that I've been experiencing probably now from the beginning of June, and it's something that I experience on a daily basis, but today there's a particular example which I can talk about today. What it relates to is it's a communication experience and it's when I'm on the telephone and I have a client calling me and I need to give out my email address. We've recently been given new email addresses and they're really difficult to say over the phone. It used to just be 'first name.surname@hotelname.com.' and that was really easy. Everyone knows how to spell 'Hotel name' and then '.com', so it was really simple.

We've now been given new ones and I think that the person that created these obviously didn't realise how they would be used in day-to-day life. Anyway, so it's 'name.surname', the email, and then it's @thehotelname.co.uk. So it sounds okay, but the 'hotel name' is the tricky bit. So it's 'the', which is T-H-E, H, the letter, A-N-D, and then 'hotelname.co.uk.' It's something that not just me has experienced, it's probably everybody in the hotel that's had to give out their email over the phone. Something that has been an invaluable tool in helping the communication is using a phonetic alphabet and being able to say, 'T for tango', etc. That's something that's really helped.

Sometimes when you're on the phone and you're speaking with ... A lot of the agents that I speak with are based in different countries, so I've got one in particular which is based in Spain. I've got another one which is based in Germany. Being able to have this phonetic alphabet has meant that everybody can understand. If I spell it out phonetically everybody will be able to get it straightaway. I know that it sounds like it's not too much of a problem, but when you're trying to give it out every day and there's quite a few people that don't understand it, it can become a problem.

Because say if I'm asking the client to send me over bank details so that I can process a payment, if I don't give out the email address and they don't understand it correctly I'll never receive them. And sometimes if it's a client phoning up directly I might not take their phone number to call them back in case they don't, so I'm reliant on them being able to take down the email address fully, because I, in quite a lot of cases, would not have the contact details to call them back. And then that would be a communication problem in itself and that would also lead to quite a lot of day-to-day problems.

> *So I think what I'm trying to say is it's really important to use and to know the phonetic alphabet, whatever job you may have. If you're customer facing, if you only speak to customers over the phone, even if you're dealing with people, colleagues and things, I think that knowing that phonetic alphabet and being able to have that communication is invaluable. And I use it on a day-to-day basis probably most times that I'm on the telephone. Maybe not most times, but at least half of the times that I'm on the telephone. Especially with my name being 'Surname', quite a lot of people would not know how to spell that. It's not something as simple as Jones. So, again, that's something where it would come into play. (Martha)*

Questions to consider from the incident:

(1) Have you ever used the phonetic alphabet when speaking on the phone? Is this easy/appropriate?
(2) Apart from the phonetic alphabet, what other tactics could you use to communicate information over the phone with a customer?
(3) This incident shows a different role in a different form of service encounter. What other roles and encounters are possible within a large hotel?

Dealing with rude customers

> *Today, I experienced a really rude client who phoned demanding to speak to my colleague who works in accounts payable regarding payment of an invoice which was overdue for payment.*
>
> *Now, we changed ownership with the hotel in June and we're now a franchise of 'Hotel name' rather than a fully managed property. Along with that changeover, there's been quite a few different things we do in the finance office to how we used to do them.*
>
> *One of those is making our own payments. Usually our 'Hotel name' head office used to make all the payments for us, but now they're going to be paid on property. There's been a changeover where all of the invoices before May have been paid by 'Hotel name' and anything after June is being paid by ourselves. As we have had this whole new changeover, we've also had brand new finance systems in place. We've had to have training over the past month of June of how to fully work the system and actually make the payments.*
>
> *There has been a delay in all of our payments which is why we have had quite a few of our clients, our suppliers, sorry phoning up*

querying why they haven't been paid. We had this one particular guest who phoned up today and spoke to me. She was just so rude.

Everything about the way the phone call went, from the very beginning, she just used a really negative tone. She was really quick and sharp. I think automatically when you speak to somebody on the phone like that, it can make you a little bit defensive. It can make you not want to help the guest as much naturally. I think it does that to a lot of people.

I know that she's been really getting on my colleague's nerves now. She's been phoning every day hounding. The thing is, it's really out of our hands, this payment. Until we get the from our finance director, until he authorises the payment, it won't go into her bank. From our side, we've done everything that we can. It's not that we're trying to be awkward and delay the payment, there is just a genuine delay in this month's payment room.

Going forward from August and going on, we'll be able to make them really easily, but because this payment is of such high value because we've got the back log, it's got to be authorised by our finance director. We were trying to relay this to the lady on the phone today. She was just being so rude and defensive. She was asking really personal questions like, 'How have you been paid? Have you been paid this month? How come they've managed to pay your wage, but they've not managed to pay me?'

This payment is 30 days old, which from a credit control point of view, I know that is not an old payment. Some of the payments on my ledger are over 90 days. Some of them are even over 120 days. There the payments that I could understand if I was having rude phone calls about, but from working in accounts receivable myself, I know that sometimes however hard somebody might try on the phone, if they can't make that payment, they physically can't do it. There's no point in being really rude to them. I just think sometimes attitudes like that, they just don't help the situation.

Myself, I know that I've found from trying to chase money myself, if you're polite and you do everything in a polite manner, you usually do get a lot further which I know goes against the stereotypes of you've got to chase that money. You've got to get it in the bank and be firm, but I do think there needs to be a balance of being firm, but also being polite at the same time.

I think that this one particular lady, I know it sounds awful, but you end up not wanting to help the supplier if that's how they're acting. That was quite challenging.

You don't know what pressure, this lady might be on commission for getting payments in below a certain amount of time. You don't know. They are doing their job which you have to appreciate, but at the same time we're doing our job and sometimes there are slight delays which are above and beyond, which in this case it was.

I think you've just got to be flexible sometimes in these situations. (Martha)

The first critical incident that occurred was on 11th January while I was dealing with customers through Facebook. As part of our marketing push for deposits and awareness, a competition was posted on Facebook where individuals could win a free place on a camp of their choice. As part of this competition it stated that flights were not included and that they were to be paid separately. As a follow on from this I received a few rude messages from a woman who strongly stated that she thought flights should be part of the competition and that she should be the one that wins. I had the task of responding to her in a way that made it clear this wasn't going to happen while also remaining polite and keeping up good customer service. This was also made more complicated as the woman I was speaking to didn't speak English and so I found it difficult to express myself in the way that I wanted to, as the women also probably felt! As a travel company there are many times that one would be speaking to customers from different countries and so understanding and learning how to express yourself effectively is key. (Beth)

Questions to consider from these incidents:

(1) What does a rude customer sound like on the phone and read like in writing?
(2) In your experience, what are the usual reactions to rude customers?
(3) What does politeness entail? How do you create it?
(4) How do you manage your own feelings as a result of rude customers at work?

Summary

(1) To present issues in the professionalisation of staff working, and academics publishing research, in tourism, events and hospitality.

As world economies have shifted from product to services, so too has the professionalisation of employment in tourism, events and hospitality. However, with the low skilled and low qualification entry routes, these sectors are still recognised as unprofessional by some. Research in tourism, events and hospitality is also seen as ranked differently, although the real-life contexts may overlap all three. Human resource management for these sectors is seen to be the location of measuring and developing skills for employment and promotion. Issues of gender, technology and lack of strategy are acknowledged within human resource management. In order for staff perspectives to be seen as utilising high-level skills, further professionalisation of employment and research is needed. Research completed in the study underpinning this book outlines how this can be achieved by utilising staff from all three sectors and ignoring the usual delineations present.

(2) To recognise definitions of, and key authors on soft skills.

Baum is noted as a key author in soft skills for tourism, events and hospitality. Spanning 35 years, his research has outlined issues in skills and operational requirements of human resource management within the sectors. Soft skills are seen to include communication, empathy, awareness, attitude, behaviour, motivation and social competence.

(3) To formulate an awareness of issues presented for soft skills development for staff in tourism, events and hospitality.

Issues in soft skilling literature included perceptions of low skill use and using service quality as a lens to consider skills from customers and not staff. These make soft skills appear as deficient in the three sectors when actually they are highly complex abilities performed consistently with a range of customers, suppliers and management. If good service is based upon customers perceiving more than adequate standards of service delivery, then it stands to reason that the skills to produce this are equally more than adequate.

(4) To examine communication forms used in customer service encounters in working contexts.

Three forms of verbal communication from an intercultural lens were offered. These were outlined and then discussed in consideration non-verbal communication presented when a lingua franca is missing. Politeness, manners and personalisation were then noted in comparing personal and professional phone conversations. As service encounters require personalisation, it was noted that both formal and informal communication may be required to satisfy customers. Gauging when and with whom informal communication is appropriate to use is a complex skill, especially in luxury high service quality businesses.

Annotated bibliography

Burns, P.M. (1997) Hard-skills, soft-skills: Undervaluing hospitality's 'service with a smile.' *Progress in Tourism and Hospitality Research* 3, 239–248.

This perspective piece offers a critique of skills needed by hospitality staff. Similarly to other papers (e.g. Nquist *et al.*, 1985 reviewed in Chapter 2), this paper identifies how hard skills taught undermine the complex ability to use soft skills such as communication. The soft skills needed in service encounters are noted as crucial to service sector businesses and that these are in fact high order skills consistently undermined by the use of 'unskilled' workforces. Although this is not a contemporary paper, it is often referenced as one of the earliest and founding works which aided the development of the soft skills debate in tourism, events and hospitality. Burns addresses how both emotional and performance skills are needed in service encounters (considered in emotional and aesthetic labour in Chapters 4 and 5, respectively) and acknowledges that these are neither simple nor static abilities for staff to create. These are both linked to the culture within which the company operates and the social norms present in service encounters. The paper concludes with suggestions for further research into the soft skills needed in service encounters to try and build acknowledgement for the highly complex skills staff require when serving customers in tourism, hospitality and events.

Question: Burns notes how soft skills used in service encounters are based upon social norms. Can you identify and list the social norms you are aware of in service encounters? How would these compare to social norms in meeting/greeting your friends and family?

Baum, T. (2002a) Skills and training for the hospitality sector: A review of issues. *Journal of Vocational Education & Training* 54 (3), 343–364.

A few years since Burns' article on soft skills, Baum here addresses the importance of service businesses to economies and outlines current issues seen in the ongoing skills debate. As a desk-based article, this piece aptly reviews the industry and education status quo for hospitality staff. The focal argument is again on recognising the value of soft skills for hospitality and that in order to gain competitive (and perhaps global) advantage, a country needs to instil education and training programmes to support these businesses. There are examples drawn from a range of countries in this article from which the reader can consider how a country can prepare a workforce for successful employment in hospitality positions through acknowledgement and development of soft skills. Baum concludes that in order for a country to be sustained as a hospitality destination and provider of excellent service 'products', government policies are needed to support national training for soft skills in service sectors.

Question: Baum refers to the de-skilling in the hospitality workforce owing to the standardisation of service encounters in fast food outlets (page 351). Why do you think scripting and standardised service leads to de-skilling? In contemporary McDonald's, customers are now required to use technology to order their food: where are the skills now required in these service encounters and is this good or bad?

Baum, T. (2008) The social construction of skills: A hospitality sector perspective. *European Journal of Vocational Education and Training* 54 (3), 74–88.

This desk-based piece directly addresses Burns' (1997) article and moves the debate forward by considering how the social distance between staff and the customer may impact the soft skills needed in different locations (developed/developing contexts in particular). Baum suggests that there is less social distance between customer and staff in developed countries in comparison with developing countries. These assertions are supported by a study reported by Baum in 2006 referred to in the article. Baum maintains that Western businesses usually have staff who have experienced similar service encounters through acting as tourists or learning from the experiences of friends and family. In developing countries, he argues that they may have limited cultural experience and therefore find managing service encounters with Western customers more challenging. In this way, Baum is noting that technical skills are easier to train across countries, but that soft skills and knowledge of customer expectations will be the defining quality differentiator for staff to learn about. Aesthetic and emotional skills are noted as part of these soft skills needed (sourcing Nickson & Warhurst). Baum acknowledges that the growth in migrant labour and availability for cultural experiences has been significant, but that training programmes need to address language, service skill and non-technical training in order for all staff to have a foundation of knowledge in the usual cultural and social norms for service encounters.

Question: Social and cultural experiences are at the heart of this paper. What would you identify as your own cultural and social experiences? Are these limited by location and nationality or who you have met and developed close relationships with? How does knowledge of other peoples cultural and social experience affect these?

Lashley, C. and Morrison, A. (2007) *In Search of Hospitality; Theoretical Perspectives and Debates*, 2nd edn. Abingdon: Routledge.

This book offers a number of useful chapters for the study of soft skills in hospitality. Its primary purpose, however, is to identify hospitality as an academic discipline emerging from hotel and catering (technical) studies. By commissioning chapters with sociological, philosophical and historical perspectives, this source offers an example of how academics were trying to legitimise and champion the complexity of working in hospitality roles. Chapter 3 in the volume is of note here as they consider the hospitableness required in producing intangible services (pages 55–72). This chapter is interesting in the consideration of soft skills as it notes how the performance of being a good host requires personality, motivation, adaptation and reciprocity in the service encounter. All of these can be directly linked to soft rather than hard skills (using Baum's 2002b definition). Being hospitable and seeing this as a moral virtue and in turn gaining enjoyment from being a good host is discussed at length.

Question: What do you think being a good samaritan involves? How do these qualities link to hosting in tourism, events and hospitality businesses? Are there clear links, and if so, could you state that soft skills have virtuous origins?

4 Emotional Labour

Chapter Learning Objectives

(1) To locate definitions of, and history on, emotional labour.
(2) To explore the surface and deep levels of acting emotions in working contexts.
(3) To assess how identity and emotion can affect the performance of emotional labour in the workplace.
(4) To critically appraise staff perspectives on performing and using emotional labour in tourism, events and hospitality contexts.

Introduction

Both the sectors skills council for tourism, events and hospitality (People 1st, 2011, 2013) and leading scholars on soft skills (e.g. Baum, 2002) identify that emotional displays and appearance are integral to offering good customer service. These areas are considered soft skills, are termed emotional labour, aesthetic labour and sexualised labour, and are widely researched in the tourism, events and hospitality industries from a customer

and human resource management perspective. This chapter assesses the literature with regard to emotional labour to further identify the components of soft skills, which are deemed necessary for successful and satisfactory service encounters in tourism, events and hospitality contexts.

Definitions of Emotional Labour

Beginning with emotional labour, Arlie Hochschild's book stemmed from her attendance at an airline training event. Her work on emotional labour is seminal and has been widely cited within tourism, events and hospitality, business, sociology, psychology and gender research since the first edition in 1983. The premise of this type of labour originated in the known training phrase 'service with a smile'. Surprenant *et al.*'s (1987) paper also noted how smiling was a necessary skill and part of a customer service encounter (as discussed previously). Hochschild noted how staff were told to use their smile – their greatest asset – to ensure that airline guests were happy and satisfied. However, this facial display was not to be a performance, but rather a 'travel experience of real happiness and calm' (Hochschild, 2012: 5). The notion that staff should not only appear happy but also *be* happy is a powerful concept when dealing with customers, who each have their own background, history and personal experiences. This smile, or positive emotional display, exemplifies a brand message ensuring that customers receive the appropriate level of service and satisfaction with their experience. Thus, emotional labour was seen by Hochschild as a commodity rather than a personal choice of feeling.

Since this initial study within a US airline, a number of publications have outlined research completed in emotional labour use for tourism, events and hospitality management. This chapter will discuss some of these, but it is accepted this is non-exhaustive of the positions presented on this topic.

Seymour (2000) considered emotional labour within fast food businesses in comparison to traditional hospitality outlets, and explored whether uniform and service scripts affected emotional labour. (Uniforms are considered to be within aesthetic labour discussed in the following chapter.) Scripted service is a service and training tool used by numerous chain tourism, events and hospitality businesses. 'Have a good day', 'How can I be of service?', 'Can I assist you with anything today?' and 'Is everything to your satisfaction?' are examples of scripted lines that staff are required to say to their customers to maintain customer satisfaction. It is important here to note that there is no research suggesting that these phrases could also annoy customers. Seymour (2000) analysed where staff deviated from these scripted lines in order to ascertain employee motivation to personalise the service:

> If you sell yourself all the time you end up losing your identity. You must hold a part of you back. You don't want to end up being just part

of the meal experience. You need to learn to keep respect for yourself. (Seymour, 2000: 167)

Like Hochschild's work with airline crew, Seymour's participants felt that the emotion communicated in conversation needed to be limited in order to ensure that their personality and identity were protected. This is an important consideration when investigating staff perceptions, as the demands from customers in the customer service encounter may conflict with their own personality and identity. For example, if a customer asks for a burger from an Islamic server, the server may find it difficult owing to their own religious practices.

From these observations, it appears that emotional labour has two axes of conflict. Vertically, emotional labour is a commodity that is produced and consumed, intangible and changing according to the interaction with and demands from a guest. Horizontally, staff have to be both robotic in communicating set scripts and individual in offering personality and flair to their service. The skills for displaying and creating emotional labour are what Stinchcombe (1990, as cited in Seymour, 2000) calls 'ethnomethodological competence'. This type of competence is seen as a core occupational skill for tourism, events and hospitality staff because they need to control interactions, which are dependent on guest requirements and organisational duties.

Employees are expected to give the appearance of enjoying their work as much as visitors are enjoying their time. (Baum, 2006a: 135)

Emotional demands are made of employees to constantly be in a positive, joyful and even playful mood. An ability to cope with such demands must be recognised as a real skill. (Baum, 2002a: 79)

Within Baum's soft skilling research he reflects on emotional labour as an important soft skill needed by workers in tourism, events and hospitality, wherein they have to show positivity and enjoyment when serving guests in order to maintain customer satisfaction. Hochschild's seminal work in emotional labour, followed by that of Seymour and Baum, identifies that emotional labour is a soft skill embedded in customer service encounters throughout the tourism, events and hospitality industries. Emotional labour can conflict with the identity and personality of the member of staff and serves to create robotic effigies of the brand that they are representing.

Within the literature on emotional labour, deep and surface emotions are outlined. Deep emotional displays relate to genuine or even subconscious emotion produced without conscious effort, while surface emotional displays are seen as consciously created in order to appease or respond appropriately to demands presented. Hochschild outlined that staff should try to produce deep acting emotional displays, as this is perceived by customers as more genuine and will aid empathy and awareness within the service encounters. However, if the guest communicates surprising, inappropriate or unusual demands in a service encounter, the staff will have to use surface emotional displays. This dualism in emotional displays outlines how emotions are either genuine or performed. The study found that surface emotional display are appropriate in some encounters because if the staff genuinely felt these emotions or empathy, they would exhibit character faults. For example, when Sophie was asked to go to the customer's room instead of paying for their bill (incident discussed in Chapter 5), she did not become upset in front of the customer, but remained calm and sought management support. Likewise, when Lucy and Jessica narrated inappropriate behaviour and communication from their management, they maintained their emotional states and reacted professionally. These serve as examples where staff should not offer genuine or deep emotional displays, but perform and produce professional emotional responses while controlling their own emotions.

This brief overview of emotional labour confirms that it is a component of soft skills for tourism, events and hospitality staff, but there are issues in producing it in customer service encounters because staff are not robots, and yet, conversely, staff are also unable to appear a complete individual so as to avoid conflict with their customers.

Identity and Emotion in Service Encounters

> The stronger the identification of employees with their organizational role, the more genuine they are when performing the role. (Yim *et al.*, 2018: 408)

This section will offer a discussion of identity and emotion present within service encounters and how these can positively and negatively affect emotional labour use by staff. Management want staff to produce genuine emotions to support service delivery, but as staff are individuals their personality and background are present and affect emotional displays. As service encounters are offered in leisure experiences, it is also evident that staff and customer emotions are present in creating the event in which the service is offered. Identity and emotions are, therefore, noted as core components of emotional labour for service encounters. Within this discussion, I will challenge the recommendations made to the management of tourism, events and hospitality businesses to train, manage and control staff emotions by instead signalling that staff themselves should be championed to reflect and develop self-awareness of identity and emotion. If staff are supported to reflect and appraise their own identity and emotions within service encounters, they will be more aware of their emotional displays and empowered to alter service delivery based on their acceptance of their own personality and abilities.

To begin, Yim *et al.* (2018) confirm that in order to perform emotional labour, staff need to feel connected and linked to the organisation. The identity of staff is, therefore, more than a personal construct in all staff, but something which needs to be similar, or linked, to the organisational goals of the company. To discuss identity in emotional labour use, gender, personal interests and culture are discussed here. These outline three aspects of individualism, but are not comprehensive of the range of individual and personality traits of staff who offer and create emotional labour.

A person's identity is based on their nationality, gender, race, dis/ability, interests, hobbies and experiences. These are all present within a person's sense of self and portrayal of self. Yim *et al.*'s (2018: 422) study on gender variances affecting emotional labour, although they refute a gender divide in performing these, outlined that 'personality' is important in the selection of tour representatives as it can negatively affect staff ability to manage and perform emotion in work. For example, if someone has strong personal views on marine conservation and is being interviewed for a tour representative for a boat tour of an area where marine conservation is an issue, it is likely they will find it difficult to praise the local area. Here, emotional labour is constrained not by the person's natural ability, but by their views conflicting with the context in which they need to perform the emotion. In every tourism, events and hospitality business, staff will need to serve guests who may evidence conflicting positions to the staff's personal opinions. As such, identity in emotional labour performance is a difficult skill as the staff will need to both acknowledge their own opinion and mitigate their usual reactions to conflicting positions offered by customers. The extent to which this is appropriate and feasible will depend on the issue and situation within which the service is being offered.

Staff working as guides for travel expeditions are also seen to need to manage their identity to perform appropriate emotions as they have to tell stories within their daily roles:

> shared modes of recognition, for example, what is said and how this connects to what is felt, sensed, and experienced. (Mathisen, 2019: 68)

This quotation from Mathison (2019) clarifies that when staff articulate a story to customers, they are also sharing a belief that there are common emotions felt about a topic, activity or local area. Staff in tourism, events and hospitality will all tell stories to customers as they will need to inform and direct them in support of service delivery. For example, concierge staff in an accommodation provider will need to clarify local attractions and ways to navigate the local area. These are not simply instructions, but are stories on how the customers can create their tourist experience during their stay. If these staff suggest activities or travel arrangements that are not deemed acceptable to the customers, the staff member is perceived negatively. This can then lead to customers perceiving the staff as offering poor service, or as being different to themselves and thus disharmonising the customer's perception of being part of the company (a key factor in services marketing and brand loyalty).

Giousmpasoglou *et al.* (2017) considered how staff culture may affect emotional labour use. One of their supported hypothesis suggests that people who are seen as individualists (Hofstede, 2006) will tend to be emotionally exhausted (when compared to collectivists) within hospitality roles. Individualist culture is seen in people who tend to prefer little to no support from others within their social networks. Therefore, this study suggests that if staff associate with the individualistic cultural dimension, they will face higher emotional exhaustion than those who may be seen as collectivists. Again, conclusions in this publication identify that management should train staff to be culturally aware of their differences in order to attract, retain and manage staff. I would argue that all staff should consider their identity and increase self-awareness in order to attribute their emotional exhaustion to personal emotional management, rather than because of a difference with others who may be deemed culturally different.

In terms of negative personality aspects that could affect emotional labour in service encounters, Walsh *et al.* (2019) identify that Machiavellianism, narcissism and psychopathy are toxic personality traits, which may lead to dysfunctional service delivery. These three personality traits are termed as the dark triad and may lead to damaging 'valuable customer relationships' (Walsh *et al.*, 2019: 12). Deep and surface acting emotional displays are affected by staff with these personality traits. However, these authors use country-specific comparisons (Japan as collectivist and USA as individualistic) without acknowledging staff nationality. Similar to publications on intercultural service encounters, this study used Hofstede's cultural dimensions and applied an understanding of these to people working in a country, rather than establishing the nationality of participants individually. This noted, this study is important in consideration of personality for emotional labour use as it clarifies specific negative personality traits that may require further support from management. The authors acknowledge that these are 'individual differences' (Walsh *et al.*, 2019: 21) rather than clinical findings, but then apply these to country to country comparisons without offering varying aspects of these presented in service delivery. For example, arrogance is noted as part of narcissism and this could be seen in a satisfying service encounter whereby the staff use their knowledge to complete the service and ignore what the customer requests:

Customer came to the bar, asked for a Coronaberg and a pint of Corona. We don't sell Coronaberg, so I obviously I double checked he meant Corona anyway, and as he pointed out, I wanted to make sure though. I said Corona, he said yeah, Coronaberg, so I said, would like you lime, he said yeah, so I gave him some. And gave him the Corona and he was happy enough. (Tom)

This example from the study outlines how Tom understood the correct term for the drink order, even though the customer noted it incorrectly. Tom not only uses his confidence to assert a challenge to the customer request, but also ignore the customer's request owing to his belief in what the customer actually wants. This shows arrogance in his management of the encounter, but it is used appropriately to deliver a service which the customer wanted, but could not clearly articulate.

It is clear from the discussion of these articles that emotional labour is affected by a person's identity and personality. In order to manage the individual elements of emotional labour displays, staff are required to manage, control and train their emotions in order to perform the deep level emotions required for customer satisfaction. Although most publications recommend that management need to train and manage these aspects, Saito *et al.* (2015) suggest that staff-to-staff support may be more beneficial. These authors considered how staff breaks and back of house conversations between staff could be used to manage emotional labour. If staff have had a difficult encounter with a customer where they had felt strong emotions about the encounter, staff-to-staff discussion on this was seen to alleviate their emotions and enable them to maintain emotional displays for the remainder of their shift. It is accepted that there will be issues in supporting this in tourism, events and hospitality as staff-to-staff discussion can be seen as a spiteful or negative conversation about staff, or that they are unable to take a break owing to the working pressures within the company. Further, if other staff do not feel the same emotions towards an incident as the member of staff, discussion of this back of house may also lead to them feeling worse about the situation. Although there are limited discussion and research on identity in emotional labour use in service delivery for tourism, events and hospitality, it is clear that this is an important tenet of the staff's ability to control and perform emotions effectively.

Now, moving on to consider emotional aspects present within service encounter performance, Lashley (2009) confirmed that:

Emotional dimensions of the service encounter have been well understood for decades. (p. 16)

Lashley (2009) outlined how emotional displays are not a new consideration in service delivery, but a constant principle supporting high service quality. As such, emotional labour theory has not created a new framework to consider staff emotions but supports an existing phenomena core to hospitality services.

They should not show negative or aggressive emotions to customers, even awkward ones! (Lashley, 2009: 16)

Here, managing emotions in the service encounter are not considered an aspect supporting service delivery, but as a core construct from which customers perceive good service. Customers want to experience positive emotions while receiving service delivery. Positive emotional experience may be perceived as more important than the products consumed within the encounter. As such, emotional labour is not simply part of the performance to offer physical products, but can be seen as the primary motivator for customer satisfaction. If staff are involved in personal or individual issues which affect their emotional states, it is likely that they will not be able to create emotionally positive environments as they are 'more concerned' in managing their own emotions than reading or supporting those of their customers (Mattila & Enz, 2002: 275).

To consider the staff emotions present within service encounters, Pabel *et al.*'s (2019) analysis of emotional labour in Australia supports the need for consideration of staff identity as they note that self-awareness of emotion can both negatively and positively affect service encounters. For example, if you are aware of feeling sad, this can either make you feel worse by reminding yourself of the reason for the sadness, or you can confront and control the sadness by changing your emotional state to a more positive one. The individual reason behind why staff may feel sad will affect their ability to change or alter this to a positive emotion. Personal issues and family situations are seen to be the most difficult surrounding contexts from which to change emotional states (Pabel *et al.*, 2019). They also note that emotions are seen as contagious and that if customers are seen to be negative, this can spread among other customers in the tour and therefore be harder to manage within the activity. Therefore, staff in these tourism locations are not simply seen as responsible for their own emotional labour control, but as needing to retain an upbeat and happy customer group on tourist activity. If staff are struggling to maintain their own emotions, due to

Through discussion of identity and emotion in emotional labour for service encounters, it is clear that recommendations are made to the management of tourism, events and hospitality businesses to hire people with the right characteristics that fit the company and lead to effective deep acting of emotions. However, in light of the personal and individual aspects of the staff present, management or control of this may be 'costly to the worker' and lead to emotional exhaustion (Pabel *et al.*, 2019: 2). If staff face emotional exhaustion through completing emotional labour, it is important for staff to be aware of this as it could lead to their desire to leave employment (Deery & Jago, 2015). Emotional labour linked to identity and emotional management should not be something management need to address, control or train, but an element of service encounter delivery which the staff should appraise and reflect upon. It is also noted that line managers of these staff have identified a need for further training on what emotional labour is and how they should manage their employees' emotional labour (Bratton & Watson, 2018). Thus, recommendations offered to management are futile without staff support to self-appraise and self-reflect on their own emotions. Self-esteem created through this self-reflection will lead to the empowerment of these staff who can then react and change their emotional displays according to the encounters and demands presented. If staff are emotionally energetic, rather than exhausted, they will also be able to create emotionally positive experiences, which may be seen as more important than the product ordered by customers in the service encounter (Lashley, 2009; Lashley *et al.*, 2004). Finally, it is noted by Laing (2018) that more research is needed in emotional labour use by volunteers in festivals, as they are not working or motivated by financial means, a position from which most emotional labour literature is discussed.

Critical Incidents with Key Questions

Review of emotional labour theory allows for clarification on why and how staff produce high customer service standards. One key element omitted from current research on emotional labour is how the staff manage their emotional displays and whether or not they like doing so.

Hochschild (2012) noted that emotional labour requires deep and surface acting when serving customers. Control of emotional displays are known to be important in face-to-face encounters, but data gathered and analysed on emotional labour in service encounters highlights problems perceived by the staff in controlling these:

- Staff utilise fake emotions (surface acting) more than deep acting owing to the personal emotions present when dealing with customers. Acting is not possible in every encounter either. For example, Lucy informed me that when a passer-by told her she looked like a pole dancer she immediately laughed and seemed to think it was a compliment. The shock at hearing this comment made Lucy unable to deal with her emotions and immediately made light of the situation instead of confronting the customer on the personal, inappropriate and rude remark.
- Genuine empathy with customers is felt by a range of staff. Incidents from Lucy, Sophie, Tom and Martha all showed empathy with customers facing a range of problems in the service encounters. Empathy helps to develop better working relationships, but they need to be real in order to fully satisfy customers.
- Smiling was noted by Jessica, but noted as 'fake smiles.' This confirmed what Hochschild (2012) identified a thin crust of display.

Staff smiling is seen as fake when customers were demanding, rude or ignorant of the communication offered from staff. Staff need to know how to control this emotion and when it is appropriate to offer emotional displays.

- Long working hours resulted in difficulties for staff trying to manage their emotions in service encounters. This was seen as a correlation for staff who struggled to manage their emotions. Management needs to be aware of this and train staff to respond appropriately even when they are working long shifts.
- If your staff feel 'You need to be "I'm perfect". Unbelievable good' (Jessica) then staff might not be fully prepared to challenge customers when they are incorrect, rude or harassing (examined in Chapter 7).

Key questions to consider on emotional labour for staff working in tourism, events and hospitality are noted as follows:

- How do staff manage their emotional displays?
- Do staff enjoy managing and performing emotions?
- Staff are often informed to satisfy guests and serve with a smile, but what if the member of staff has personal, relationship or emotional issues?
- What if the customer is acting inappropriately?
- What if the company does not have service standards and the staff is unsure of which occasion to smile and enthuse with the guest?

These questions still require further research and consideration, but for clarity in working environments, the incidents offered below enable readers to critically appraise emotional labour from staff perspectives.

Comforting guests

Today, I'm back to the restaurant post. I served a French customer today and I found it's so difficult to hear their accents and I nearly failed to get their order for the meal. And he even asked for some kind of food that 'Hotel name' do not provide, and he was so stubborn to have that food. I told him we do not provide this food, and he asked me why. So I said that it's not in the menu, and I'm not sure with the chef, so he asked me to suggest to the chef to have this dish, because this is kind of the common dish in the Western style. To comfort him, I said, yeah, I will pass this message to the chef and ask him to consider about it. So he settled down. Some customers are really stubborn on what they want. They thought they were the person who paying, so they have their rights on everything. But it's our job to comfort them as well, in a polite way, because customer has always the right person when comes to problem. (Sophie).

Questions to consider from this incident:

(1) Do you agree with Sophie's response to this customer request?
(2) Is it usual for guests to request food from their own hometown area?
(3) How do you think Sophie used and showed emotional labour in this encounter?

Scripted service and emotions

My first observation at 'Restaurant name' the restaurant I work is one of the scripted service. For example, apologising to a guest for a complaint that you do not feel is warranted. At 'Restaurant name' we did a two-week training course when I first started, which was a couple of months ago, on the guest experience. It was drilled into the host to create a warm, friendly environment for a customer at the first point of contact. As a host I'm required to greet potential customers at the menu board and ask them if they're okay, make small talk and ask them if they've done any shopping or if there are any good sales on. Ask them if they've ever been to 'Restaurant name' before and if they've ever had tapas before. If they haven't then explain that tapas are a traditional Spanish dish made to share, that we recommend for three to four people.

I feel uncomfortable doing this because in my opinion I don't think shoppers want to be bombarded with a load of questions when standing in a door trying to read the menu. The whole 'Are you okay?' question is ... I just feel it is unnecessary and really no real sincerity to it. I also think that asking people if they've had tapas before ... that's ... I think that some of the people might think that you think that they're uncultured and take it personally. These observations have come from me using a combination of what I've been asked to say and what I've chosen to say myself and seeing the different reactions.

When I've greeted people with the requested phrases there is a bit of an element of panic. On many occasions I was interrupted with a very abrupt, 'I'm just looking,' or completely ignored by the person. Or they'd continue to look at the menu board and avoid eye contact with me. It was just pretty awkward. On a few occasions it even made people walk off without considering us. It wasn't the way I was saying it, it was just the fact that people were being instantly sort of harassed.

In comparison, when I was left to my own devices and just said what came naturally, I was giving a warm smile or saying hello, just being genuine, customers were a lot more receptive and a lot more at ease.

They didn't feel like they were being conned into something or being sold something and gave them more of a sense of control I think. Same applies to seating really. We're told to put them in this specific seating, different areas so that each waitress obviously gets a turn and nobody's swamped with loaded tables.

We're supposed to ask if they want to sit inside or outside and then take them to a specific table. That's another thing that I've tweaked because from my observations if ... You can still lead someone into a certain area but then just to give them a pick of the five tables in that area makes them feel in control and makes them feel more at ease. It generally gives them more satisfaction than when you take them to a specific table, which might not be one they'd like.

Again, any of these sort of scripted behaviour, I think you lose a lot of sincerity and my observation was just that the more freedom we're given or ... the more scope we're given really, of being told that we want to get people into the restaurant and we want to seat them in certain areas but being given the opportunity to work that the way we feel is best is probably a lot more beneficial than having these ... being forced to seat people in specific areas and having to say ... churn out the same sort of few lines that they think are going to get people into the restaurant. That's my first observation. (Lucy)

Questions to consider from this incident:

(1) What are the benefits of using scripted service in tourism, events and hospitality?
(2) Why do you think Lucy feels more comfortable left to her 'own devices'?
(3) Why do you think Lucy feels customers do not like her using scripted service?
(4) If you were Lucy's manager, how could you support her in adhering to company procedures and also use her own initiative in communication?

Summary

(1) To locate definitions of and history on emotional labour.

Emotional labour for tourism, events and hospitality is usually linked to the work of Arlie Hochschild. She defined this term as being genuine service offered by staff displaying real, deeply felt, positive emotions.

(2) To explore surface and deep levels of acting emotions in working contexts.

Surface and deep levels of emotional displays are outlined in the literature as dual elements of emotional labour. Existing research informs management to support deep and genuine displays of emotion, but this does not reflect demands or situations in which staff face inappropriate situations. Within problematic encounters this book advises that staff utilise surface acting to perform appropriate emotional displays. Staff therefore need to use both deep and surface emotional displays, in the appropriate contexts, to both support the service encounter and maintain professionalism.

(3) To assess how identity and emotion can affect the performance of Emotional Labour in the workplace.

Staff identity was discussed using gender, culture and personality. This outlined how individual elements of staff will affect the delivery of deep acting in service encounters. Instead of recruiting or managing staff who fit the company culture to fit the emotional labour required, it is recommended that staff actively reflect on their personality and identity in order to self-appraise their identity. This will not only lead to increased self-esteem and motivation but enable staff to consider why their emotional states differ within encounters with different people. In consideration of emotions in emotional labour, staff are seen to need to create positive emotional experiences and develop emotional resilience in the delivery of services. Both of these rely upon an active interpretation of customers' emotions, as well as a consistent performance of positive emotional displays. Again, it was argued here that this is an individual self-managing aspect in service encounter delivery, which staff require support and facilitation, rather than management and training.

(4) To critically appraise staff perspectives on performing and using emotional labour in tourism, events and hospitality contexts.

This chapter juxtaposes discussion of emotional labour by offering staff perspectives on the use and reflection on the need for emotional display in service encounters. When staff face rude or inappropriate comments from customers they need to know how to react professionally, confidentially and without reprimand from management. Likewise, as staff may have personal health and well-being issues, producing emotional displays will not always be possible. Management needs to be sensitive and aware of staff capability in producing the emotions and support staff that may not be capable of deep acting throughout their shift. The incidents offered from participants in industry showcase a range of techniques used by staff to perform emotions and identify and these are not noted as being from education or industry training, but from individual ability and previous life experiences. Active reflection on emotional use is noted as key to supporting the use and development of emotional labour for staff in service encounters.

Annotated bibliography

Hochschild, A. (2012) *The Managed Heart: Commercialization of Human Feeling with a New Afterword*, 3rd edn. London: University of California Press: California.

This is considered as the founding text on emotional labour and Hochschild is cited as the creator of this well-known term. Based on her observations in airline training contexts, Hochschild noted the term 'emotional labour' owing to the airline training requiring staff to offer service with a smile. This book considers this term and the implications it has for staff and management in creating an authentic and real performance of positive emotion in service encounters. Hochschild refers to a range of case examples, which are useful for understanding the contexts within which emotions need to be portrayed to customers and how they can affect and enhance service standards. A core component to the definition of emotional labour is how it needs to be interpreted by customers as authentic, and how it can be performed as surface or deep acting. Hochschild maintains that in order to offer real (authentic) service, staff must act emotions from a deep (or genuine) motivation. If positive emotions are acted from surface (or superficial) positions, customers may not believe in the sincerity of the service.

Question: Where might service with a smile be inappropriate in service contexts? Apart from warmth and happiness, how else can service with a smile be interpreted in tourism, events and hospitality contexts?

Seymour, D. (2000) Emotional labour: A comparison between fast food and traditional service work. *International Journal of Hospitality Management* 19 (2), 159–171. DOI: https://doi.org/10.1016/S0278-4319(00)00009-8.

This paper reports a study on emotional labour in a traditional versus fast food hospitality business. Participants were staff working in two establishments and Seymour reports on the findings from interviews conducted with 24 participant hospitality workers. The findings identified that regardless of how the staff felt, they always knew they had to appear and act cheerfully and courteously. They also had to restrain and maintain their inner feelings in order to satisfy guests in both establishments. The conclusions note that although the study is limited in size, it identifies how standardised and personalised service both require management and production of emotional labour. It highlights problems felt by staff in creating and performing these emotions as they may differ from their own natural response to customer demands made. One flaw in this paper is that being professional (maintaining your own emotions) is required in every workplace and not simply hospitality.

Question: Seymour advocates for restaurant staff who may find performing emotional labour difficult when working with customers who come with a range of complicated demands. What other workers or professions, external to tourism, events and hospitality, have to maintain their own emotions to remain professional in front of customers or people they work with?

Surprenant, C.F. and Solomon, M.R. (1987) Predictability and personalization in the service encounter. *Journal of Marketing* 51 (2), 86–96.

Although based in banking and within a marketing journal, this article is of note regarding emotional labour as it considers how emotional labour supports the personalisation of service encounters. The authors conducted a quantitative study based on role plays completed in a banking context. They wanted to identify how customers and staff perceive personalised service and how this affects service quality. Emotional labour is present here due to the effects of personalisation manipulation where they note perceptions of friendliness, warmth, trust and sociability from the service encounter. The conclusions identify that personalised service does not always result in higher customer satisfaction and that as a construct, it is multidimensional (due to a lack of a script and based on an individuals skills, understanding and awareness). This paper is important when considering emotional labour as it is a component part of communicating friendliness and warmth to customers. This paper accepts these as important to build successful relationships and foster loyal customers.

Question: Apart from smiling, how would you communicate warmth and trust and sociability in a service encounter?

Witz, A., Warhurst, C., and Nickson, D. (2003) The labour of aesthetics and the aesthetics of organization. *Organization* 10 (1), 33–54. DOI: https://doi.org/10.1177/135050840 3010001375.

This article is one of the authors' early publications which began their establishment of aesthetic labour as a term and field of study. As they base their definition on emotional labour, it is salient to consider this paper in the study of emotional labour in order to understand how emotion can also be seen as styled in a service encounter. Quite a substantial part of this paper critiques Hochschild's book owing to the authors' perception that emotions cannot be separated from the embodied physical self in which they are seen and understood. They contend that Hochschild dismisses the body and corporate display (body and uniform) in which the emotions are performed. They conclude that in addition to personalised service (communication) and emotional labour (performing emotion), the body from which these are offered also affects service quality and standards. They term this corporeal display, aesthetic labour (reviewed in the following chapter).

Question: Using a gendered example, how would you interpret a smiling female member of staff differently if she had no make-up versus a full face of make-up? Does the colour of lipstick affect your interpretation of the emotion performed also?

5 Aesthetic and Sexualised Labour

Chapter Learning Objectives

(1) To consider definitions of aesthetic and sexualised labour.
(2) To understand the dimensions of aesthetic labour.
(3) To explore locations of sexualised labour.
(4) To examine issues linked to aesthetic and sexualised labour in customer service encounters from staff perspectives.

Introduction

From the work completed on emotional labour, aesthetic labour emerged as a term that describes how tourism, events and hospitality staff need to present themselves physically. This chapter will offer information on both aesthetic and sexualised labour. Both of these terms grew from the literature on emotional labour and have been previously

examined from customer and management perspectives. Here again, staff perspectives are championed to offer counter-perspectives on creating and maintaining these in tourism, events and hospitality businesses. By offering a critique through a staff lens, issues in identity and sexuality are also raised as concerns not noted in current literature.

The Appearance of Staff in the Service Encounter

Aesthetic labour is seen as the visual presentation of staff within service encounters (Witz *et al.*, 2003). As customers are presented with staff appearance within service delivery, it is accepted that this plays a part in the satisfaction and success of the encounter. This section will offer consideration of some positions on aesthetic labour, but a full review can be sought from Minaham's (2007) book, which offers an overview of the key debates in this field. To discuss the definitions and dimensions of aesthetic labour, surface and deep acting, staff uniform, personality and attitude in appearance and personal talent management are considered.

Seymour's (2000) research (noted in the previous chapter) also considered uniform and appearance when discussing emotional labour, as they enable 'surface acting' to portray their role in the company (Seymour, 2000: 164). Aesthetic labour was later conceptualised by Witz *et al.* (2003) as follows:

> we feel that the concept of Emotional Labour foregrounds the worker as a mindful, feelingful self, but loses a secure conceptual grip on the worker as an embodied self. (Witz, 2003: 36)

Witz *et al.* critiqued Hochschild's text, as they felt that the separation of surface and deep acting diminished the visible and innate bodily functions surrounding emotional labour. For example, a person's body is tall, short, fat, thin, etc., regardless of their own personal feelings and performance in a customer service encounter. A company makes use of these 'embodied capacities' (Witz *et al.*, 37) in recruitment and training to transfer staff appearance so as to portray their brand and style within the service. Their conceptualisation of aesthetic labour refers to the control that managers have over employee hair, makeup, uniform and weight, and how this is controlled to create high service levels and aid employee emotional labour.

Witz *et al.* (2003) compare employee aesthetics with the aesthetics created by the organisation in their marketing, branding and outlet styles. When comparing staff aesthetic labour to the company's aesthetics they note that aesthetic labour is like:

> the inanimate elements of the corporate landscape, corporately designed and produced. (Witz *et al.*, 2003: 44)

Their conceptualisation of aesthetic labour seeks to diminish an employee's personal feelings when made to look part of a business (ultimately an intangible and corporate object), but highlights an important aspect of business priority in creating a styled labour force to portray a brand and offer a specific level of service to guests. Furthermore, Witz *et al.* (2003: 35) suggested that uniform and staff appearance offer customers a 'distinctive mode of exchange beyond contract'. This suggests that uniform/attire is a mandatory practice even if it is not within the employment contract. If it is also seen as an exchange, then it is clear that staff aesthetics are part of the service and received by customers. Ultimately, Witz *et al.* (2003) classify aesthetic labour as a skill which is learned through recruitment, but fail to mention the incompatibility between a person's identity and feelings and being made to look a certain way.

Warhurst and Nickson's (2007) research in hospitality and retail noted that employers prioritise attitude and appearance as vital aspects of their staff, but that on-the-job training focused on hard and technical skills and expected the recruitment process to control for appropriate appearance and attitude skills in new staff:

> For those staff who had received appearance related training 62 percent had training in dress sense and style, 60 percent in body language and nearly a third in make-up and grooming (29%). (Warhurst & Nickson, 2007: 114)

This confirms that soft skills are pre-eminent, as they focus on these in recruitment and follow-up with on-the-job training. Again, their work in aesthetic labour fails to mention staff feelings when being trained or encountering customers using these communication devices. They do not consider how effectively aesthetic labour is implanted or how it could be communicated to staff in tourism, events and hospitality and retail courses, and they do not address personal sensitivity issues when staff are being made to look or communicate in specific ways. They conclude that businesses are allowed to discriminate in recruitment practices if there is a business case concerning appearance. Even if it is lawful, aesthetic labour research does not account for how staff feel or how it affects their ability to learn soft skills and produce them effectively in the 'styled labour market' (Warhurst & Nickson, 2007: 107). As Tsai (2019) confirmed that self-confidence is required for effective aesthetic labour, it is apparent that staff perceptions on aesthetic labour are important in order for them to appear confident, capable and willing to complete the demands made in service encounters.

Personal talent management is the final aspect to be discussed within aesthetic labour. This is not explicitly linked in current fields of discussion, but is seen as linked owing to research publications noting that management needs to seek and retain staff with talent and nurture this to improve service performance. If management should attract and retain staff who look good and sound right, then it stands to reason that this is a dimension of aesthetic labour extending to their personal fitness and retail habits (Langmead & Land, 2019). Retail staff are often linked in aesthetic labour theory (for examples, see Hall & Van den Broek, 2012; Pettinger, 2005, 2008, 2017), as they have to wear clothes being sold in shops and department stores. Retail staff are seen to be living the concept and culture of the retail company and embodying its function in order to sell to customers. Staff in tourism, events and hospitality can be perceived similarly, as they may be completing the activity at the same time as customers (see the examples from Mathisen, 2019; Pabel *et al.*, 2019 discussed in Chapter 4).

As such, talent management can be used as a lens to consider how staff not only fit within the organisational culture of the company, and portray the brand in their uniform, but are themselves personally groomed and understanding of the aesthetics of the service delivery. For example, a beauty therapist in a hotel spa facility would be expected not only to supply and advise on beauty treatments, but also use and advocate for their use. Concierge and reception staff working in this hotel would likewise be expected to inform customers of this facility and are seen as part of the chain of service delivery. Firth (2019) noted how hair, clothing and personal hygiene are all important in order to obtain employment in tourism, events and hospitality, but here I am advocating for these to be maintained as personal assets to conduct service encounters with appropriate aesthetic labour also. Protocols in staff uniform will support this to an extent, but as Marinakou (2019) notes, this is also a talent management element and so needs to be continual and checked.

This section has offered a brief overview of how staff are seen as aesthetic or are aestheticised as labour within tourism, events and hospitality employment to support service encounter delivery. This has clarified how appearance is both in uniform and bodily presentation and will affect customers' perceptions of the service delivered. However, personality and attitude on aesthetic presentation need consideration in order to ensure staff not only look the part, but feel confident in their roles and are content to be perceived in an aesthetic way. In light of this, talent management was linked to aesthetic labour as not only a recruitment decision, but a consideration in understanding staff lifestyle choices and continued personal grooming and hygiene. Staff in tourism, events and hospitality should be supported to maintain and appreciate their appearance inside and outside of work as this will lead to improved motivation and confidence.

Sex Appeal in the Service Encounter

Sex appeal and sexual undertones are prevalent within tourism, events and hospitality. As noted in Chapter 1, Lashley and Morrison

(2007) noted how tourists may ask for sexual services (in their quotation, fellate a customer) in hospitality businesses without consideration of the requests inappropriateness to the staff. Here, similarly, sexual labour is seen in the sex appeal of staff and how this can aid selling the service, but without consideration of the staff's acceptance or willingness to be seen in this light. There are businesses that specifically cater to sex appeal (e.g. Hooters bars) and there is significant economic support for sex tourism (for examples, see Oppermann, 1999; Ryan & Kinder, 1996; Yeoman & Mars, 2012), but here, discussion is offered on how service encounters utilise sexual labour in staff appearance and communication in order to satisfy customers and create a sexual element to service encounters. This section will define and identify locations of sexualised labour and outline why harassment and gender are seen as a current issue in this strand of knowledge.

Seminal authors, Warhurst and Nickson's (2009) considered sexuality and sexualised labour to be components of aesthetic labour. Employee appearance, including flirting and sex appeal, is seen as a core aspect of serving and satisfying guests in a tourism, events and hospitality service encounter. They note three levels of sexualised labour. These range from being sanctioned by management to being a specific strategic element of the business. Hooters bars in America are an example of strategic sexualised labour, as their uniform consists of:

> short shorts and a choice of a tight tank top or crop or a tight T-shirt to deliberately make up female employees as sexy waitresses. (Warhurst & Nickson, 2009: 396)

Warhurst and Nickson do not explore how being sexy or sex appeal is defined, understood or consumed. Instead, they critique how it is seen and trained through aesthetic labour. Specifically, they identify how staff use this sex appeal between colleagues to improve their working environment:

> As such, appealing to the senses of other staff, through flirting, for example, is behaviour used to create less boring and less bureaucratic, more exciting and more personal workplaces. (Warhurst & Nickson, 2009: 391–393)

Sexual harassment and unwanted sexual advances must be a concern to managers and employees using this form of aesthetic labour. The flirting conversation is understood and produced with a range of intentions. If people are not aware of the motivation behind this behaviour, then it could be misconstrued and lead to problems between staff and customers. Equally, with the retention issues in tourism, events and hospitality as identified by (People 1st, 2011, 2013), sexual harassment could be seen as a reason for staff leaving their roles in the sector. The article even notes how tour reps in holiday destinations use alcohol to increase sexualised labour. Here, the danger of sexualised labour is made clear by Warhurst and Nickson, who note how female workers choose to drink less alcohol to ensure that they 'remain in control' (Warhurst & Nickson, 2009: 400). This article does not underline the dangerous elements of sexualised labour in employee harassment, discrimination and illegal behaviour. It only seeks to label the types of sexualised labour seen in aesthetic labour and identify how they are used.

Gender is seen as an issue in sexualised labour as this term often refers to how female staff are seen as attractive to male customers. Women are recruited as being attractive or are sexualised through their uniform in order to meet 'men's sexual desires' (Ren, 2017: 395). This was accepted as a component part of airline advertising in the 1970s in Western business (Lessor, 1984), but is maintaining pace in Chinese airline recruitment practices, whereby even beauty contests are used to identify new attractive female staff (Ren, 2017). In this article, Ren notes that aesthetic labour is dominant in service delivery in China, but most notable in airlines:

> particularly acute in the Chinese airline industry in which women are dominant in low-skilled, feminised, sometimes sexualised service roles. (Ren, 2017: 396)

This quotation supports the consistent low-skilled perspectives taken on service encounters in tourism business, as staff are seen to be employed for their looks and not their competencies and competences. Gendering aesthetic labour in airline work leads to further problems, as outlined in Neal-Smith and Cockburn's (2009) article, as female pilots encounter sexism owing to not being seen as the appropriate gender in the role and being 'ignored' (Neal-Smith & Cockburn, 2009: 42) by their male co-pilots. Sexism in the workplace is a discrimination and harassment issue managed by the human resource department of most tourism, events and hospitality businesses (for examples, see Baum, 2006; Van Der Wagen, 2014) but is outlined here as part of recruitment practice for aesthetic labour. If aesthetic labour recruitment leads to sexualised labour and sexism in the workplace, how are staff then protected when customers act inappropriately towards them?

Finally, within the issue of gender noted from sexualised labour, it is clear this currently refers to heterosexual (and not homosexual) labour. Female staff being dressed or employed to appear attractive to male customers is the usual lens from which sexualised labour is presented. This ignores male staff being attractive to female customers and female-to-female and male-to-male positions also. Warhurst and Nickson (2009: 401) note this is deficient of supporting the 'pink pound'. Seeing sexualised labour as important to meet and exceed business profits is again from a customer satisfaction position. Do staff want to be viewed as sexual? Are they happy to be flirted with and respond to sexual demands made by customers? Answers to these questions are noted, in part, by the incidents in this chapter.

The texts on sexualised labour noted here clearly raise some concerns when considering the staff perspective. The literature discussed positions this term from aesthetic labour theory, but the publications analysed do not explain how staff could be trained, or identify staff awareness and ability to deal with this aspect of soft skill use in their roles. Evidence of empirical research into sexualised labour in tourism, events and hospitality is limited, but papers by Spiess and Waring (2005) on airline marking using sexualised labour and Wikesinghe's (2009) review of hotel reception staff using sexualised labour in encounters with customers are of note (discussed in the annotated bibliography at the end of this chapter).

Critical Incidents with Key Questions

Before we consider incidents relating to aesthetic labour and sexualised labour, it is pertinent to offer some discussion here on what the critical incidents surrounding these terms identified.

Aesthetic labour was defined by Witz *et al.* (2003) as a corporate display of appearance. It combines staff uniform and body image to market a company. This text suggests that discrimination may occur as a result of aesthetic labour. Jessica noted that she received inappropriate comments about her attire that was not overtly 'abusive', but made her feel uncomfortable. Lucy also noted disliking her uniform, which consisted of a short skirt, red lipstick and a red flower in her hair. As well as contradicting her own style of dress, Lucy felt it gave the 'wrong impression' to customers. Previous literature on aesthetic labour related mainly to female requirements and issues in appearance, and not male attire. None of the male participants used in this text related service encounter demands to their appearance and none of the other participants mentioned male colleagues' attire either. It is noted here, though, that this dimension needs further consideration and review in order to clarify all staff perspectives.

Sexualised labour is present in customer service encounters and this results in insulting and discriminatory comments from customers to staff (Sophie and Lucy noted this in particular). The uniform stipulated by management can also contradict the staff's usual style or choices in clothing, making them feel uncomfortable at work and thus making emotional labour more difficult to perform. The demands noted from critical incidents highlight heterosexual demands made of female staff from male customers. More research is required to consider female customer comments towards male staff, and homosexual comments or demands in service encounters and how all of these affect staff, colleagues and management. Lucy noted that she does not like wearing a uniform that enhances her attractiveness. If this makes staff feel uncomfortable, how can they complete their work in a professional manner? One of the participants who faced a sexual demand in her workplace has decided they will no longer work in a bar again as the experience was too stressful.

Uniform as a character

During my internship, I noticed a difference in my own behaviour and with customer behaviour towards me when I was in my uniform, I was performing different emotions whilst at work. An example of this was especially clear one day when using the guest kitchen in my work uniform I got asked questions and I had conversations with customers, displaying a positive attitude and facial expressions even though I was on my lunch break. However, that evening I used the kitchen without my uniform on and did not get asked any questions I also didn't feel the need to make any conversation like I had earlier in the day. (Emma)

Further details to support knowledge of this incident include Emma worked in a hostel in a European city. Guests and staff would access the kitchens in order to prepare food. Emma also lived at the hostel and so she had to prepare her own food in the kitchen as well as work in the hostel to support paying guests.

Questions to consider from this incident:

(1) Do you think Emma changed her own attitude and outward facial expressions when in or out of uniform in this incident?
(2) How does a uniform affect staff? Does it enhance or hinder service standards in encounters with customers?
(3) If customers and staff are working in the same location, does this change the power balance and attitude between these people?

Suited and booted

At 'company name' the dress policy is suits for both men and women, with the option of wearing a tie. This is to keep a professional environment when clients and other companies come in for meetings. However on a Friday, they allow employees to wear casual clothes to keep them motivated after a long week. The only rule is that if you are attending a meeting with external people such as clients and insurers you must wear suits even on dress down day. I was offered to sit in on a meeting with a client to outline problems that may have with them. This meant that my line manager told me that I had to dress in a suit and tie as we had a meeting even though it was a dress down day. As a result this made me feel slightly uncomfortable as everyone else was wearing casual clothes. (Phil)

On the first day of my internship with the management team, I was advised to look professional and dress smartly as the managers throughout 'company name' wear their own smart attire. As advised, I wore a suit jacket and skirt on my first day. However, it almost came apparent that I had dressed too formal than expected and I was almost laughed at. Not only by managers who probably assumed I would dress more casual but also by colleagues who I have worked alongside for 2 years on the floor during my contracted weekend hours. They often made comments in joke form such as, 'look at you, acting like a manager now'. Within this environment, there were clearly different expectations and I needed to make adjustments towards them. (Katy)

My second critical incident occurred on my first day, when I first received my work placement contract it was specified that the dress code was 'smart casual' this can have many interpretations so when I turned up on my first day I was dressed very smartly. When I arrived at the office it was obvious that everyone was dressed in casual attire in trainers and jeans and I stood out of the crowd in what I was wearing. I had to adapt the way I presented myself to my environment, this actually benefited me as it meant I could wear clothes I would normally wear in day-to-day life.

Another incident that occurred which follows on from the previous occurred when I was asked to sit in on one of their client meetings. The client was 'client name' who are a private bank company who offer wealth management for customers with large amounts of money. I was not informed I would be sitting in on this meeting before so I was wearing much more casual clothes when the other Account Handler team were more dressed up. The clients were very formal and I felt like I was slightly out of place. With the more formal style of meeting I was unsure how to act and greet the clients or if I should just stay in the background. This resulted in an awkward encounter between one of the clients and I when they went for a handshake and I was not expecting it. (Taylor)

Questions to consider from these incidents:

(1) How would you define and differentiate smart, formal and smart casual attire? Do the contexts in which these are required change their composition?

(2) If colleagues are wearing one form of uniform and you wear another, does this change how you feel and act in work? If so, how?

(3) How is female and male formal attire in work different? Why do you think they are different?

(4) Are there any industry contexts within which staff uniform is incongruent with customer expectations? If there is a discrepancy, how does this affect the service encounter?

Sexualised labour

Today I'm in the bar section, and it's the late night shift. A drunk guy asked for bill and I get the bill to him. While I passed the bill to him, he tried to get my hand with him and ask whether I'm interested to have one night stand with him and he would pay for me for that. And I said, I'm not interested, I do not need that money and ask him to just pay for the bill. He did not let go my hand and the bartender saw it so he asked the manager to come over, so the manager come over and bring me away and ask the drunk customer to behave or the waiter to bring it up back to his room. It's so scary when I got this incident. It's my first time and I found that it's really, really scary. I request a manager saying that may I not work for a late night shift in the bar section because it's quite scary for the girl, and the manager have say yes. (Sophie)

Questions to consider from this incident:

(1) What in this incident does Sophie find scary? Why?

(2) Working in a 5* international hotel, Sophie's uniform was a standard skirt and shirt outfit. Do you think the uniform affected the customer's actions and behaviour?

(3) If you saw this incident, what would your reaction be?

(4) What are the usual staff discussions around customers flirting, offering their phone number, or asking them out on a date? Is this always appropriate?

Summary

(1) To consider definitions of aesthetic and sexualised labour.

Aesthetic labour is defined as both the uniform presentation of the staff and the bodily attractiveness of staff. Sexualised labour is defined as male customers finding female staff attractive and enabling higher service quality by looking attractive.

(2) To understand the dimensions of aesthetic labour.

Aesthetic labour is constructed using uniform standards and recruitment practice. Staff uniform enables workers to represent a brand whilst maintaining a homogenous appearance. Recruitment practice may favour attractive female staff over male staff as this is seen to aid service quality and customer expectations. From a staff perspective, issues of personality and attitude were outlined to clarify how uniform standards may conflict with staff preferences making it more difficult to complete Service Encounters as it can lead to lower self-confidence. Personal talent management was outlined as an area to support staff aesthetic labour as this may lead to improved self-confidence and professional appearance.

(3) To explore locations of sexualised labour.

Sexualised labour is most notable in airline locations. Female air stewardesses are of particular note as recruitment practices across the world still require beautiful and attractive staff for these roles. Gender and sexuality were outlined as issues in current research as these lead to discrimination and harassment for staff in these roles.

(4) To examine issues linked to aesthetic and sexualised labour in customer service encounters from staff perspectives.

This chapter has highlighted how companies and brands use uniform and staff appearance to aid customer service encounters. Through the review of staff incidents in these roles, it is evident that further support, training and advice is required for staff to deal with the reactions and consequent behaviour customers and colleagues may have towards them. Warhurst, Witz and Nickson's critique of emotional labour speculated that emotions cannot be devoid of the bodies in which employees portray and complete their duties. Their creation of aesthetic labour allows researchers to consider appearance soft skills and how these are used in the recruitment and training of employees. From this, they link sexualised labour to aesthetic labour and advocate that employee sex appeal is needed so as to sell and maintain guest satisfaction in the tourism, events and hospitality industries. Although emotional labour, aesthetic labour and sexualised labour are all noted as soft skills, current literature focuses on how this serves to make a tourism, events and hospitality business successful and not how staff learn these skills and manage their feelings in situations. As these clearly play a part in every customer service encounter, it is concerning that little evidence of staff opinion on these is available.

Annotated bibliography

Warhurst, C. and Nickson, D. (2007) Employee experience of aesthetic labour in retail and hospitality. *Work, Employment & Society* 21 (1), 103–120. DOI: https://doi.org/10.1177/0950017007073622

Warhurst and Nickson are colleagues at the University of Strathclyde and are synonymous with aesthetic labour in hospitality and tourism research. This later paper of theirs addresses the employee perspectives on dress codes and appearance. The study they report on used a survey and focus group with students who had worked in retail or hospitality roles. Using university students is a limited group, however, as these sectors are made up of transient student workforces this is also an inappropriate sample to research with. The recruitment and selection of these staff are interesting, as it identifies the informal nature of these processes in retail and hospitality. Management seemingly had an informal face-to-face chat with the students and they were then offered work. Within their employment, the uniforms and dress codes further aestheticise the participants to develop their appearance to conform to the organisational culture. The authors concluded that aesthetic labour requires training and understanding of appearance as a skill, which can be developed and commodified, and not simply gained with the employee.

Question: What would an aesthetic training course involve? Pick a suitable tourism, hospitality or event business and identify the skills and knowledge staff would need to effectively look the part.

Warhurst, C. and Nickson, D. (2009) 'Who's got the look?' Emotional, aesthetic and sexualized labour in interactive services. *Gender, Work & Organization* 16 (3), 385–404. DOI: 10.1111/j.1468-0432.2009.00450.x

These core authors on aesthetic labour offer a conceptual paper on how sexualised work is also present in emotional and aesthetic labour. Their previous studies sought to extract aesthetic components in emotional labour and this piece then moved to conceive how sexualised work is also inherent in aesthetics. They defined sexualised work as being in work and of work whereby sexual harassment, relationships in work and staff sex appeal are present in organisations regardless of the management strategy and policy around these. In a service encounter context, they noted that if a service is going to be perceived as satisfactory, the package (body) in which it is provided can be improved, if a customer perceives it to be sexually attractive. This piece concentrated on the verbal and body language aspects of sexualised work in flirtatious language, hugging and compliments with colleagues and customers as being an advantage for maintaining working relationships and loyal customers. The physical attractiveness of staff was only noted for companies such as Hooters in the USA (where they specifically advertise and sell service with a sexual core). Caveats important in this piece, but not fully addressed, are the subjective nature of sexual attractiveness and the homosexual and transgender nuances to sex appeal. The sourced articles seemingly assumed what being attractive is (without full definition or clarification) and the levels of sexuality and gender appear binary between male and females only (prominence was paid to attractive female staff).

Question: The authors suggest that physical contact (hugging and cheek kissing) and flirtatious conversation from staff to management is an attempt to challenge authority in the workplace. What are your thoughts on this position?

Wijesinghe, G. (2009) A display of candy in an open jar: Portraying sexualised labour in the hospitality industry using expressive phenomenology as methodology. *Tourism and Hospitality Planning & Development* 6 (2), 133–143.

As a report of a phenomenological study, the author clearly outlined her positions as an academic in Australia, but also as a previous worker in hospitality positions. As a Sri Lankan female, she noted how her own experience in hospitality led to her study of sexualised encounters in hotels. It is interesting that she noted how her culture would not allow her to talk to strange men outside of her family and yet working in hotels automatically requires and presumes this as acceptable. The verbatim stories offered in this paper are illuminating and alarming as they evidence sexual harassment, bullying and poor management support for front-line staff. As the paper's aim was to evaluate a method, rather than conclude on theory in empirical research, the conclusions are limited to review of the methodology. The paper offers some interesting points in sexualised labour, most notably in how female staff are treated by male customers who use their purchasing power and satisfaction as a reason to expect flirtatious and sexual behaviour from the female staff.

Question: Read the story of Janaki offered in the paper. How would you react in this situation and how would you expect your own staff to respond to such customer demands?

Spiess, L. and Waring, P. (2005) Aesthetic labour, cost minimisation and the labour process in the Asia Pacific airline industry. *Employee Relations* 27 (2), 193–207.

Based at the University of Newcastle, Australia, these authors offered a desk-based review of airline policies relating to the aesthetics and sexualisation of airline staff. They identified how airline commercials and marketing tend to position of female air stewardesses being sexually attractive and that the industry has sex appeal in employment and service experience. They offered a range of interesting discussions on marketing campaigns and training policies surrounding aesthetic labour, which identifies how body shape and attractiveness are integral to the service offered. In the conclusions, they noted how organisational culture needs to support staff in these positions and that staff can become bored with the sexualised labour within their roles, particularly if they are on low salaries. This discussion did not go further to address the discriminatory and heterosexual elements of sexualised labour in the airline industries. They simply stated that this component of competitive advantage is more difficult to manage.

Question: What airline advertisements can you find for airlines? Do people on these address a range of body shapes, genders and sexualities? How are they evident?

6 Intercultural Sensitivity

Chapter Learning Objectives

(1) To outline definitions on intercultural communication and intercultural competence.
(2) To understand forms of verbal and non-verbal communication.
(3) To review models of intercultural competence and apply these to customer service encounters.
(4) To analyse intercultural sensitivity training for tourism, events and hospitality and identify its use for staff completing customer service encounters.

Introduction

Intercultural sensitivity is of vital importance when serving guests from transnational backgrounds. Tourism, events and hospitality businesses naturally embrace multicultural encounters as they produce services in a plethora of contexts. Whether it be a fine dining experience on a suspended dinner table in Dubai or takeaway fish and chips in Blackpool, the staff and customers could be from anywhere in the world. The context within which the service is created is rarely the home for either staff or customer present.

This chapter follows on from the discussion on intercultural service encounters in Chapter 1 and also offers more on the communication skills noted in Chapter 2. It considers alternative definitions of 'intercultural' to the Hofstedian one noted previously, and evidences models of intercultural competence and awareness from which to situate the development of intercultural sensitivity. Intercultural sensitivity is the focus of this chapter, as this has been noted as a priority for employers in tourism, events and hospitality (People 1st, 2013), lacking in current applicants and under speculated for service encounter theory.

Intercultural Communication and Competence

Before the review of intercultural sensitivity theory, this section will offer information on intercultural communication and intercultural competence. These two terms have origins in anthropology, sociology, linguistics and communication studies. With such an array of disciplines using these terms, this section offers details from key publications pertaining to this body of work.

Chapters 1 and 2 offered singular definitions on culture and communication in order to establish positions on these from theory located in the tourism, events and hospitality locale. This section will now identify alternative definitions and perspectives from research completed in other disciplines to offer a more reflective and critical lens.

The term intercultural has been defined and debated frequently in academic literature. Whether situated in language or cultural studies, the term alludes to distinct and divergent meanings dependent on the epistemology of the researcher and foci of the research. The Hofstedian definition noted in Chapter 1 identified culture as being limited to a person's nationality or citizenship. This was criticised as being minimalistic, but also problematic in its application, since prior research has used the geographic location of the participant to infer this culture rather than verifying their specific nationality (see Chapter 1 for a full critique of this). To expand on the Hofstedian definition, Holliday (2011) and O'Sullivan's (1994) definitions of intercultural will be noted to widen the possible application of the term.

> popular narratives of 'culture' lead us easily and sometimes innocently to the reduction of the foreign Other as culturally deficient. (Holliday, 2011: 9)

The quotation above supports criticism of Hofstede's definition of culture noted in Chapter 1. By establishing culture as a label of difference, people can easily reduce aspects of a person's character or behaviour to their nationality, rather than the complex contexts within which they are situated. Holliday's definition of intercultural addresses the complexities of this by positing culture as either small or large.

Small cultures are identified through groups of people being associated together in, for example, social or economic groupings, and that their behaviour is emergent rather than predefined. A group of customers attending a wedding, for example, will all create a small culture within the wedding event. Their behaviours and actions at this event will all conform to a culture expected and directed by the bride and groom. Similarly, a group of tourists going on a day excursion together will all conform and perform group norms according to the activities in which they are completing. Large cultures are then defined by Holliday as being the ethnic or national groupings related to the birth and background contexts from which a person has grown. These two aspects of culture defined by Holliday are not opposites; they are to be used in tandem to explain and interpret people's actions and behaviour. Further, Holliday notes that culture is:

> something individually constructed, based on a person's ideology, and used in situations where people identify or relate to others via a common situation. (Holliday, 2011: 97)

This quotation establishes that culture is not simply about the groups that a person can associate with, but is individually created by a person and is therefore emergent and ever-changing. O'Sullivan's (1994) text offers further support for this notion of individuality and suggests that intercultural communication is focused on effective communication between *any* two people in *any* given situation.

Defining intercultural communication as being about any interaction between any two people in any given context is a more appropriate foundation to consider service encounters in tourism, events and hospitality. It is deemed more appropriate, as the staff and customer could be from any background, working or visiting for a range of purposes and motivations, and be located in a collection of social groups which each inform their reactions and behaviour in each encounter completed.

Publications on intercultural communication allow for a more flexible definition of culture when applying the concept in service encounters. As the encounters are composed of people from transnational backgrounds and perspectives, viewing the people present as individuals made of complex cultural facets is more relevant when used in contemporary tourism, events and hospitality business settings. Within publications on intercultural communication, further detail on non-verbal and verbal communication is offered. This is of particular use in consideration of service encounters as it allows for full dissection of the forms of communication completed. These are summarised in Tables 6.1 and 6.2.

Tables 6.1 and 6.2 offer a clear framework from which to identify and assess the communication completed in a service encounter. Each

Table 6.1 Non-verbal communication

Area	What does this look like?	What does it suggest?
Proxemics	The distance between people communicating	Brazilians (for example) speak more closely to each other
Chronemics	The time between speech acts	Pause = thinking?
		No pauses = urgency?
Kinesics	Facial expressions and gestures	Emotion, familiarity or instruction
Adumbration	Body language or breathing cues	That behaviour or speech is about to happen
High context culture	Taking more meaning from the person's knowledge, situation and relationship between the people	The context of communication is more important than the words spoken
Scripts	The order in which situations are completed	Some restaurants require you to pay for food, then order food and then sit. Others need to you to sit first, then order and then pay on exit
Frames	Explanation of a procedure	One person has authority over another and describes the way something operates
Schemata	Complaining to someone	A certain social understanding of a situation

Source: Based on Hall (1959), Scollon *et al.* (2012) and Clyne (1994)

element of non-verbal and verbal communication can help to identify the individual and national cultural differences present between the two people completing the communication. This assertion is divergent from the application of intercultural differences noted in Chapters 1 and 2, where the difference is simply labelled as national or geographic. It is an important assertion, however, as a culture can be inferred from a single word or action perceived by another person in a fleeting encounter. Acknowledgement of this individual, time and context-based definition of culture is important in tourism, events and hospitality, as customers often act differently away from home and the staff are also in a performative role aiming to satisfy each guest. In this way, service encounters in these contexts are always unique, evolving and dependent on the two individuals completing the encounter.

A final consideration before the review of intercultural sensitivity training is intercultural competence. Like intercultural communication, intercultural competence is applied in a range of disciplines. Most notably, it is used in language education contexts whereby students are required to reflect on their competency when speaking in other languages and with people from different cultures. This term, again, hinges on varied definitions of intercultural, this time dependent on the location in which the competency is assessed. For an overview of the models applied in intercultural competence research, see Table 6.3.

The models referred to Table 6.3 enable researchers to analyse the level of competency exhibited in intercultural interactions. The forms

Table 6.2 Verbal communication

Area	What does this sound like?	What does it suggest?
Linguistic relativity	Communicating the same word in different languages	Speech influences how we view things (world view). Germans use maternal aunts, English speakers use just Aunt as the name
Communicative relativity	Language used when communicating with different people	Informal language on Facebook. Formal language in written assignments
Language inferences	Meaning from words used can create an inferred belief, intention or understanding	People can misunderstand language owing to inferred meaning
Speech act	Situation in which communication occurs	That two people want to communicate something to each other
Speech event	The phrase of communication offered to another person	A person wants to request or state something to another person
Low context culture	The interpretation of the exact words spoken to mean all communication	Communication relies on language solely
Involvement	A statement or question that identifies empathy or awareness of another person's involvement: 'I know just what you mean'	Awareness of other people having the same background or familiarity with a subject or action
Independence	A statement or question identifying an understanding of independence: 'It would be nice to do something, but I am aware you may be busy'	It does not take ownership from the other person. It communicates awareness of independence
Prosodic patterns	Intonation when speaking	Intonation can suggest emotion, position and familiarity with the other person or situation.
Discourse system	Words and language used based on an individual's background	Each and every person will use different words and phrasing to communicate to another person

Source: Based on Piller (2011) and Scollon *et al.* (2012)

Table 6.3 Models of intercultural competence

Model	Authors	Component
Compositional	Deardorff (2006)	Lists of knowledge, skills and behaviour used to identify a pyramid of effective intercultural competence
Co-orientational	Fantini (2001) Byram (1997)	Linguistic processes and skills to achieve effective intercultural competence
Developmental	King and Baxter Magolda (2005) INCA (2004)	Competence evolves and develops over time. Moving from ethnocentric to ethnorelativism. Intercultural sensitivity
Adaptational	Kim (2008)	Refers to intercultural communicative competence development via encounter and adaptation. It is something that develops through stages and where each person adapts to suit the interlocutor
Causal path	Arasaratnam and Doerfel (2005)	A linear process in which communication variables are examined individually

(*Source:* Based on Firth, 2019)

of competency, level of ability and context in which these have been applied vary according to the discipline and focus of the communication. Application of these models in service encounters for tourism, events and hospitality is unknown and present focus on intercultural tenets of service remains fixed on customer satisfaction through intercultural service encounter theory. Use these models in consideration of the critical incidents at the end of this chapter to outline how competence for intercultural sensitivity is evident in staff completing service encounters.

Intercultural Sensitivity Training

Intercultural sensitivity training theory is widely based on Bennett s (1986) model of intercultural communication between people of different nationalities and assessing a person's intercultural competence in this communication. His definition of intercultural states that there is a perceived difference between one person and another, but that this difference is not labelled or categorised, but rather 'a learner's subjective experience of difference' (Bennett, 1986: 181). The intercultural sensitivity training model is shown in Figure 6.1.

Bennett's use of ethnocentrism and ethnorelativism (the latter created as an antonym to ethnocentrism) is taken from a chapter on intercultural communication as written by Samovar and Porter in 1982. Samovar *et al.* (2013) define ethnocentrism as a worldview in which each person perceives their own culture as rigid and central. This model for intercultural sensitivity training suggests that students can complete progressive learning, development and accomplishment from ethnocentrism to ethnorelativism.

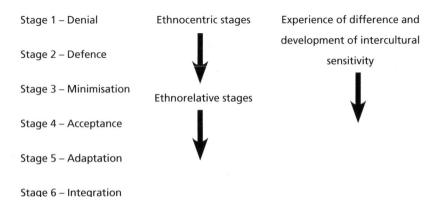

Figure 6.1 Bennett's model of intercultural sensitivity training
Source: Based on Bennett (1986: 182)

To understand how ethnocentrism and ethnorelativism are situated in tourism, events and hospitality contexts, Lashley and Morrison's book offers a further explanation:

> European waiters create fewer problems than American waiters because the former are more accustomed to class differences and low social mobility and therefore less resentful of social distinctions. (Lashley & Morrison, 2007: 264)

This quotation suggests that tourism, events and hospitality staff's nationality can affect service because of their worldview and understanding of differences. However, the quotation does not identify whether staff are located in that context or merely a national of that area. For example, a European waiter working in the USA may actually conform to the supposed US ethnocentric tendencies owing to assimilation of the host culture. Furthermore, restaurant tourism, events and hospitality businesses often create cultural experiences that specifically require staff to act or perform in respect of nationality (e.g. staff who may be ethnically labelled Indian or Chinese because they work in ethnic restaurants). Therefore, ethnocentrism and ethnorelativism may be part of the expected performance by tourism, events and hospitality staff, as well as being a frame through which to ensure that they can serve a range of other cultures. Clearly, consideration of cultures and differences in these staff is complex and multidimensional.

Two papers on application and adaptation of Bennett's model of intercultural sensitivity will now be critiqued to identify the types of encounters where intercultural sensitivity development and application are required in tourism, events and hospitality.

Medina-Lopez-Portillo's (2004) doctoral studies suggest that students benefit from study abroad programmes of a certain length, whereby they increase their intercultural sensitivity. Here, she applied Bennett's model to explore whether Maryland students who went to Taxco and Mexico City thought of themselves as individual cultural beings or belonging to a culture grouped by nationality. Participants completed a survey akin to Barron and Dasli's (2010) later research, but they also conducted interviews and offered student journal entries on their intercultural experiences. Results from this research suggested that study-abroad programmes specifically aided student intercultural sensitivity development (31% in Taxco and 67% in Mexico City). Longer periods of time abroad led to increased intercultural sensitivity. Cultural differences analysed were located in both nationality and individual behaviour. These points noted, there were interesting conclusions drawn when considering how this could apply to tourism, events and hospitality education. They identified that if a student had a rigid understanding of culture to begin with, it was more difficult for them to progress through Bennett's stages of intercultural sensitivity. When considering this paper from a tourism, events and hospitality education perspective, it could be argued that all tourism, events and hospitality experiences would offer similar intercultural sensitivity improvements. Tourism, events and hospitality work itself brings together people from all nationalities and backgrounds, so students could encounter and reflect on differences without necessarily going to a different geographical location. Moreover, student groups themselves are inherently global; therefore, the class itself may already be in a different location from their home or national culture. Clearly, this paper feels that geographical movement is needed for intercultural sensitivity development, but i would argue that tourism, events and hospitality education and training already do this.

As noted, Medina-Lopez-Portillo's (2004) paper situates intercultural differences in national and locational differences. It is odd, therefore, that the author also considers the individual understanding of intercultural sensitivity. If it is accepted that students can perceive differences on an individual level, why question large cultural differences from geographical locations? The individual tenets of culture as identified by her participants are as follows:

I think it's really just what people are used to in a different culture. I think it's just the little things that you take for granted, that you accept as part of your everyday life, that everybody does that it's so obvious that those little things that change when you go to another culture. I think that's the real cultural differences. It's the part of everyday life that changes from society to society. (Medina-Lopez-Portillo, 2004: 188)

These individual tenets of intercultural sensitivity infer adaptive personality, behaviour, attitude and motivation. This has parallels with the skills required for emotional labour and aesthetic labour as well as the individual service types offered in the industry. Cultural differences in a multicultural society should not assume that the geographical location of the person infers their nationality. In this study the nationality of participants is not confirmed; instead, their own culture is inferred by their geographical movement from Maryland to Mexico. Moving geographical location is not the only way in which cultural differences can be encountered to assess intercultural sensitivity. If you visit an ethnic restaurant (e.g. Chinese, Indian or Asian) or attend a cultural event (religious, national or societal), you will also interact with people from other nationalities and experience cuisines, language or behaviour different from what is usual.

Moving on to tourism, events and hospitality education research in the UK, Barron and Dasli (2010) completed a quantitative study with their tourism, events and hospitality students at Edinburgh Napier University to investigate their intercultural sensitivity. In this study, the 'difference' taken from intercultural was attributed to whether students were classified as either home or international. As noted earlier, any university classroom can be viewed as a multicultural setting within which students could analyse their own ethnocentric and ethnorelative perspectives. However, this research suggested that classrooms do not inherently allow for this training. Instead, it was noted that international students tended not to integrate with the home students, which led to a division in the groups. The reason for this division was attributed to language problems, wherein the home and international students could not communicate effectively. These language problems made group work assignments difficult and home students became less empathetic towards the international students. Results from this study identified that intercultural sensitivity problems in a classroom were addressed and resolved easily, as the classroom context already engendered open debate through which to resolve differences in opinion and perception. The perceived differences noted by these students lay in behaviour and expectations of 'normality', which actually suggests an individual and behavioural intercultural divide rather than solely language problems. Evidently, intercultural sensitivity education in tourism, events and hospitality focused classroom can have positive outcomes, but the authors did acknowledge that they were uncertain whether the intercultural sensitivity developments would be replicated outside of the classroom's protected space.

These outcomes from Barron and Dasli (2010) show how tourism, events and hospitality academics have interpreted Bennett's use of 'difference' to mean nationality within students' enrolment status. By applying this definition to an examination of intercultural sensitivity, they unveil a range of skills present. Willingness, adaptation, empathy, understanding and respect are all noted in how their students address cultural differences. However, as 'the students do not engage in sufficient culture learning opportunities' (Barron & Dasli, 2010: 14), it was noted that UK students tended to be ethnocentric rather than ethnorelative. Again, I would argue that classifying students as either home or international and using this as the parameter of national difference is inappropriate. A student is classified as a 'home' student if they have UK or European citizenship. Living in or having parents from a geographical location does not mean that all of these people have the same perspectives or backgrounds. For example, West Indian families who came to the UK in the 1950s are now in their second or third generation, but may still speak Patois.

Evidently, intercultural sensitivity has been considered within general education and tourism, events and hospitality classrooms to explore whether students have the necessary skills for intercultural encounters on graduation. The skills identified include personality traits, behaviour, language, motivation, understanding and awareness.

Critical Incidents with Key Questions

Intercultural sensitivity was another area noted as being needed by employers, but not fully supported by new applicants into tourism, events and hospitality roles. Using Bennett's (1986) definition of intercultural sensitivity, research for this book found that participants showed high intercultural sensitivity, but their customers and colleagues did not. Jessica was consistently asked about her own nationality in encounters which did not warrant this probing from customers. Lucy witnessed ethnocentric behaviour from her colleagues about Irish customers, whom management referred to as English. Tom and Jessica were both requested to change their pronunciation according to Mancunian or Irish accents and language.

These data confirm that ethnocentric beliefs and behaviour were present in customer service encounters. However, the incidents offered to identify customers and colleagues as ethnocentric enabled the graduates to educate and communicate ethnorelative positions clearly.

When I probed Sophie about her incidents relating to intercultural sensitivity, she noted that culture is about:

> different things. You know about others, and not just focus on yours and think that you are right.

This ethnorelative position (Bennett, 1986) was seen in all participants' accounts of culture and difference. As noted earlier in this chapter, Bennett (1986) defined intercultural sensitivity as being on a scale from ethnocentric to ethnorelative. All participants used for this book appeared to have an ethnorelative perspective on culture based on knowledge of a range of people and nationalities. In this way, their intercultural sensitivity was seen as high, as Bennett (1986) identified that intercultural sensitivity education is focused on developing people to move from an ethnocentric to an ethnorelative perspective.

An analysis of intercultural service encounter theory with data collected for the study, it was also clear that intercultural sensitivity has parity with tenets of intercultural service encounters. Participants experienced culture shocks within the incidents offered. Examples of these from the data include Sophie, Jessica and Tom all being questioned by customers on her nationality and Lucy was called a 'racist' by her colleagues owing to a stereotype associated with her nationality. These culture shocks seen in the data support Strauss and Mang's (1999) research on intercultural service encounters. However, staff had these shocks as a result of customer comments or questions and not simply because of perceived cultural differences. Further, and as the study analysed the staffs' perspective, it is clear that culture shocks are not merely 'ascribed stereotypes' (Barker & Härtel, 2004: 4) viewed by customers and hindering service quality, but based on customer intrigue at notice of transnational employees within a Tourism, Events and Hospitality business.

Intercultural sensitivity was noted in data from the study within the following skills and knowledge present:

• Communication around culture, nationality and difference.
• Knowledge of difference (menu, drinks and linguistics).
• Empathy with different service preferences based on culture.
• Negotiation on service types and processes requested.

These findings have been added to the model of customer service encounters offered in Chapter 2 and expanded to include intercultural sensitivity:

Figure 6.2 adds intercultural sensitivity to the model of customer service encounters to clarify the previous (traditional) and new dimensions as a result of data offered in this book. By including this, it is clear that due to the acknowledgement of 'others' in this encounter, intercultural sensitivity is not only needed of staff for their customers but also for their colleagues, management and suppliers also. The communication and interaction viewed across this model embrace all verbal and non-verbal communication forms noted for Intercultural communication and that the competencies drawn from this communication can also be classified as intercultural competencies. This is a contribution to existing knowledge in customer service encounter theory and is acknowledged in Chapters 9 and 10 with further additions offered to the model.

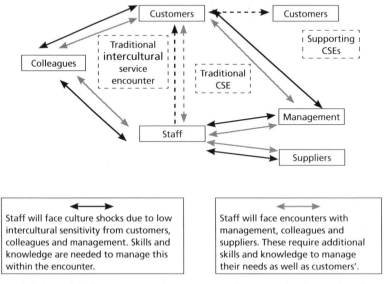

Figure 6.2 A model of customer service encounters incorporating intercultural sensitivity
Note: CSE, customer service encounter

Misunderstanding language

I worked the evening shift from 3–11 with another person on the reception and the bar. During this time the alarm for the hostel had broken and was constantly beeping, therefore the repair man was needed to be called in order to stop the noise. This was around 9.30 pm therefore we were worried that someone would not be able to come out to the hostel, and we were already getting complaints by the customers, we had to tell them that the beeping was going to be fixed within the evening and had to remind them that the noise should not affect them in their dormitory rooms. When the engineer finally arrived he could only speak Portuguese and the other person who was working on reception was busy, therefore I had to deal with him and try to explain the situation which was very difficult. At the same time as trying to speak to this man, I heard a women behind me shouting 'oi, oi' – in England this would be a rude way to get somebodies attention so I turned around and wasn't pleased because I thought the women was being rude whilst I was clearly busy with the engineer. However, when I had said 'can I help you' to the women, and she continued to speak in Portuguese then the misunderstanding was instantly resolved, due to 'oi' being the Brazilian Portuguese way of saying 'hey' – this was one time where a language barrier had caused confusion in the role as well as frustrating feeling for myself. (Mary)

Questions to consider from this incident:

(1) How do you think Mary felt when the customer was shouting 'oi oi' to her?
(2) Do you know of any other usual phrases in different languages which could sound insulting or rude to others?
(3) In a situation where neither customer nor staff speak the same language, is it possible to meet all service standards and customer expectations?
(4) Using the list of non-verbal communication forms tabulated in this chapter, identify how each one was present in this incident and why.

Educating customers on cultural difference

As usual, I go to work. I work as an event helper or waitress in the 'Hotel name' that located in Manchester. Today there's no event, so I assigned to the restaurant to serve customers. I saw a couple walking into the restaurant, so I decide to serve them to a table, and start to help them to order their meal. Once they sit down, the man asked whether I'm local or international student, because I speak fluent English, but I do not look like a European. So I say that I'm an international student from Malaysia. The reason why I can speak fluent English because we do English from high school, and I do all my modules in college with English. So the guy was so surprised, and he said, he thought that Malaysia is a Muslim country and does not have other culture as Chinese, and can speak fluent English. So I told him that although Malaysia is a Muslim country, we do have Chinese and Indian culture, I'm sorry, religion, and we do not have to become a Muslim. We have our own rights to choose our religion.

And we talk quite the long time, and the customer was quite happy and he said he got something new in his head now, and saying thank you to me to change his perception to Malaysia. Talking so much with the customer made me feel that not all the European racist on Asian, some are really friendly to accept Asian and wanted to know more about Asian. (Sophie)

Questions to consider from this incident:

(1) What could it have been about Sophie that suggested to the customer that she was not European? Is this a correct assumption?
(2) Using the forms of verbal communication tabulated in this chapter, write and perform key phrases Sophie might have used in this incident.
(3) If Sophie was English, how might this customer question have felt to her?
(4) How did Sophie make this encounter a positive and educational incident for the customer?

Tipping cultures

Today I have had an incident relating to communication, more linked to cultural knowledge I suppose. It's an observation that's probably daily conversation, but when at our restaurant you seat an Asian, Indian-Pakistani or Chinese table, you quite often get some sort of feedback from the waitresses that you seat in their section. Normally joking, but a lot of time there's sort of an element of truth to it. Well there is. Basically, waiters and waitresses generally and especially in this restaurant, the Polish staff don't like being seated Asian tables.

And I've been told and experienced it myself over the years that first and foremost, they don't tip. That's obviously a cultural thing, it's not anything personal. But it's quite difficult for people who are used to a tipping culture to get used to because a small, as a waitress you rely largely on your tips. And a small tip even 2% of the bill feels like a bit of a slap in the face, but it helps. And when you don't get any tip, generally they get sort of ... what's the word ... well my experience and from what the waitresses told me that you quite often have to change dishes, make sure something's taken out, try to get these meals to come out with these meals, just go out of your way for a lot of the Asian people that come in. And then to not get a tip, it annoys staff and it yeah. It makes them unhappy.

And so that observation, one of the Polish girls I work with, I seated her a couple of tables, two tables of Indian-Pakistani origin and a Chinese table. And she came up to me and asked if I didn't like her. And she was completely joking, but she wasn't. She was joking saying I didn't like her, but she wasn't joking about the fact she wasn't happy about the tables she'd been seated. And that was, we spoke about it afterwards. And it's actually generally Polish staff that feel more comfortable telling me how they feel I think. And they said that with especially mainly with Chinese tables that they don't tip. They're quite rude, which is also maybe a lack of understanding their culture on our part. And quite demanding.

And I can't actually say that I completely agree with that statement. I'd never tar a whole nation with the same brush or just say anything negatively about a whole nation of people. But when seating people, most people let me finish my pitch at the door sort of 'hi, how's it going, how are you, table for four? Would you like to sit inside or outside?' That's what I try to keep it down to. And when I've had Chinese tables come through, they've asked, well they've not let me finish my sentence. They've sort of barged past me, not listened to me, and just been difficult to manage.

And so they have a, maybe not all of them, but a lot of them have a culture of clicking to get your attention. And that a lot of people find offensive, which is also maybe something that they just do. It's normal to them. But it's annoyed a lot of people, well it annoys our staff anyway. The staff at the restaurant I'm working at. And what else, what else did they say.

I think basically just the impatience and not tipping. My dad went to Japan, and he's been to China on business trips. And he's told me it's just you get treated like royalty, especially Japan actually. Where there's staff there ready, waiting. It's obviously in the more business-type lounges and it might not apply to everything, but the staff waiting to light your cigarette. As you lift your cigarette box, there's someone there with a lighter. And they've got hand towels and it's a great guest experience. So maybe they're not used to sort of it being so, staff not being as efficient maybe. (Lucy)

Questions to consider from this incident:

(1) If you remove the nationality, noted by Lucy, of the customers and staff in this incident and replace them with other descriptors like men/women/tall/old/thin/pretty could the issues present in the encounter still be valid and usual?
(2) What judgements does Lucy acknowledge and then challenge according to her own perspectives?
(3) What intercultural competences has Lucy used in this incident? Pick one of the models noted and identify her level of competence portrayed.
(4) How could management tackle staff judgements on these customers?

Summary

(1) To outline definitions on intercultural communication and intercultural competence.

Intercultural communication requires staff to consider verbal and non-verbal tenets of communication and adapt these appropriately when conveying information to another person. Intercultural competence is the level of ability a person has to manage intercultural interactions.

(2) To understand forms of verbal and non-verbal communication.

Proxemics, chronemics, kinesics, adumbration, high context cultures, scripts, frames and schemata were noted as part of non-verbal communication which may be formed or inherited from a person's nationality or family upbringing. Linguistic relativity, communicative relativity, language inferences, speech acts and events, low context culture, involvement, independence, prosodic patterns and discourse systems were noted as components of verbal communication.

(3) To review models of intercultural competence and apply these to customer service encounters.

Compositional, co-orientational, developmental, adaptational and causal path models of intercultural competence were outlined. Using the incidents at the end of this chapter, apply your knowledge of these to consider all competences required for intercultural sensitivity in service encounters.

(4) To analyse intercultural sensitivity training for tourism, events and hospitality and identify its use for staff completing customer service encounters.

The literature on intercultural sensitivity for tourism, events and hospitality was found to use an ethnocentric lens as it classified culture using nationality and not small cultures. A key issue noted was that these publications fail to accurately ascertain the nationality of the student, customer or staff. The geographical location was again used (similarly to intercultural service encounter literature discussed in Chapter 1) as a way to identify culture. By using a large culture approach in current studies, staff perspectives from small culture experiences and identity are missing. Using the critical incidents in this chapter, consider whether large nationality is present, or if intercultural sensitivity is due to their individual competences in communicating and completing service delivery. Intercultural sensitivity was noted by People 1st (2013) as a key skill required by tourism, events and hospitality employers, but consistently lacking in applicants put forward for roles. This chapter has moved discussion forwards on the definition and use of intercultural by addressing intercultural communication, competence and sensitivity. These areas have shown the diversity of application and use of the term intercultural and has enabled a more flexible, critical and contemporary definition which hinges on two individuals meeting and communicating effectively. Forms of communication have been identified in more detail to enable readers an insight into how linguistic and communication studies experts analyse speech patterns and communication. Models of intercultural competency have been outlined to clarify how competency can be both measured and assessed in these encounters. Regardless of citizenship and nationality, the staff and customer completing an encounter are part of a range of social and economic groups which all inform their action and behaviour. Acknowledgement of the individual identities in these situations allows for a more ethical review of intercultural encounters and supports ethnorelative intercultural sensitivity development.

Annotated bibliography

Hall, E. (1959) *The Silent Language*. New York: Doubleday.

This text is widely cited for discussion and research on intercultural communication. Hall worked in the army for a number of years and this text comes from his experience of working in Europe and the Philipinnes during World War II. His famous quotation from this text 'culture is communication and communication is culture' (chapter 5: 186) identifies how culture is not simply explicit knowledge to be repeated, but it is emergent through spoken communication. As an anthropologist, Hall saw communication as being a tool to develop and understand culture in a linguistic frame. Hall has written a number of texts on intercultural communication, but this one is of note as he identifies how culture can be polychronic. Polychronic cultures show how a situation can use a number of events simultaneously. For example, an office worker can complete singular tasks in a linear fashion (monochronic) or can be polychronic in responding to a variety of demands all at once.

Question: Using the example of a waiter in a restaurant at a tourist destination. How does their work require polychronic communication and evidence of polychronic culture?

Barron, P. and Dasli, M. (2010) Towards an understanding of integration amongst hospitality and tourism students using Bennett's developmental model of intercultural sensitivity. *Journal of Hospitality, Tourism, Events and Hospitality, Sport and Tourism Education* 9 (2), 77–88.

These authors from Edinburgh Napier University use Bennett's (1986) model of intercultural sensitivity to explore students levels of intercultural sensitivity. They administer a survey to students in the tourism department to ascertain if there are any differences between home and international students level of intercultural sensitivity and if there are themes in their levels according to their status as a home or international student. As the survey is not presented within the paper, it is not possible to identify if the authors established the nationality, family experience of country of residence for these students. It appears as though they simply use the university label of home versus international as the determining factor to analyse their intercultural awareness. This comparator is rendered irrelevant when you consider that international students could have moved to the UK at a young age and spent their time living in the local area of the university. Equally, that home students who are nationals of the UK could have moved abroad for their earlier education. If you consider these points and presume the authors did not pose this question, their analysis and data might be seen as flawed. Conclusions suggest that home students seem to be more ethnorelative than international students, but there is no rationale for this finding. The authors do note limitations in the study owing to the sample and location of the study, but the issue of the prior location of living and educational experience is not acknowledged.

Question: During your studies, how you noticed differences in how you and your colleagues work within the classroom? Are the groups of friends who sit together easily grouped or defined and is this in physical cultural differences?

Bennett, M. (1986) A developmental approach to training for intercultural sensitivity. *International Journal of Intercultural Relations* 10 (2), 179–196.

Bennett was based at Portland State University in the USA and researched in speech communication. This paper is a conceptual piece outlining her model for training in intercultural communication. Her model identifies how people are either ethnocentric or ethnorelative in their cultural sensitivity. Within these two levels there are three levels of understanding: denial, defence and minimization in ethnocentric; and acceptance, adaptation and integration in ethnorelative. By noting stages and levels of intercultural sensitivity it is suggested that this is fluid and moveable, but that there are also cues to being rigidly integrated or in denial of other cultures. Written in 1986, this paper is symptomatic of the time and location of its author. In 2019, it can be argued that the transnational flows of people mean that integration or denial is no longer present. If they are, they may not be necessary or obvious in service encounters either. For each of the stages in the model, there are diagnosis and training strategies noted to combat the perceived problem in intercultural sensitivity.

Question: Which level of intercultural sensitivity do you think you are in? Has this ever changed and if so, why?

Byram, M. (1997) *Teaching and Assessing Intercultural Communicative Competence.* Clevedon: Multilingual Matters.

Byram is a Professor of Education at Durham University in the UK. His research and publications on intercultural communicative competence (ICC) education and training are extensive and widely cited. This text offers an excellent overview of his thinking for teaching ICC including models of ICC and positions on communicating culture in face-to-face encounters. Although the publication focuses on foreign language teaching, there are links to be drawn to tourism as service encounters in these locations require effective communication between two people of different nationalities, local dialects or colloquial phrasing, all of which need to be clearly communicated and understood.

Question: On page 13 in chapter 1, Byram offers examples of non-verbal communication which clarifies culture. How do these differ between people of different cultures?

Deardorff, D. (2006) Identification and assessment of intercultural competence as a student outcome of internationalization. *Journal of Studies in International Education* 10 (3), 241–266. DOI:doi/10.1177/1028315306287002.

Based in Durham, North Carolina, Deardorff is Executive Director of the Association of International Education Administrators. As an adjunct professor at local universities and international visiting professor, her expertise and publications on intercultural competence are extensive. Similar to Barron and Dasli's article noted earlier, this article examines the intercultural competence of students in higher education. The paper identifies definitions of intercultural competence, establishes how this is perceived by scholars and students in higher education, where and why it is required in higher education and the levels that students portray this. Conclusions accept that intercultural competence is not limited or simplistically defined as it requires action, behaviour and attitude in different situations in order for it to be individually assessed. A new model of intercultural competence is offered alongside new research questions to consider.

Question: Use figure 4 on page 256 in a service encounter situation and identify how the staff will use their intercultural competence to perform the service.

7 Co-production and Co-creation

Chapter Learning Objectives

(1) To appreciate and understand definitions of co-creation and co-production.
(2) To understand how co-production requires customers and staff to work together in creating service encounters.
(3) To identify how customers and staff create service encounters in tandem using their communication skills.

Introduction

Co-creation and co-production are important terms in emergent literature from service quality theory, which is the driving force of service encounters in tourism, events and hospitality. This chapter will define these terms and identify problems when comparing them with the service encounter literature noted earlier in this book. They serve as a counter perspective to the customer/management dominance in theory noted in service encounters, and acknowledge that service is produced and consumed bilaterally. Customer-to-customer positions discussed in customer service encounter literature also links to this chapter as they are component co-creators and co-producers of the experience.

Co-creating the Service

Co-creation can be defined as when a customer becomes a 'co-producer' of a service (Gummesson, 1991: 68). This is seen within service-dominant logic and was based on the marketing and service quality literature from the 1980s. Literature on co-creation is primarily found in tourism publications, since tourists are seen to both participate in and actively create the tourist experience. The work of Pine and Gilmore (1999) is also heavily linked to the term, because the experience economy has driven customers to become creators and not simply users of service. Similarly, Rihova *et al.* (2015: 356) identify that co-creation occurs owing to the 'social contexts' in which tourist services occur. Co-creation links to service quality since researchers have perceived that the expectations customers came with were actually being moulded in the service encounter owing to their participation and production of the experience. Co-creation is therefore also seen as 'co-creating value' in a service encounter (Rihova *et al.*, 2015: 357). Binkhorst (2005) and later Binkhorst and Dekker (2009) identify that it is simply the humans involved in the service that creates the value of the experience. In this way, co-creation is opposed to previous research on service quality as:

> staged experiences that are considered too commercial, artificial and superficial and therefore not always suitable to attract todays customers. (Binkhorst & Dekker, 2009: 312)

This work suggests that customers in the 21st century no longer want managed experiences and that they desire to create and participate in the service in order to be satisfied. Thus, co-creation is rooted in marketing and service quality literature, but addresses new forms of tourists wanting to produce the experience themselves.

The work of Navarro *et al.* and Harkison is also relevant to the discussion here. Based primarily in the hotel sectors, this work is emergent in co-creation and offers insight into hospitality contexts where staff are required to serve tourist and event customers.

Starting with Navarro *et al.* (2014), this research considered how hoteliers prepare for the arrival of and support the experiences of disabled customers. In this research, they are explicit about descriptions of the customers, but vague on the particular staff supporting their arrival, as they are noted homogenously as the 'hoteliers' (Navarro *et al.*, 2014: 815). As such, the hotelier participants could be one or more people working in the business. These could have had a variety of experience with disabled customers and their own personal life or experiences with disabled customers are unclear. One outcome of the research is that people with a disability do not feel their comments or feedback are treated as equal to customers who do not have disabilities. Advice to management from this research suggests they should be more:

> engaging, collaborating with and learning from customers. (Navarro *et al.*, 2014: 817)

This quotation could be applied to any management in tourism, events and hospitality, as learning from customer feedback leads to improved service delivery. Further, they recommend that 'if staff members had received suitable training' (Navarro *et al.*, 2014: 818) they would have offered higher levels of service. Similarly to the training recommended to staff on culture noted in Chapter 1, training on disability could lead to othering these customers or making incorrect judgements on them based visual appearance. This book suggests that utilising current staff knowledge and experience will aid their management of all customer requirements, regardless of disability. Where customers require particular support or advice to co-create an experience, it would be more genuine if staff are encouraged to ask customers for advice directly. Supporting staff to be inquisitive about the various customer differences and how this will lead to alternative co-created experience will not only show the customer care, but also lead to increased staff knowledge.

The following two papers from Navarro *et al.* (2015, 2016) are still located in hotels, but are concerned with disabled customers (2015) and spa guests (2016). Navarro *et al.* (2015) outlined that disabled customers require effective relationships with staff, staff training and a supportive environment (in order of ascending importance). In terms of staff training, they noted that staff should be 'more aware of disabled customers' needs' (Navarro *et al.*, 2015: 1634). Staff should be supported to be aware of all customer needs, as well as their own. Further, the staff perspective is offered from:

> eight experts on accessible tourism and tourism for disabled people, each from a disability association. (Navarro *et al.*, 2015: 1631)

Again, instead of reviewing specific front-line staff interactions to support co-creation with disabled customers, Navarro *et al.* (2015) sought advice from experts who advise on tourism for people with disabilities. Therefore, the advice was not sought from staff perspectives working and communicating with disabled customers. Staff with disabilities were also missing in the discussion on support for these customers. If staff with disabilities are employed within these hotels, their advice should be sought in aid of other colleagues completing interactions with this customer group.

Within Navarro *et al.*'s (2016) study of co-creation in hotel spa experiences, they identified that satisfying service was due to customers:

> who either help other customers and are tolerant, or those who have a positive relation with the employees. (Navarro *et al.*, 2016: 1339)

The personal qualities noted in this quotation can also be seen as elements of good citizenship (Firth, 2011). Part of being a good citizen means being someone who helps others and has positive relationships. These are not specific to service in hotel spas and are a component part of training staff through human resources management in tourism, events and hospitality (Baum, 2006).

None of the participants in the study noted incidents with disabled customers. This does not confirm that these particular service encounters are devoid of the issue, but that they were not noted as important to participants to offer as demands found in employment. Also, some of the customers could have had disabilities that participants were either unaware of or were not evident in affecting the service creation. Being a customer with a disability or experiencing leisure facilities in a spa is a form of customer and location of service, but are not seen as different from the intercultural encounters completed by all front-line staff.

Now to consider the work of Harkison and three articles from her research (Harkison, 2017, 2018; Harkison *et al.*, 2018). Her 2017 paper notes how co-creation requires customers to create the value in experiences as well as interpret value from the experience. Instead of using a personalised service provided by staff, this publication recommends the increased use of technology in service interactions. The photo used at the beginning of this chapter is of an international restaurant chain who have implemented technology in the ordering process of their meals and this service has been increasing across the service sectors. The shift from services marketing literature in the 1980s, which supported staff delivery of the service, to customers co-creating the service using computer interfaces is important. As technology is faceless, an encounter solely using technology may negatively affect brand perceptions. Technology is also inconsistent in its operating abilities. If technology fails to work, local staff may be blamed for this failure. As it is unlikely local staff will have created the operating programs, this will lead to further issues for staff in service encounters.

Harkison (2018) further supports the use of technology in customer interactions and notes how this may be linked to societal changes. People now increasingly communicate with others virtually, rather than face-to-face. This study offers customer, management and employee perspectives equally to consider how luxury hotels co-create value. In terms of how staff can improve their support for co-creation she notes:

> encouraging staff to visit producers of local products and wine will enable them to talk informatively to the guests about these topics, (Harkison, 2018: 16)

Development of staff product knowledge is common practice in tourism, events and hospitality businesses. Learning about items on a menu, rooms in the property or tickets available are all examples of business practice required to complete service delivery. By considering staff perspectives, this research approaches co-creation in acceptance and inquisition of all potential positions. However, in Harkison *et al.* (2018: 1735) management are recommended to offer:

> training, creating standards of procedure, introducing incentives to the employees and using communication tools that will enhance the guests' and employees' perception of the property.

Again, this is a recommendation for staff to be trained and create service for customers, rather than reflect on how staff can aid co-creation with their own individual positions. People within the encounters are termed actors and are seen to offer a 'performance' (Harkison *et al.*, 2018: 1735). This mirrors emotional and aesthetic labour theory, whereby staff are required to act a part instead of offer service as an empowered professional completing their duties.

Co-producing the Experience

Co-production was coined by Lovelock and Young (1979) and relates to the service quality created by customers, but using services already on offer. Chathoth *et al.* (2013) use a self-service buffet in a hotel as an example of this. In this example, the customer creates the service by taking the food from the buffet, but there is a limit to this creation because of the number of dishes on display. Therefore, co-production is seen as more passive than co-creation as customers can only use what is at their disposal.

These two terms evidently relate to service encounters as they note how service is created with 'face-to-face' encounters (Gummesson,

1991: 67). Although these terms relate to a wide range of experiences in tourism, current research on these terms again neglects the staff involved in creating the experiences. Grissemann and Stokburger-Saure (2012: 1490) recommend that travel agencies need 'highly trained staff' in order for co-creation to occur. In this paper, they note that the staff handed out surveys to customers, but they do not ask how the staff completed this part of the service. Binkhorst and Dekker (2009: 314) note how customers are 'partners' in the service, but again fail to acknowledge the other person in the partnership. Rihova *et al.* (2015: 357) also note that co-creation is a 'joint value realising process', but link the company as the other part of co-creation with customers and not the staff involved in creating the service encompassing value.

In terms of educating staff to co-produce and co-create these experiences in tourism, no current literature was found (it mainly relates to training and managing them). Binkhorst and Dekker (2009) note that education is an important quadrant for tourist motivation and demand, but this is only one component of the experience economy (Pine & Gilmore, 1999) and not seen from the position of educating the staff involved in the experience. Evidently, these two emergent terms are important in tourism services and tourism, events and hospitality marketing, but by ignoring the staff involved in creating the experiences again neglects the other position contributing towards the encounter. The study used in this book looked at the service encounter from the staff's perspective and so addresses a current gap seen in co-production and co-creation literature to identify how staff help to create the service.

Discussion from the Study Data

Co-creation and co-production are part of emergent literature from service quality theory and publications on the experience economy. Two key points are highlighted below from an analysis of the incidents offered by graduates in the industry:

(1) Staff are a vital component in creating customer experiences and have their own needs and expectations which need to be met. This is not currently acknowledged in the co-creation and co-production literature. Humans, customers and management are acknowledged in the texts, but the needs of staff are not fully outlined. For example, Holly consistently narrated how she needed her customers to sign contracts so that she could confirm events to venues holding spaces on her behalf. Holly was liaising between both customers and venue managers in order to create successful events. Incidents gathered from staff show that customers needed more empathy and understanding of staff needs in order to create successful experiences for their guests. This was also seen in Martha's incidents

where she needed to consistently inform her guests of the financial terms and conditions of their stay in the hotel in order to complete her role effectively. Without considering the staff perspective in co-creation literature, current research omits to mention how staff also have needs and expectations of the customers. This is important so that graduates are able to reflect on their participation in the experience and inform customers about the actions and information they require from their customers.

(2) Again linking to the lack of consideration for staff in current literature, this book suggests that co-creation and co-production need further analysis of how staff specifically contribute to the experience. Looking from a staff perspective, staff motivation and willingness is a crucial element in creating the customers' experience and without this, the service would fail. For example, Sophie encountered a customer who demanded a typical French dish. Instead of simply informing the guests this was not possible, she offered to inform her head chef and request the item on the menu in future. This offers an example of how motivated and willing staff are able to create a more effective experience for their customers. This response was not due to scripted service either, it was a personal response from that member of staff. Alternatively, Martha narrated about a very rude customer who was demanding changes to her bill over the phone:

There the payments that I could understand if I was having rude phone calls about, but from working in accounts receivable myself, I know that sometimes however hard somebody might try on the phone, if they can't make that payment, they physically can't do it. There's no point in being really rude to them. I just think sometimes attitudes like that, they just don't help the situation

This excerpt from Martha identifies how demanding customers made the encounter difficult for the staff and that poor customer communication hinders successful service. Staff motivation and willingness in the creation of experiences is therefore negatively affected by customers in some encounters.

These two findings noted from the analysis of participant data again exemplify how the staff perspective is crucial in completing effective customer service encounters. Both co-creation and co-production literature currently fail to consider these perspectives. Without acknowledgement of staff perspectives, current research omits the other person(s) involved in creating the service. Training management and staff on these elements and ensuring the use their empathy and patience to navigate the various customer demands will ensure they co-create and co-produce experiences in mind of customer needs and business requirements.

Critical Incidents with Key Questions

Supporting colleagues in co-creation

Yesterday was Wednesday. In regards to work I would say it was quite a stressful day for two main reasons. The first one was, one of my colleagues that I've been working with closely had a training day today, which meant that I had to take over all her work as well for that day, as well as all my work for that day. One of the clients in particular was a woman who wanted a conference for next week, so I had a very, very short lead time and she couldn't decide what she wanted. She kept ringing up and making changes and when I received the brief from my client yesterday, she had just added a lot more changes to the whole booking as well as added a load of bedrooms on, which proved to be a bit of a problem because in Bristol at the moment, which is where she wanted the conference, there is graduation going on. So they don't actually have enough space for everyone.

We managed to find a few hotels that actually could accommodate what she was looking for, and then she decided in the afternoon she wanted to change it again. Obviously my colleague was in her training session, so I have to solve it. I managed to find other rates for her, however after persuading venues to keep holding on to the rooms for longer than they actually would have done for us, and actually one of the venues actually went above their regional manager to their director to try and secure this busy booking.

When coming back from my afternoon break, me and my colleague who was back from her training day saw that the woman had actually called and cancelled the event, so the whole thing was now cancelled and I'd done three hours work on it for nothing, and my colleague had been fretting about it in her training day for nothing. (Holly)

Questions to consider from this incident:

(1) When working in a team like Holly and her colleague, how can you ensure each other has the same information on a specific client?
(2) How do you think Holly felt as a result of this incident?
(3) Are there any business practices that could inhibit customers cancelling events at the last minute?

Customer querying prices

One of my main roles within the hotel is to send out all of the invoices which relate to any events, any bedroom reservations to all of our clients who have an account set up with this which allow for the invoicing facility to be there. I send these invoices out and then the client has up to 30 days to pay. One thing that I can get quite often is clients phoning up just to check what charges are relating to, just to get a bit more information, see if they've got a charge for their guest services. They might want to know what's that for. You have all your notes and things there to tell you it might have been flowers, it might have been chocolates or whatever. That's usually fine and then they're happy to make the payment.

Today I had one particular client who was calling to query the prices of the car parking and the internet at the hotel. These charges are clearly displayed all through the hotel. It was for an event that she had. She basically said that she thought the prices were too high and she didn't want to pay for them.

The thing is with that, it's a tricky one because my main role at the hotel is to make sure we get all the money in. I wouldn't want to be taking charges off unnecessarily when I don't think that there's a valid reason to do so. It was for an event and this client, our sales team, I'm really confident that they will have clearly told them all about the pricing structure. The prices will have also have been in a contract which they will have signed. It then would have been on an event sheet which again they will have signed.

When they got to the hotel, reception will have probably informed them at that time of the charges. They'll have had to log into the internet and pay the charge to add it onto the room then finally after the event has taken place, we have a meeting with the client where we review all of the bill. Our F&B guys do that, check that they're happy with the bill. They do a final signature, then that's their way of saying, 'We're happy for you to invoice us everything that's on that receipt' which then gets passed onto me. I give it a final check and then we send it out to the client.

To me, that's a lot of different times when the client has been made aware of the prices. They've signed to agree to them. To come and query the charges that late on, it's something that I wouldn't really be prepared to do. It's important to stand your ground on these things. We can't just be rebating everything and giving it away. Otherwise we'd make no money.

I had to explain this in polite terms to the client and make sure that we got the money at the end of the day. I think one thing that you get told is that the customer is always right. I think that that's a really important thing to know, but I think you should always take it with a pinch of salt and you shouldn't always put that into every single situation.

In this scenario, the client had just thought it was too high. She'd still agreed to pay to it and she'd signed to agree, she just thought it was a bit too expensive, which each can happen. I could walk into Marks and Spencer's and pick up a jumper and think, 'It's a bit too expensive, but I'm still going to buy it.' I wouldn't be able to go back to them two weeks later and say, 'Actually I've worn the jumper twice now and I think it's a bit too expensive.'

I think a lot of the time the problem in the hospitality industry is that because it's a service and it's not a product as such, people don't threat the money and the payments the same way. You would never order some things online from a shop and then decide, 'Oh actually I've got them, but I'm not going to pay for them.' That's something that we're all very conscious of. Car parking and internet are things that might not necessarily cost us directly as a hotel, but there are costs associated with them. We have to pay for the extra land, we have to pay for the internet connections.

I do think it's important that as well as always trying to make sure the customer's happy, but also look at from a business point of view. If every client said that they thought the prices were too high, then we would never make any money if we had to refund it for everybody.

We had a difference in opinion. I tried to explain it to her. We are a City Centre hotel. There's lots of reasons why we have to charge the prices that we do. They are competitively priced within our competitive set of hotels. The client has agreed to pay at the end of the day. It's all fine, but there was that confrontation there which did have to be dealt with in an appropriate manner. (Martha)

Questions to consider from this incident:

(1) Although the customer was informed of the prices for Wi-Fi and parking, this customer still queried these after checking out. Why do you think customers do this?
(2) Martha notes she dealt with the customer in an appropriate manner. How would you respond to a similar customer querying prices of services already taken?
(3) What support did Martha have in clarifying the costs for the services taken by this customer?

Being the middle person

Today I wanted to talk a little bit more about the importance of ... I think what I'm trying to talk about is communication and the difference between experience that I have with agents and clients, who are basically the two main people that we would liaise with. So we would either speak to the client directly, or the agent would book on behalf of the client and we would have all of the contact with the agent and then the agent would have contact with the client.

There are quite a few different ways in which we need to communicate between the two. I had an agent phone up today and she was querying a few invoices that we'd sent over, and basically what she was saying was is that she couldn't process any of the invoices because they didn't have the agent's reference number on. They still had the booking confirmation attached to the back of the invoices, but because they weren't actually printed directly on the invoices they wouldn't accept them.

It can sometimes be quite computerised the way that you have to interact with agents because if you don't do everything one certain way then they'll just reject everything. It's like sometimes there's no human input, even though they are humans, there's no human input into what they do. So they might just say, 'That's not on there, I can't do that', or, 'You've missed off this so I can't process it'. It can affect the payments, it can make me miss a payment batch and then they'll say, 'Right, well we've not had it so we're not going to pay until next month now', which will then make my payments really overdue and won't look good on my ledger. Which then can affect quite a lot of the debts and things at the hotel.

I just think it can be quite funny. What is important for me is now, from a sales point of view, when they send me all of the documentation I need to make sure that they put all the reference numbers in the right places, because otherwise I'm sounding like the robot that's sending it all back to them saying, 'You know, I need the reference numbers.' So it can also be like a pattern, their behaviour makes me feel a bit robotic in the fact that I have then got to pass it on to other people in the hotel to make sure that we're all complying in the same format. Whereas if you are sending it to a client directly, as long as you know you've got the main details on there, they're pretty much usually happy to accept it and process it. Sometimes they might just phone up and say, 'Oh, you know, I've received an invoice, I'm not too sure what it's for.' You can tell them over the phone and they go, 'Oh yeah, I know exactly what you mean. I'll process it now.'

Whereas with an agent if you don't have those certain criteria on it when they need it then it can be quite hard and quite difficult. I've only worked in the ... Well, I've worked in the job now since the end of March so I'm still coming to terms with some of the agents that we don't work with as often, their ways and their patterns and how we have to send everything out in a specific way. Some agents, we have to fax all of our invoices to. Some of them will only accept them by post, some won't accept them by post. So it's kind of like getting to know each agent, finding out how they want everything done and then making sure that you adhere to it. And then that way you can pretty much guarantee that you're going to get all of your payments on time, and that's you as a credit controller doing your job correctly. (Martha)

Questions to consider from this incident:

(1) What aspects of Martha's role makes her feel like a robot?
(2) How do agents work differently with Martha? How does this affect her daily duties?
(3) Working in a supportive role, such as finance, how can you maintain service standards when you are not the person booking or delivering the service?

Summary

(1) To appreciate definitions of co-production and co-creation.

Co-creation where the customer actively participates to make the service encounter. Customers do not simply request usual services but seek to define the experience and create the activity. This was noted in Chapter 4 on emotional labour where tour guides needed customer support to create and enhance the experience, as well as Chapter 9 where performance from customers aided the creation of humorous incidents. Co-creation is mainly considered from the customer lens so that management can consider how to support their participation within the service.

(2) To understand how co-production requires customers and staff to work together in creating service encounters.

Within co-production, customers use the tools and facilities given by management and staff to build or generate their own unique product or experience. This differs from co-creation as the customers receive the elements required to make individual products. Co-creation is whereby the experience is co-created with the staff and may lead to unique experiences or products.

(3) To identify how customers and staff create service encounters in tandem using their communication skills.

Co-creation and co-production have been considered in this chapter to address the gaps seen in service encounter theory. Chapter 1 identified how service encounter theory addresses management and customer perspectives of service quality, without a full review of the staff who produce and perform the service. Co-production and co-creation move this forward to confirm that the staff are important within the service, but again fails to promote staff opinions and perspectives in the creation and production of services. Through incident reflection, it is clear to see that staff are not simply invested in creating good experiences for customers but are often emotionally reflective on how they are treated by customers, colleagues and management. Communication (face-to-face, via email or on the phone) is noted as vital to deliver these aspects of service provision. Research papers discussed in this chapter have outlined how technology may decrease usual staff service encounters. If this maintains pace, it is essential staff in tourism, events and hospitality businesses acquire knowledge of these operations in order to facilitate and support their use.

Annotated bibliography

Binkhorst, E. and Dekker, T. (2009) Agenda for co-creation tourism experience research. *Journal of Hospitality Marketing & Management* 18 (2–3), 311–327. DOI: doi/abs/10.1080/19368620802594193

European authors from Spain (Binkhorst) and The Netherlands (Dekker) offer this conceptual piece to identify how tourism requires research into how co-creation can offer competitive advantage. Acknowledgement of the growth in technology and tourists booking experiences online rather than through a single travel operator identifies how the tourist customer is both recipient and creator of their own holiday itineraries. Using pictorial figures of the networks within which tourists operate allows clarification on how tourists are not in a simplistic line of service purchasing and consumption. The paper identifies that a new agenda in research is needed to consider tourists as co-creators. Based on Pine and Gilmore (1999), this paper acknowledges how economies are increasingly reliant on co-creation to enable consumers to actively participate in new and exciting experiences.

Question: review the tourism experience network on page 322 and identify if you use all of these elements when booking and completing a new tourist experience.

Grissemann, U.S. and Stokburger-Sauer, N.E. (2012) Customer co-creation of travel services: The role of company support and customer satisfaction with the co-creation performance. *Tourism Management* 33 (6), 1483–1492.

Based in Innsbruck, Austria, these authors reasearch strategic management and tourism. This paper addresses the high-contact context in which tourism operates (notable service encounters are not explicit in the paper). Using empirical research in a travel agency, the authors sought to understand customers' opinions on the interactions completed and whether they were allowed to be an integral component in the creation of their holiday booking. Using co-creation in travel agencies increased customer loyalty owing to the company offering consultation and discussion with customers on a one to one basis. This was noted as important for customers to understand their options and make personalised decisions on their travel arrangements.

Question: Online travel agencies, such as Expedia, often offer customers online chats to discuss their bookings when using the internet. How often do you think these are used and do you think they are regarded as beneficial as speaking to a travel adviser in a travel agency?

Lovelock, C. and Young, R. (1979) Look to consumers to increase productivity. *Harvard Business Review* 57 (May–June), 168–178.

Lovelock was an established scholar in services marketing who, although born in Cornwall in the UK, mainly worked in the Harvard Business School in the USA. This article is from the *Harvard Business Review*, an online and print news publication. Although not a book or journal article, this review is regarded highly by business scholars due to its prominent authors. Lovelock and Young are prime examples of these. In this opinion piece, they note how productivity in services requires consumer integration and action. Without noting co-creation or co-production, this article clearly identifies similar requirements of customers in order for services to be operated efficiently. A range of case study examples is illuminated in this piece from a range of industries where services and service encounters are paramount. In their concluding remarks, they identify how service companies need to stop perceiving customers as a nuisance and embrace their ability to support the creation of services and not simply that they consume these as robots.

Question: This article refers to case study examples in banks. Identify five forms of service encounter from tourism, events and hospitality and link each of these to other industry encounters which are similar. For example, a bank teller meeting a customer is similar to a receptionist at a hotel.

8 Legal Frameworks

Chapter Learning Objectives

(1) To analyse employment contracts used in tourism, events and hospitality.
(2) To discover forms of employee sickness and absence law.
(3) To illustrate health and safety legislation present in tourism, events and hospitality to support customers.
(4) To assess how these legal frameworks apply to customer service encounters.

Introduction

Although staff in tourism, events and hospitality are protected in law, it is commonplace for these rights either not to be exercised by the staff or adhered to by management. This chapter considers employment contracts, staff sickness and absence, employee protection for personal and sensitive issues, and customer health and safety. These areas of

legislation are paramount for staff well-being and welfare in all working conditions. When applied in the high pressure, long working hours and fluctuating industry contexts of tourism, events and hospitality, they are all the more important in order to maintain staff morale, motivation, productivity and retention in customer-facing positions.

Employment Contracts

This opening section considers employment contracts used in tourism, events and hospitality. An employment contract is a legal document clarifying the relationship between an employee and their employer (Simon, 1951). This document should specify the terms and conditions of this relationship considering the following elements:

- Type of contract (permanent/fixed term/agency/casual. All discussed below).
- Hours of work per week.
- Rate of pay and frequency of pay.
- Holiday entitlement and sickness policy.
- Job description or usual duties.
- Location of work.
- Other job specific details (e.g. if career professional development certification is required to maintain position).

Before drawing comment on the types of contracts used in tourism, events and hospitality, it is useful to set out the context of general employment in these industries within whole economies. Statistical evidence on workforce jobs' growth of key industry contributors in the UK from 2004 to 2017 shows that tourism, events and hospitality roles occupy 29.51% of the total workforce jobs (ONS, 2018b). With an increase of total workforce jobs of over 18% between 2004 and 2017 (ONS, 2018b), it is clear that the tourism, events and hospitality industries offer a large portion of working positions for the UK economy. Looking internationally, the World Travel and Tourism Council (WTTC, 2017) found that 9.6% of all employment was completed in tourism roles worldwide. The area with the highest number of tourism roles is seen in the Asia-Pacific region (WTO & ILO, 2014). Average working weeks are around 41 hours in the tourism industry, but there is a disparity in the genders, with women working nearer 39 and men working over 44 hours per week (WTO & ILO, 2014). In the USA, hospitality employment contributes 7.42% of total employment (ILO, 2010). These employment data clarify the need for a sustained labour force capable of working in a range of positions. It should also be noted that although the figures reported above are specific to tourism, events and hospitality, these do not confirm the total number of workers in these industries. For example, cleaners working in tourism, events and hospitality businesses may be subcontracted from external companies and be accounted for in other business categories such as support services or professional industry businesses.

So now to review employment contracts. It should be acknowledged here that these differ according to the country within which you are employed. In the USA, employment contracts define work as being 'at will'. This means that employees and employers can terminate the contract at any time, without forewarning or reprimand. Conversely, UK employment contracts are more formal, since employees and employers are required to give notice of any contract termination or change. As there are such discrepancies between these contracts, this section will consider different forms of the employment contract. Although based on UK types, the four employment contracts discussed below identify how formal and informal contracts are used to manage staff across the tourism, events and hospitality sector. Discussion on employment contracts is then followed by international perspectives of tourism, events and hospitality employment contracts. It is widely accepted and known that these industries consistently require and rely on temporary/casual employment contracts so that management may deal with the fluctuations in customer demand, as well as the transient nature of staff working in these businesses. This temporary nature of the work is highlighted as an issue for maintaining business standards, but also creating a cohesive workforce that supports and nurtures new colleagues.

Employees and workers in the UK are required to have a contract stipulating their rights, responsibilities and terms of employment (UK Gov, 2018a). These employment contracts have different forms: full/part-time, fixed-term, agency, freelancer and zero-hours (UK Gov, 2018b). Full- and part-time contracts are seen as permanent and will specify the hours of work and pay contracted for the staff on a weekly or monthly basis. This is accepted as the most stable form of contract, since the employee is paid a set wage and is expected to complete usual tasks in a specified role (usually clarified in a job description). Fixed-term contracts are whereby the employee also receives full- or part-time working hours, but they will only work for a set period of time. For example, an employee with a full-time fixed-term contract might work for 38 hours per week until 30th August in a determined year. This form of contract supports businesses with fluctuating income and demand, since they have a clearly defined end date at which the employee ceases employment. It is also clear to the member of staff and they are able to plan ahead and know when they too will need to find further employment. The permanent and fixed-term contracts noted here ensure staff are trained and inducted into a company in order to maintain customer satisfaction and brand standards. These are the more preferable contracts for staff as they offer the most security, but they are also difficult in businesses that have fluctuating customer demand and income.

Agency, freelance and zero-hour contracts are seen to be less supportive of staff well-being, since they do not offer consistent work nor consistent training and development. Agency work is whereby staff are contracted to temporary positions in a range of companies through a recruitment business. There are a number of these supporting tourism, events and hospitality in the UK (e.g. Sodexo and Berkeley Scoot). Staff working for these agencies will be informed of their shifts one week in advance and they could be working in a number of different tourism, events and hospitality businesses during a week. They are paid by the agency instead of the company they complete the work in, and usually, the agency obtains commission per hour from the company they send the staff to. This form of contract and employment can offer enhanced career professional development opportunities for these staff. Working in a range of positions and locations will offer a quick succession of experiences gained in service standards and protocol for service encounters. However, with more variety in working conditions and standards, there is also less focus on team development and consistent training for each role.

Freelance work (also called portfolio careers) is whereby staff operate as a self-employed worker and manage their own contracts with businesses. These staff will work alone and develop a portfolio of employment contracts with different businesses throughout the year. For example, an independent wedding planner is seen as a freelancer as they are paid by the couple planning to get married; they also liaise with tourism, events and hospitality venues and destinations in accordance with the couple's requirements.

Finally, zero-hour contracts are the most flexible, but least supportive form of contract used in UK law. They contract a member of staff to work at one specific business, but the hours of work vary from week to week. This means that the company can align staff working hours to match peak levels of trade, but that staff will not know if they will be working 0 or 50 hours in a week. This contract, perceptibly, is unstable for staff. Table 8.1 situates the employment contracts noted above in tourism, events and hospitality contexts for further clarification.

Table 8.1 Usual roles completed per contract type in tourism, events and hospitality

Full-/part-time	Fixed term	Agency	Freelance	Zero hours
All roles, but as a minimum, management and core operations jobs	All roles, but usually used for early business development whereby staff funds require management	Usually, customer-facing roles. Often in large venues where they do not have a core set of temporary staff. Sports stadia, local government events, private functions	A role that is not considered core for operations nor management of the business. For example, the stage manager wedding planner photographer graphic designer	Customer-facing roles in all businesses. Usually, roles requiring little to no training

From a brief description of the usual types of employment contract used in tourism, events and hospitality in UK businesses, it is salient to now quantify these to evidence usual management practice of employment contracts. The UK is used as an example here, but world averages are also compared for further context. In 2017, 6% of the UK working population had an employment contract within the tourism, events and hospitality industries (ONS, 2018a). The majority of these contracts were full time, with only around a quarter completing part-time roles. When comparing the tourism, events and hospitality contracts with national averages, there is a notable +2% difference in part-time contracts in these industries compared with the national average. This could suggest that tourism, events and hospitality businesses are making use of the different forms of contracts to support the different levels of trade and customer demand. In comparison with EU averages, 19% of EU hospitality workers have part-time contracts (ILO, 2010). This statistic would suggest that the UK offers comparatively more stable and longer working hour contracts than neighbouring countries. However, in 2011, People 1st (2011), the sector skills council for these industries found that almost half of the tourism, events and hospitality employment contracts were part-time, 19% higher than the national average. This is a significant difference to the reported +2% difference from the government reports noted above. The different samples used for these reports and methods of data collection taken cannot fully explain this stark difference in reported part-time contract percentages. It could be that the UK government reporting combines other working roles supportive of the tourism, events and hospitality industries and People 1st maintains focus on traditional tourism, events and hospitality roles only. Either way, it is clear that the reporting of these employment contracts in the tourism, events and hospitality sectors is neither transparent nor accurate. This review of percentages of full- and part-time contracts used in these industries evidence that businesses are supportive of permanent contracts. However, they do not publish on fixed-term, agency, freelance or zero-hour contracts in the same publications.

To consider less stable forms of contracts for staff, zero-hours contracts will now be discussed. It is accepted across tourism, events and hospitality research that the workforce consists of an unusually high number of employees working casual or zero-hour contracts (Deery & Jago, 2002; Duncan *et al.*, 2013; Richardson, 2009, 2010). People 1st (2013) also noted a significantly higher, and increasing, number of zero-hours contracts used in these industries. One reason stated for the use of more zero-hours contracts is that these industries require a more 'flexible workforce' (People 1st, 2013: 31). The tourism, events and hospitality industries require a more flexible workforce owing to the seasonal and fluctuating demands placed by customers using the businesses associated. Internationally, it is noted that tourism businesses require a flexible workforce owing to the 'labour intensive nature' of the industry (WTO and ILO, 2014: 2). The perceived overuse of temporary or zero-hour contracts in these businesses is not only damaging to potential applicants who may see the work negatively, but harmful to staff who require more stable pay and working conditions.

Zero-hour contracts are legal under UK law within the EU Working Time Directive of 1998. These are the most flexible forms of employment contracts available in the UK. Staff are entitled to a minimum wage and statutory annual leave, but their working rota will vary according to the business demands. In this way, the employee and employer will consistently change the numbers of hours worked by each employee.

Staff Sickness and Absence

Staff sickness and absence is supported by law in a number of countries by either paying staff when they are off work because of poor health or supporting absence owing to other commitments (e.g. family illness). This is important in tourism, events and hospitality work as staff traditionally work long unsociable shifts. Staff can incur medical problems owing to the manual nature of the work, or they may suffer from stress and emotional exhaustion owing to a lack of acceptable work/life balance. This section outlines key legislation in supporting staff sickness and absence to evidence the support available in tourism, events and hospitality employment contexts. For clarification, Table 8.2 outlines examples of the diversity of support for staff absence.

Table 8.2 Examples of international sickness and absence law

Country	Legislation	Paid leave	Unpaid leave
Australia	National Employment Standards	Sick leave for all employees. Does not cover casual staff. Maximum of 10 days each year	Two days allowed for carer responsibilities once the paid leave has been used
Canada	Canada Labour Code	No provision. The Employment Insurance Act may offer some pay as a benefit but this is not paid by the employer	Any absence up to but no longer than 17 weeks. The role is protected for the employee to return to work only
Germany	Continued Remuneration Act	Six weeks paid as long as the employee has been employed for 4 weeks	Ten days of unpaid leave allowed for care responsibilities of family members
Hong Kong	Employment Ordinance	Four/five of usual salary paid for sick leave. Two days of sickness allowed per month of employment up to a maximum of 120 days	If the employee has not accrued enough days for the leave then these will be taken unpaid
USA	None	No provision for paid leave. Insurance with the Family Medical Leave Act can support where necessary	

Source: See list of key websites for legislation data in the reference list at the end of this chapter

Examples of sickness legislation offered in Table 8.2 clarify the diversity of legal support available for staff absence when working in tourism, events and hospitality globally. From the days allowed, to the amount payable, to who pays the wages during the absence, the differences in this law are stark. In the UK, all employees are permitted to take time off work because of sickness. Medical proof of this illness is only required in the UK after an absence of seven days (UK Gov, 2018c). Other countries noted above tend to require illness from three days leave. If an employee is unwell for less than seven days in the UK, the employer can ask the employee to complete a 'fit for work' form to confirm they are well enough to complete their duties (HSE, 2010). This form is not mandatory and the pay is regulated within national insurance and tax taken per month from each employee. In the examples shown in Table 8.2, they mainly require a doctor's certificate rather than self-certification, and this is required in a shorter period of time also.

Similarities in sickness or absence law are seen in staff with temporary contracts and for absence related to carer or family duties. If staff are on temporary contracts, they are not usually paid for absence owing to the provisional nature of the work required.

One reason why this legislation is important when considering service encounters is that the work itself often leads to the absence. For example, workers in catering and tourism, events and hospitality services in the UK have proportionally higher absence rates in the UK than other industries (ONS, 2017). This can be seen as a trend since the Chartered Institute of Personnel and Development (2005, cited in Nickson, 2007) also noted these industries as having higher sickness percentages. However, Nickson (2007: 244) notes how employees in these roles may not be seen as having 'genuine' reasons for these absences. This suggests that the staff working in these roles are more likely to take a day's absence for unreasonable reasons rather than because of legitimate illness. This trend could be due to the younger demographic make-up of the sectors and their more social lifestyle in that they call in sick for work as they have other plans or are ill due to a heavy social lifestyle. This is perhaps where the UK legislation can be seen as lacking in comparison to other countries. The requirement of a doctor's note maintains the legitimacy and severity of absence from work and so staff cannot simply self-certify the reason. This noted, there may be instances where staff feel stressed and might not be able to attend a doctor's appointment to be able to gain such evidence.

In the UK, when staff return to work after any period of absence, their manager should conduct a 'chat about their absence' (HSE, 2010: 2). This is when they can complete the self-certification for their absence and verbally discuss the reason and management of the issue surrounding the absence. This informal chat should remain confidential and be held privately between the manager and the staff member.

This section has highlighted a prevalent issue in staff management in the tourism, events and hospitality sectors, that is, absenteeism. Legal support available in a range of countries has been offered to clarify the variety of payment, processes and conditions within which this absence is managed. As tourism, events and hospitality staff may face work-based and personal issues, the next section will now consider how these are supported in law to also combat absenteeism.

Staff Protection for Personal and Sensitive Issues

This section pertains to two important areas of employment law: discrimination and equality. These components of the law are created in order to support staff well-being. Table 8.3 offers examples of laws in support of staff facing these issues in work:

Examples offered in Table 8.3 clarify how equality is supported worldwide and that discrimination against staff is challenged with the support of national laws. Although applicants and staff are protected owing to certain characteristics (e.g. gender/age/sexuality/religion) there is less evidence of legal support for harassment, bullying or victimisation of staff. In the UK, all discrimination and harassment is covered under one piece of legislation, the Equality Act 2010. This not only protects staff with certain characteristics, but it protects all staff from bullying and harassment.

Staff protection is maintained in UK law against the following:

- 'spreading malicious rumours
- unfair treatment
- picking on or regularly undermining someone
- denying someone's training or promotion opportunities' (Gov. UK, 2018d)

The list above clarifies the type of undesirable behaviour in the work-place and staff who may feel themselves the victim of these forms are

Table 8.3 Examples discrimination law for tourism, events and hospitality

Country	Legislation	Support contained
France	Labour Code	No discrimination surrounding staff medical conditions
China	Employment Promotion Law and Labour Law	Equal treatment for all applicants and employees
EU	Labour and Equality Laws	All staff should be protected against discrimination, harassment and victimisation in the workplace. Individual countries have to apply for the same protection in national law
USA	Civil Rights Act	Each state has its own range of laws to protect staff with certain characteristics. The majority of states protect age discrimination of staff, but there is a wide discrepancy of support for all other characteristics. No law on bullying or harassment

Source: See list of key websites for legislation data in the reference list at the end of this chapter

able to challenge management practices. In the UK, if staff feel they are being victimised they can raise a complaint against staff and management, and if this is not resolved satisfactorily, they can then go to the Advisory, Conciliation and Arbitration Service (ACAS) for further support. Going through ACAS can result in legal action against the company responsible for the staff/manager, which in turn could lead to negative press surrounding an entire brand. This extensive staff support available in the UK is free and available to all staff working with any employment contract. This noted, charities such as Hospitality Action, are still necessary in the UK to support staff welfare.

Additional support is required for staff's personal and sensitive issues. These are present for every employee in every industry, but as tourism, events and hospitality businesses demand long working hours, performed happiness, presentation of brand messages and consistent service quality, management of staff emotions in these positions can be seen as more difficult. Working in tourism, events and hospitality can often feel like you work with a family, rather than colleagues. This is in part due to the long hours where you might spend up to 100 hours a week in the business, but it is also due to the organisational cultures of work (familial) within tourism, events and hospitality businesses. Whether the service is business or tourism, events and hospitality focused, there is always an element of entertainment or celebration within the encounter. As staff co-produce and co-create the service, they, in turn, will feel part of this service, and thus naturally have feelings on the occasion also. If staff are going through a particularly difficult time in their own life outside of work, this working atmosphere can often be incongruous to staff well-being. For example, a receptionist at a hotel could serve a guest attending a funeral, wedding or conference. That member of staff could be going through bereavement, divorce or career professional challenges at the same time. As staff need to perform and enquire about customer happiness and occasion, these encounters will always challenge staff's own personal situations, as they will naturally reflect on their own situations in tandem. Dealing with these contexts and managing their responses if the situation is highly emotionally charged for them, is again, a difficult proposition requiring higher order skills and abilities.

Discrimination against staff and ensuring equal treatment is maintained in legislation in most countries. The examples offered in this section identify how key characteristics are protected to ensure equal opportunities are adhered to in all working environments. Staff protection against bullying, victimisation, harassment and sensitive issues is not currently as well supported in international law, however. A brief description of how these can manifest and affect staff has been offered, but this is an area requiring further attention to support staff retention and satisfaction in their roles.

Customer Health and Safety

Customer health and safety is not only a legal requirement for all businesses, but is also considered imperative for customer satisfaction. Customers across the tourism, events and hospitality sectors are frequently asked to give feedback on their experiences within recent tourism, events and hospitality stays, and their health and safety is a crucial aspect of their experience. As customers can photograph problems they perceive in the business, the visual aspect of health and safety is now of more importance and weight. Photographs of a building site next to the hotel, poor sanitation in the toilets and staff appearing unwell or unhygienic are all examples of how customers can perceive and prove health and safety issues to future guests and local law officials. If a business is found lacking or infringes health and safety law, they can be closed by local officials within moments. Clearly this is unfavourable to management in tourism, events and hospitality.

In terms of how this affects staff, poor health and safety management can result in the termination of their employment contracts, or even staff fatalities. For example, in licensed venues, staff who serve alcohol to underage customers can face fines or termination of their employment contract. In working kitchens, chefs need to manage shelf life dates for all consumable products as well as maintain safe use of cleaning chemicals in order to avoid fatalities of customers or colleagues.

Critical Incidents with Key Questions

There were evident problems and demands present in several incidents, which I saw as being directly linked to people not following current employment laws. The majority of these were offered from Jessica, but as other participants also noted discrimination, bullying, harassment and victimisation, it is clear that employment law was not fully adhered to in the incidents offered. Jessica's incidents were most notably related to how legal frameworks do not always support staff as she was 'punched' by management, told her holiday form should go in the 'bin', asked to work over 35 hours in three days, not allowed holiday time when it had been accrued and ridiculed by management in front of other staff for having a day off sick. Clearly, Jessica's incidents could suggest that the management at her work needed further training, but as other participants had similar incidents it is seen that this is an important issue from the data. Staff in tourism, events and hospitality need both pieces of knowledge of the law and skills to deal with problems linked to employment law. Employment law should support them in the workplace and if it is not being adhered to, they need to know how to react professionally to any situation that could arise.

Holiday request

Today I had a very interesting issue going on and it was between me and my supervisor. I recently took a week off and I had three paid days off during that week and I'm on zero-hour contract that doesn't state how many days off I'm able to have, I can have as many as I like in a certain period of time, so I took just the week off for my graduation, my degree graduation, and explained it, and I filled out the forms, and then they all been accepted with my line manager and supervisors and managers.

So I also wanted to book a holidays for my future time in August, and I just came in the office to ask him for me to print the form that I will need to fill in and leave with my manager. And I filled it up. He asked me when I'm going, and I said, 'I'm going in the, in August, for just two weeks, I'm going home, home back to my country.' And when I fill it in, there was two supervisors at that time in the office, and it was just only me working so it was two supervisors supervising one person, that was a little bit weird and awkward, but I didn't say anything and I was doing my job.

In that moment when I filled out the form and I asked David (supervisor), 'Where would like me to place it?' Or, 'Where is best place for me to put it because my manager needs to see it and accept it?' He said the best place for my form will be in a bin, in a trash bin. He didn't said it so it's in form of a joke or anything like that, he said it quite seriously. There was no kind of laugh or smile on his face or anything like that.

In the same time, the other supervisor next to me turned around and asked me like, 'Oh, how was your holidays? Was everything okay?' It's like, 'Yeah, I was, the holidays was fine and good but I couldn't understand why "Supervisor name" said that to me.' And I asked him like, 'Excuse me, are you sure? Maybe I should place it somewhere else?' 'No, no, no. Nobody is going to, nobody is going to read it anyways.'

So I thought it was a little bit unfair and I just left it on a desk and I left to finish my shift and we never discussed it. Since that time nothing really happened. In the end of the shift nobody came to me and said that my holiday's been accepted but I think with the time my manager will say something about it. If not, I just go fill up another form probably or, I don't know, but I felt that they don't care about me and I felt unfair. I felt that the situation was so unfair because they can have 30 paid days off. I didn't even ask for paid days I just basically filled up the form saying I'm not going to be able to do my work for two weeks.

This was just one of the times that I just didn't say anything and then I left because I thought that whatever I going to say, they're not going to hear it or they're not going to listen to me. I didn't want to put my ego or my character in the situation and make a fight or make myself in trouble. Because there's two supervisors and just one worker so I don't really think it's fair. (Jessica)

The incidents offered from Jessica here clarify how management action and behaviour can negatively affect staff. Holiday entitlement and company processes for completing holiday requests are ridiculed by management and the member of staff is evidently upset by their response. By not saying 'anything', as Jessica is in a situation where she may feel bullied or intimidated it is possible she has not used her employment rights to confront management. Her dissatisfaction in the workplace is not due to her lack of knowledge, but due to poor organisational practice within this particular business.

Questions to consider from this incident:

(1) What holiday rights does Jessica have with her zero-hours employment contract?
(2) Which aspects of her management's behaviour are seen as unfavourable? How could the response have been more professional?
(3) If Jessica was unsatisfied with management in this situation, what could her reaction have been? Who could have offered further support?
(4) Looking to the final paragraph starting 'This was just one...' how do you think Jessica feels as a result of this incident? Do you think it will affect her work? If so, how?

Sensitive issues in work

So it's 3:15 in the morning and I just recently came home from work. Today I had a couple of situations that I can report off and most of them would be against just some situations with my supervisor. Basically, what I wanted to explain that I didn't work yesterday and I called in sick three hours before my shift starts. For a certain reason, I could not turn up to work; and today as soon as I came to work, a supervisor starts to ask me questions. In front of all the staff members, why I wasn't at work. He did it in front of chefs as well. Which is kind of funny for like, did I have the diarrhoea and I couldn't stand up and I couldn't get to work or something like that.

So I just told him that if he really wants to discuss why I didn't turn up to work, we can go and discuss it between me and him, privately. Then not just to take it out of the team in the middle of food service. In the middle of food service for a wedding. So, he started to laugh about it and just made me feel uncomfortable. Because, I think that there was some personal issues involved, and he was not supposed to bring it out in the middle of work. In the middle of the team, my colleagues. So that was the first issue.

The second issue was with another supervisor that come on a shift. I don't even know how to explain. He was just all over the place and whatever we were talking between me and my friends were because we worked for a while together. So, we have some personal issues and we talk about many different things when we have the time or we are on a break. So, he was basically coming to me and then saying to me that something is wrong with me, and if I would like to discuss it, I need to go and discuss it with him. But, I don't really know why I should.

Because, firstly, he's my supervisor and whatever he's given me tasks to do, I complete the tasks and I don't really think that something else should be involved, and he said to me that there must be something serious, because I usually smile; and I don't smile today. I don't really know. What is it personal because he likes me or just because he really wants to be my friend. But, he's not the best supervisor in the world, I'd say, and he doesn't do all of his job correctly. So, I don't particularly think that there must be something else involved. Except work between me and him.

He also asked me why I didn't turn up to work in the middle of my conversation with some other people and it was just weird and inappropriate in that moment. Yeah. It was just nosey and then them nosey about many things. He was not supposed to be. And asked me about my personal private life. That if I want to discuss it with him, I need to go and talk to him, and we never discussed it before so, I don't really think that I should.

Yeah that was my day. Ten-hour shift with no break. He asked me do I want to have a break at 1:00 in the morning, when we were finished in an hour time. So, I said, 'No, I'm fine,' because there's no point having break at 1:00 in the morning when you finish almost in an hour and a half, and everyone else is working and you would be just having a break. That's just the busiest time and you set up for next day weddings.
(Jessica)

Questions to consider from this incident:

(1) If staff are unwell and cannot work, what are the usual practices for confirming illness and checking they are safe to return to their duties?
(2) What was specifically poor about management behaviour in this incident?
(3) How did Jessica control the situations where she was asked personal and sensitive information? Are there better ways to have dealt with the requests made by management?
(4) If a member of staff is unwell and returns to work the following day, what are the possible reasons for this?
(5) If you were a member of staff overhearing these situations, how would you feel and what would you do?

Customer health and safety

Thursday the 11th of July a regular customer was quite intoxicated. Had been at the bar for a few hours. Having known he's had a few relationship issues recently have obliged him. He's a well-known and a well-liked regular, however I found him asleep. 15 minutes later sat within view of the entrance so I had a bit of a joke with him. Told him to cop on, that he couldn't be sleeping in the pub. Went back 10 minutes later he was dozed off again, offered to ring him a taxi but he said it was time to leave himself, so all sorted. (Tom)

Additional information about this incident: Tom informed me that he knew the customer not only as a regular visitor to the pub, but also as a former teacher at his school. The customer had been served alcohol before Tom started his shift that day. On the following day the customer returned to the pub and apologised to Tom for their behaviour on the previous day.

Questions to consider from this incident:

(1) Are there any laws specifying alcohol service to inebriated customers? If so, what does this state?
(2) What reason is given in this incident for Tom serving the customer more alcohol?
(3) If the customer had become seriously unwell, what consequences could have occurred for Tom?
(4) When faced with customers going through personal issues, how should you treat and serve them?
(5) If you knew a customer personally, would this affect how you serve them? How and why?

Cleaning up after customers

A group of lads who I'd known for quite a long time came in. They'd been out for one of their birthdays and they were quite intoxicated but not really too bad, obviously having a good night. However, towards the end of the night, I noticed one of the lads sat in a chair, dozing off. It was about half one, quarter to two. So I gave him a nudge and told him to wake up, which he did. However, I went over ten minutes later, well I was called to go over, and he was asleep with a big pile of sick underneath him.

Cleaning up the sick wasn't really a problem, as it's something you've got to do. However, trying to get him out the way to move was a bit of an issue. So I spoke to his friend who I've known for quite a while, and suggested they move him. They didn't tell me that they didn't know him, but I was quite strict with him and told them that they had to get him to the kitchen, get him to the toilet- the bathroom, sorry, or out the door, just to get him cleaned up while we could get rid of the sick. Didn't make any trouble out of it, as there's no need to. Happens to quite a lot of people. So... Anyway, his friends picked him up and brought him and cleaned him up, and we sorted out the pub. (Tom)

Questions to consider from this incident:

(1) Whose responsibility is it when a customer becomes inebriated and unwell on business premises?
(2) Was it acceptable for Tom to ask the other customers to deal with the poorly customer?
(3) If becoming unwell and sick in a pub is usual practice, what processes would you suggest are appropriate for dealing with them as a standardised practice?
(4) If you were unaware of 'pub culture', how might you react and feel in this situation? How would you manage a member of staff facing this?

Summary

(1) To analyse employment contracts used in tourism, events and hospitality.

Staff employed in tourism, events and hospitality are known to have full-time, part-time, fixed-term, freelance or zero-hours contracts. Staff experience, knowledge and skills will vary according to their contract employment history and current contract of employment. Being able to develop relationships with regular customers and usual customer market groups will enable staff to complete service encounters effectively.

(2) To discover forms of employee sickness and absence law.

Participants in the study noted feeling pressure to attend work owing to limited resources available to support their absence. It was noted that any employee will require days off work in order to recover from illness and that this should be supported. This section sought to clarify different legislation supporting tourism, events and hospitality staff when taking sickness absence. Legislation from five countries was outlined to clarify frameworks of staff absence support. As there is a high proportion of staff completing zero-hours or temporary work in these sectors they will not be financially supported if they are ill. With long working hours and emotional exhaustion being commonplace for these staff, management should not only reward them for punctuality and presenteeism, but support their return to work and seek to use their feedback to assist other staff who may face similar issues.

(3) To illustrate health and safety legislation present in tourism, events and hospitality to support customers.

Discrimination and equality were discussed in this section to outline frameworks to support staff's personal and emotional issues. Once employed in tourism, events and hospitality, staff may face encounters with other staff, suppliers, management or customers which lead to emotional distress. It is plain that staff, therefore, need support to manage and reflect on incidents which may be discriminatory or show unequal treatment.

(4) To assess how these legal frameworks apply to customer service encounters.

This chapter has offered legal contexts within which customers and staff in tourism, events and hospitality are protected and supported. Laws discussed in this chapter are similar in name and form across countries, but their application and management will differ according to the company and service offered. Within the service encounter incidents, staff and management disregard for the law has been noted. The consequences for this disregard are not only felt by staff, but are potentially life-threatening for customers. Using the staff perspective on these, it is also clear that management does not always show a positive lead on these matters. As such, it is important that staff are not only aware of the law in support of their working environment, but equipped with how to tackle any illegal activity or behaviour they witness.

Annotated bibliography

Deery, M. amd Jago, L.K. (2002) The core and the periphery: An examination of the flexible workforce model in the hotel industry. *International Journal of Hospitality Management* 21 (4), 339–351.

These authors, who were based in the Department of Hospitality and Tourism Research at Victoria University, Australia, offer a report of an empirical study completed in hotels in Melbourne. They sought to understand employees' perceptions of training, promotion and job security. Understanding employees' perceptions of the internal labour market were deemed necessary in order to understand their career path intentions, to further support hotel human resource policies and aid staff retention. The sample focus was also on peripheral employees who may feel marginalised within a company (noted as casual or zero-hour staff in this chapter). Three hundred surveys from six hotel businesses were analysed to understand these employee perceptions. They conclude that further model analysis is needed to adequately address peripheral staff's career ambitions and morale in service sectors. Staff perceptions are complex and their ability to use internal labour market support is limited due to the other levels of an employment contract and opportunity available.

Question: In your experience or research, are all new employees offered the same induction programme when starting in a tourism, events and hospitality role? If they differ, how does this affect staff morale and intention to remain?

Richardson, S. (2009) Undergraduates' perceptions of tourism and hospitality as a career choice. *International Journal of Hospitality Management* 28 (3), 382–388.

This author was based in the Department of Tourism, Tourism, Events and Hospitality, Hotel and Sport Management, Griffith University, Queensland. Richardson investigates student opinions on whether tourism and hospitality offer suitable career paths for them after their studies in hospitality and tourism courses at eight universities across Australia. As students in this study are completing courses in tourism and hospitality, it seems odd that an author would raise this question to students who have already chosen this path. It is noted, however, this may be due to a long-standing issue in these industries: the professionalisation of these sectors needs supporting and championing. If students are aware of the benefits of these industries, they will seek and continue employment. This article is both a useful education exercise and industry reporting consideration to ascertain current student motivations to move into careers in these industries, regardless of their current focus of study. Conclusions are drawn from the parametric analysis of quantitative data yielded in the study point to two important considerations. First, that students are not fully aware of the variety of roles and careers possible from their studies; and secondly, that they perceive the working conditions in these industries as less supportive than others in terms of pay and working conditions.

Question: With knowledge of the fluctuating customer demands made in tourism, events and hospitality, how can management in these businesses offer more attractive roles and employment conditions? Would portfolio and self-employment routes be seen as more enticing if the pay and conditions were higher than in other sectors? Would commission work support this?

Duncan, T., Scott, D.G. and Baum, T. (2013) The mobilities of hospitality work: An exploration of issues and debates. *Annals of Tourism Research* 41, 1–19. DOI: http://dx.doi.org/10.1016/j.annals.2012.10.004.

The authors in this article span the globe. Duncan was at the University of Otago in New Zealand, Scott was at Southern Cross University, Australia and Baum works at the University of Strathclyde, Scotland, UK. This conceptual piece seeks to challenge common narratives on the hospitality and tourism workforce. The counter arguments presented in this publication are that the workforces in these industries are not simply a homogenous group who can be trained and developed in hard and soft skills. They suggest the adoption of a mobilities framework, which acknowledges employee experience and lifestyle as an individual. By suggesting that this workforce, similar to the customers being served, is mobile and shifting according to individual factors, they identify that companies need to review training and motivation strategies to maintain an effective workforce.

Question: Classifications of workers as 'migrant', 'tourist', 'worker' and 'local' are noted in this article (14) as problematic owing to the transnational flows of people with a range of life experiences. What benefits are there to removing these labels on staff working in hospitality and tourism?

Notes

(1) Full time (85%) versus part time (15%) for national average and 83%/17% respectively for hospitality, events and tourism employment (ONS, 2018a).

(2) 2.7% compared with a national average of 1.9%.

Country sources for legislation

Australia: https://www.fairwork.gov.au/leave/sick-and-carers-leave/unpaid-carers-leave.

Canada: https://www.canada.ca/en/employment-social-development/services/labour-standards/reports/sick-leave.html.

Germany: https://uk.practicallaw.thomsonreuters.com/3-503-3433?transitionType=Default&contextData=(sc.Default)&firstPage=true&comp=pluk&bhcp=1.

Hong Kong: https://www.labour.gov.hk/eng/public/wcp/ConciseGuide/EO_guide_full.pdf

USA: https://www.dol.gov/general/topic/benefits-leave/fmla.

Look at Thomson Reuters for further details on legislation present across the world: www.thomsonreuters.com.

9 Using Humour in Customer Service Encounters

Chapter Learning Objectives

(1) To appreciate fields of study linked to use of humour in the workplace.
(2) To identity how humour is perceived in tourism, events and hospitality.
(3) To evaluate the use of humour in service encounters and identify if this is appropriate and professional in every context.

Introduction

This chapter offers an emergent perspective on service encounters: the use of humour. This was identified as an important aspect of service encounter production from the incidents submitted by workers in industry roles. Recently, and more colloquially, this could also be

noted as being 'banter'. Humour between staff is discussed as being a usual aspect of working life in tourism, events and hospitality, but that this can lead to negative effects on staff and customers. Humour use also unveils the front/back of house dimensions prevalent in these businesses and how gossip, informal discussion and ultimately bitching can lead to entertaining work environments for staff. The need for this entertainment is desirable to staff owing to the often-monotonous tasks completed in their roles. Relief is also sought in the face of consistent customer queries, negative feedback and demanding customers who all need satisfying regardless of staff opinion.

Common Frameworks in Humour Theory

The consideration of humour in personality, communication and psychology theory has been documented variously. As humour relates to one's understanding of difference, incongruence and self it has also been noted by many established experts in their fields (notably Freud, Allport and Maslow). Discussion of three definitions of humour will be presented here for clarification on potential motivations for humour use. These are from philosophical positions and are used as definitions on humour by researchers in tourism, events and hospitality papers discussed later in the chapter.

Descartes's (1989 translation of 1649 text) quotation below outlines the first position on humour: the superiority theory:

> Derision or scorn is a sort of joy mingled with hatred, which proceeds from our perceiving some small evil in a person whom we consider to be deserving of it; we have hatred for this evil, we have joy in seeing it in him who is deserving of it; and when that comes upon us unexpectedly, the surprise of wonder is the cause of our bursting into laughter. (Descartes, 1989: 178–179)

This quotation outlines how people use humour to show superiority (or to mock others or ourselves). Mocking humour described above also involves hatred or dissatisfaction with the observed behaviour or action. Stating that something is inadequate can be amusing if the other person or self is able to reflect and understand the point is not an insult, but it can easily lead to interpretations of insult.

> observing the imperfections of other men. (Hobbes, 1651, part one chapter 6)

The above quotation from Hobbes simplifies Descartes' definition by noting that this form of humour is through awareness of the inadequacies of others. In order to create this form of humour, you need awareness of a status quo from which any deviancy can be noted and mocked.

For example, if a worker arrives at work with a creased shirt and their colleague states 'did your iron run off today?' (stated with a laugh) the colleague is mocking the employee by pointing out that their uniform is below standard. This example also uses sarcasm, since an iron cannot run. By stating something that is impossible, about an action (ironing) which the colleague could have done, they are also mocking their knowledge and ability to use irons.

The second definition of humour relates to the need to relieve stress or tension. This observation was made by Lord Shaftesbury in the 1700s when he wrote a paper on how humour and wit enables the release and venting of tension. Freud (1905) developed this earlier definition and concluded that humour is needed to release nervous energy to support psychological well-being. In this way, humour is used as a medicine to relieve psychological stress or anxiety. For example, if a worker states 'I think I need to go on another training course to learn about time management, but I think I'd be late to that also!' This example uses both superiority and relief theory in that it allows the worker to relieve their stress at being late to work through making a joke, while also acknowledging their lack of time management (superiority). May (1953 cited in Kuiper *et al.*, 1993: 2) suggested that humour has the function of:

> preserving the sense of self ... It is the healthy way of feeling a 'distance' between one's self and the problem, a way of standing off and looking at one's problem with perspective

This confirms Freud's writings on humour used for psychological well-being, as it allows a person to self-reflect and acknowledges problems in a light-hearted way. Finally, in Plester's (2009) article on relief humour, swearing is acknowledged as a key linguistic tactic used here. They even warn readers of the profanities contained in the article in case readers are offended by the strong language used. If a customer or worker was to use swearing in this form it may again be perceived as insulting, rude or provocative.

The third and final definition of humour to be discussed here is that of incongruity. This is where someone notes something as humorous owing to the odd or unusual behaviour or action noted. Kant (1790: 133) uses a hospitality situation to describe this:

> *An Indian at the table of an Englishman in Surat, when he saw a bottle of ale opened and all the beer turned into froth and overflowing, testified his great astonishment with many exclamations. When the Englishman asked him, 'What is there in this to astonish you so much?' he answered, 'I am not at all astonished that it should flow out, but I do wonder how you ever got it in.*

This example is humorous, since the speaker is insinuating that it is difficult to put the beer back into a bottle as it flows out and therefore would not pour back in. Equally, the appearance of froth would make it seem as though there is more mass to put back into the bottle. The statement is a redundant one as they are drinking and would not want to put the liquid back. Here, humour is seen in the odd suggestion, which would not be necessary considering their situation. Another example could be if a customer has been asking for lots of additions to their meal order and the worker asking if they need him to join them at the table while he narrates the remainder of the order. A worker sitting at the table with a customer is incongruous to the social norms of the situation and the worker would not do this, but they acknowledge a humorous situation by suggesting an unusual action to complement the unusual customer requests.

Superiority, relief and incongruity theories of humour have been briefly noted here to offer clarification on the academic framing given to humour use. This is limited, but is important to acknowledge positions from which humour is researched and perceived.

Researching Humour in Tourism, Events and Hospitality

In terms of knowledge and research into humour used in tourism, events and hospitality, there has been relatively little studied and published. Although Frew (2006) notes that a study was conducted on baseball humour (Katovich, 1993), the earliest mention of humour use in tourism, events and hospitality is by Ball and Johnson (2001). These authors consider the use of humour in hospitality owing to the friendliness and relationship building requirements in service encounters. They accept that humour has been scarcely considered in hospitality publications, and so address this in consideration of how it is defined and manifested in communication. Ball and Johnson (2001) define humour as being something that is present in all communication forms (verbal and non-verbal) and that it usually attends to the unusual or incongruent positions one can perceive. They note that it is culturally bound and that different cultures will perform and understand humour in different ways. An example drawn is that Americans use one-liners, whereas British people base humour on personality or character traits. The acceptance of a variety of humour offered for a variety of reasons leads these authors to note that it is therefore difficult to offer appropriately in service encounters.

The reason asserted for humour use in hospitality, according to Ball and Johnson (2001), is that you need to show care and attention to customers who are going through potentially stressful events. A tourist visiting a new city and suffering from jet lag or a bride anxious about her wedding day are both examples of hospitality guests in tourism and events contexts whereby staff need to show empathy and understanding by making light or comforting these guests. Ball and Johnson (2001) suggest that these traumatic events can be mitigated through staff's use of humour in conversation. Although these authors note humour use can be perilous owing to staff needing to 'preventing (sic) offence' (Ball & Johnson, 2001: 223), they do not fully consider this problematic element. Using appropriate language in transnational contexts can be difficult. Using appropriate humour is therefore even more problematic. As such, humour use in hospitality can be seen to be an attempt to lighten or make a situation friendly regardless as to whether the customer understands the nuances of the humour used. For example, if an anxious bride noted how she was unsure if her wedding cake arrived in time, suggesting that she could get one from a local supermarket would not make the situation humorous, it would worsen the situation.

Ball and Johnson (2001) offer links between humour and aesthetic labour also. They note that in creating uniform standards, some companies allow for humorous appearances of their staff to make customers feel at ease in a situation, while also allowing staff to show individual flair in their attire. Humour is therefore noted in this chapter as part of a competitive advantage, which could be used by hospitality companies to show a caring, less formal and more human stance towards professional services. Showing a humorous side to your company is also accepted as a common position in marketing or TV campaigns. Figure 9.1 offers examples of how hotels have used humour in their signs to aid the marketing of their business.

The examples in Figure 9.1 showcase how hospitality businesses can use humour to attract customers by seeming to have a personality.

Figure 9.1 Humorous hotel signs
Sources: Listed in the References with other photo sources

Customers will immediately be made aware that the staff or management operating these businesses have a sense of humour and therefore may be someone you would want to get to know or develop a business relationship with. As noted previously, humour humanises a business by showing personality and flair to what may be a normal or mundane business operation.

Humour can also be witnessed within a hotel:

> Dogs are welcome in this hotel. We never had a dog that smoked in bed and set fire to the blankets. We never had a dog that stole our towels and played the T.V. too loud, or had a noisy fight with his travelling companion. We never had a dog that got drunk and broke up the furniture. ... So if your dog can vouch for you, you're welcome too. The manager. (sourced from photo taken of a sign uploaded on pinterest – URL in reference list)

This sign does two things: it identifies a sense of humour from the management and reminds customers to behave appropriately while staying there. If a member of staff were to tell a customer not to steal towels, fight with their companion or break any furniture, they might be interpreted as being rude and overly bossy. By using humour, this sign communicates how management expects customers to behave in a light-hearted and amusing way.

Unlike the service quality and service encounter texts, Ball and Johnson's (2001) chapter on the use of humour addresses the staff-to-staff dimension of humour use, as well as customer perceptions of this in service encounters. They state that it can have numerous positive effects on staff and management when they are faced with stressful situations in work. Figure 9.2 is offered to consider how humour use between staff can have positive and negative effects.

Figure 9.2 clarifies how humour use can positively affect staff and management working in hospitality. From productivity to morale, it can offer a significant improvement in staff motivation when working long shifts. However, when used inappropriately, it can lead to conflict and even dismissal. Further reasons for organisational humour noted include tension relieving, enhanced team spirit and checking common beliefs.

Implicit hints or vague assertions suggesting to wit or humour can also be perilous, since they can suggest or underline the stupidity of a customer if they are seen to not understand the joke being made. Done too lightly and the joke will be rendered mute, but if you over-assert an implicit hint the other person can be left confused and unsure of what is expected as a reaction.

The final area considered in Ball and Johnson's (2001) chapter is that of unintentional humour. This element of humour is most notable by tourists visiting, reading or understanding language written or spoken in

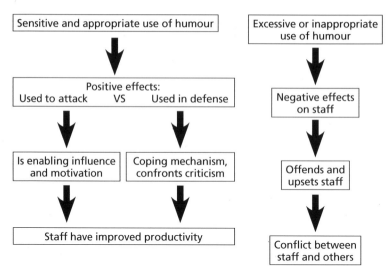

Figure 9.2 Use of and effects of organisational humour
Source: Based on Johnson and Ball (2001: 232)

tourist destinations. Some examples of unintentional humour owing to translations to the English language on signs offered by these authors are shown in Figure 9.3.

If tourists view signs such as those shown in Figure 9.3 at destinations, they will perceive humour in the signs through the lack of knowledge in language translation. This noted, Ball and Johnson (2001) do not address those who do not speak English and who may find these confusing and concerning. If a non-native speaker of English read these signs it may lead to concern about the services offered and raise further queries with staff in service encounters. If the staff are not aware of how they could be interpreted, it could lead to service failure and guest

---

In a Yugoslavian hotel: 'The flattening of underwear with pleasure is the job of the chambermaid.'

In a Norwegian cocktail lounge: 'Ladies·are requested not to have children in the bar.'

In an Acapulco hotel: 'The manager has personally passed all the water served here.'

In a Tokyo bar: 'Special cocktails for the ladies with nuts.'

On a Polish hotel's menu: 'Salad a firm's own make; limpid red beet soup with cheesy dumplings in the form of a finger; roasted duck let loose, beef rashers beaten up in the country people's fashion.'

Figure 9.3 Humorous written signs
Source: Ball and Johnson (2001: 235)

complaint. This is not identified as a potential problem by Ball and Johnson (2001).

Following Ball and Johnson (2001), the next paper found to explore humour used in tourism, events and hospitality is an article by Frew (2006). Here, humour is discussed as a benefit to customer satisfaction in tourism management as it can ensure 'the experience is a positive one' (Frew, 2006: 644). Again, the focus for humour research is on how it can positively affect and support service quality for the consumers; however, neither staff nor management interplays are documented.

Humour in tourism has since become more prominent, owing in part to Pabel's PhD thesis in 2014; since then, Pabel and Pearce have published widely on this topic from a (see Pearce & Pabel, 2013, 2015, 2016, 2018). Pearce and Pabel's (2015) book is of note as it summarises their research and discussions succinctly. Like Ball and Johnson (2001), they acknowledge the humorous side to signs translated incorrectly and witticisms by tourists who respond in service encounters in incorrect ways. They add to the humour debate in service encounters by acknowledging humorous storytelling in tourism, the dark side to humour and how humour can be co-created.

Storytelling the study supporting this book is founded upon. The critical incidents allow the theory to be situated and contextualised in order to understand the practical and workplace scenarios in which the theory can be explored. In tourism blogs, reviews and posts, humour is noted being used in order to gain larger readerships (Pearce & Pabel, 2015). Within these stories of travelling, 65.5% of the blogs referred to conversational humour. This suggests that even though written communication can be unintentionally funny, the majority of memorable humour comes from spoken encounters when visiting a place. Within the re-telling of humorous stories, Pearce and Pabel (2015) note that there are key narrative traits necessary to make them humorous: a naïve author, a stereotypical or known element of the context that is unknown to the author, the emotional discomfort of the author and using speed to identify panic or uncertainty in the situation. These narrative cues enable travel bloggers and writers to re-tell incidents ensuring the humorous core maintains appeal and clarity. Pearce and Pabel (2015) do not acknowledge whether humorous travel blogs are used in other languages nor whether the readership uses the stories to then go in search of their own humorous adventures. These are key considerations for service encounters, because, if tourists re-tell them in service encounters, or expect them in service encounters, the humour could be lost in translation with people of other cultural experiences and identities.

By using humour in tourism writing, stories in blogs and travel books can appear as fiction writing rather than honest accounts of real experience. In fact, Frew (2006) noted above is also a comic who completes stand up performances to entertain. The use of humour in tourism writing is of note in this book, as tourists may refer to reviews, travel books and blogs in order to decide which experience they want while visiting a destination. The crucial difficulty from these is that customers may then expect humorous incidents and if these are not confirmed in service encounters through staff showing a sense of humour, or placing them in a similar situation whereby they end up the naïve tourist, they may deem the experience as unsatisfactory.

Next, Pearce and Pabel's (2015) discussion on the dark side of humour is discussed. Here, they address the problems associated with interpreting humour (noted in the discussion of Ball & Johnson, 2001). As incongruence is important in understanding or perceiving humour, there is always a potential for humour to be misinterpreted or for people to be confused or offended. There are social norms to be considered, usual tastes in conversation topic, decency of opinion and political correctness all inherent in conversation. If these are not adhered to effectively, a joke or humorous comment can not only offend but belittle and humiliate a person. If humour fails, the person trying to be humorous can also be embarrassed and lose confidence in their own communication abilities. Acknowledgement of this dark side to humour is rife with problems. In terms of recovery from failed humour, Pearce and Pabel (2015: 107) cite Bell's (2009) five usual reactions to humour failure as follows:

(1) Polite or sarcastic laughter (37.1%).
(2) Metalinguistic comments[1] (32.3%).
(3) Interjections such as 'okay' or 'mmm' (19.4%).
(4) Evaluative comments such as 'that's stupid' or 'you are being silly' (15.0%).
(5) Rhetorical questions to challenge the joke teller such as 'are you drunk?' (8.1%).

The above five responses to humour failure all imply politeness and acceptance of an attempt to be humorous. They do not address potential upset or insult felt by either party, which could lead to emotionally charged angry or violent reactions.

In terms of common reasons for disliking humour in tourist situations, Pearce and Pabel (2015) note results from focus groups on dissatisfying humour use. Here they identify the following five reasons for disliking humour use:

(1) Too much humour used.
(2) Staged humour.
(3) Not understanding humour.
(4) Taken literally or misinterpreting.
(5) May cause offence.

In review of the dark side to humour, Pearce and Pabel (2015) refer to cultural and social norms in humour use. They note that people are sensitive to unusual of unexpected behaviour and although these can be seen as humorous, there is a tendency for this to offend or insult.

The final area of humour to consider from Pearce and Pabel's (2015) text is that of the co-creation of humour. This links to co-creation theory noted in Chapter 7. Pearce and Pabel (2015) also cite Pine and Gilmore (1999) and the experience economy as the underlying motivator for this form of humour in tourism. Three forms of co-created humour are discussed in Chapter 3 of their book:

(1) Creating humorous experiences through requiring tourists to clap, sing or chant.
(2) Placing tourists in a performance situation where they interact with actors during the experience.[2]
(3) Asking individual tourists to go on a stage to support performance.

These three forms of co-creating humour require tourist participation in order for the humour to be successful. They rely on tourists being willing and open to humiliation and incongruity in a situation in which they are acting outside usual social customs and norms. The contexts need to be staged in order for both the tourist's comfort and humorous event to be played out in full.

In acknowledgement of Ball and Johnson (2001), Frew (2006) and Pabel and Pearce's various publications, it is clear there is limited but supported the use of humour in service encounters. Ball and Johnson (2001: 238) noted the 'dearth of scholarly material' related to this topic and that they hoped their chapter would support further exploration of this in service environments. From the review completed for this chapter, it is noted that little scholarly attention, nor research, has resulted since. However, the discussion offered in this chapter has alluded to examples of humour use in service encounters and how it can be both beneficial and enhancing for customer satisfaction and staff morale. It is therefore noted as an important element of communication used in service encounters, particularly where customers may feel traumatised at being away from home, or where unusual or incongruent behaviours are witnessed.

The papers discussed above offer useful positions in which humour has been researched and used in tourism, events and hospitality. Seemingly only one source considers this from a hospitality perspective; the majority is seen through a tourism consumer lens and there are no events management papers found at the time of writing. Other examples of publication and research in working contexts can be found in nursing (Åstedt-Kurki *et al.*, 2001), medical (Tanay *et al.*, 2013) and sex (Sanders, 2004) working conditions.

Misuse of Humour in Service Encounters

First, using humour as a coping mechanism is prevalent in the incidents gathered. Encounters where participants were insulted, discriminated against and ignored were all seen by participants as humorous. This was also clear in the stimulated recall where I was able to probe further to illuminate their feelings:

> I get called a racist every day. (Lucy)

> So, generally people are just trying to have a good time and anything that's funny, or anything that's remotely entertaining, we all let each other know and we all tease each other about it. That's what we do. (Lucy)

Data suggest that the use of humour was in encounters where their emotions were high, or they were stressed and that humour was used to release tension in the situation. However, owing to the gravitas of incidents where humour was seen, this book raises it as a key finding to be addressed. Staff and management need to be aware of appropriate and inappropriate humour use to support their colleagues in the industry.

From the discussion offered above, it is clear that participants viewed some types of harassment, including racist and sexually exploitive demands, as being humorous. Even in Sophie's incident, where she was scared of a customer's sexual advances, she found it humorous and referred to other colleagues' similar experiences to identify how it is common and usual to make light of sexual demands made by customers. In particular, Sophie noted how her colleagues would 'brag' and 'laugh' about customers who tried to initiate personal relationships with staff. When you consider that the resulting impact of the incident for Sophie is that she will no longer work in a bar again, perhaps this needs to be challenged further, rather than continued to be accepted. The data also suggest that staff need to be aware of how humour is used so that they can understand the culture of the industry and react appropriately.

To evidence and discuss this emerging aspect of service encounters, incidents will be offered, followed by discussion and key questions to consider:

Critical Incidents with Key Questions

Making fun of customers

This wasn't actually something that happened particularly to me, but it happened to the other staff on the floor today. There was an elderly couple that came in with a pram and a blanket covering the top of the pram. This is quite a crazy incident really. This couple that had come in with a pram and something covering it, and Tracy (waitress), she's in her forties and quite a bubbly and interesting girl; and she's worked for the 'Restaurant name' now for 15 or 16 years.

So, Tracy was serving this couple and she's, as is said, quite bubbly and I asked if she could see the baby, and obviously they said that was fine. When she lifted the blanket it was covering the ... I don't know. The opening of the pram I suppose it's called. There was a doll. An actual doll, not a baby in the pram; and obviously she was shocked and tried to react as normally as possible. But, was just obviously odd, just isn't couldn't really believe it. That they brought a doll out with them. I suppose we'd all do it, but her initial reaction was to tell all of us.

Then she went as far as telling a manager that the couple on this table had a really cute baby. So, Theresa (manager), our shift manager went over and did exactly the same thing. Asked if she could see this really cute baby and also just was completely shocked when she saw it just because Tracy was obviously just playing a bit of a prank. But, I suppose that was highly unprofessional and quite insensitive. But, in the hospitality industry an observation of mine is that we're always just, you know, there's long hours and bad pay. So, generally people are just trying to have a good time and anything that's funny, or anything that's remotely entertaining, we all let each other know and we all tease each other about it. That's what we do.

Yep, that was an awkward situation. Which probably could have been handled a bit better. A bit differently. And, probably, for the couple, I mean if you're going to bring a doll out and pretend it's a baby, I suppose they've had all sorts of reactions and they're probably used to them too; and maybe weren't even aware that Tracy had played a joke on Theresa and told her to come look at this doll. But, it's something to think about and it was an awkward situation. These things do happen quite often, where, you know, you get some many people that come in and out all the time. You do get lots of really strange customers or customers with really strange requests. It happens quite regularly, but this was something in my 15 years of waitressing, I'd never seen something quite as surprising. (Lucy)

This incident showed a situation where Lucy's colleague made fun of her manager by using customers in the restaurant. In this incident, an 'elderly couple' had sat in the restaurant with a pram and, when Lucy's colleague had asked to see the baby, she discovered there was a doll in the place of a baby. Lucy's colleague decided to make this a humorous occasion by telling their manager that there was a 'lovely' baby in the pram and that the manager should also go and ask to see it. Evidently, once the manager did this and saw the doll, Lucy's colleague laughed at the manager's reaction. Lucy narrated this incident as a voyeur, but it was clear that Lucy did not find the incident amusing. In the stimulated recall, Lucy noted how 'horrible' it was for the manager and that it made her feel uncomfortable.

Questions to consider from this incident:

(1) Which of the three forms of humour discussed in the chapter is seen here (superiority, relief or incongruous)?
(2) How would have felt if you had witnessed a colleague and manager in this incident?
(3) What could Lucy have done after this incident to protect other customers in the future?

Lucy noted in another incident that her manager made fun of other staff by giving them nicknames. Lucy noted that a new member of bar staff called Dave was given the name 'little Dave' owing to him being smaller than the other Dave who already worked there. Lucy noted that 'management have a good laugh about' that and that nicknaming staff was seen as humorous. This is inappropriate behaviour witnessed by Lucy, which she not only accepts and reports on, but does not challenge either. In consideration of bullying legislation noted in the previous chapter, calling staff alternative names based on their appearance is not only harassing but illegal. At no point in our discussions does Lucy acknowledge this illegal action, but it is clear from her offering the incident that she is both aware of and concerned for the use of humour with this colleague.

As previously noted in Chapter 4, Lucy offered an incident where a woman walked past the restaurant and said she should work on a pole. Lucy found this amusing when she narrated the incident, but on reflection in the stimulated recall, it was clear she was concerned with this response to her visual appearance. Working in uniform prescribed by management, Lucy felt the uniform was incongruous with her own style, but this comment from a passer-by made her more concerned with how she was made to look and feel. One element from this incident suggesting why Lucy found it humorous was that the customer was an 'old lady.' If the customer had been a younger male, Lucy noted she would have reacted 'differently' owing to her perceptions that the comment would appear sleazier.

It is clear from Lucy's incidents and stimulated recall that she saw humour used inappropriately by her colleagues and the management. What was interesting though was that Lucy did not confront the inappropriate use of humour and concluded that this form of humour is usual in the hospitality sector; it is part of a 'teasing' organisational culture. This chapter seeks to challenge this position and underline the negative, dangerous and illegal ramifications of using humour in these businesses.

The teasing aspect to tourism, events and hospitality roles was also noted as inappropriate by Jessica. In her first incident when she asked her manager to approve her holiday request, he 'joked' that the form should go in the 'bin', suggesting that he did not want to approve the holiday time. Later in Jessica's fourth incident, her manager also threatened to 'fire' her if she did not try and speak to customers with a Mancunian accent. Jessica saw the first incident as unacceptable and yet the fourth incident as 'funny'. Again, it is interesting how Jessica's manager uses humour in these incidents to communicate their feelings about Jessica and how Jessica does not appear to confront this. This could be because the humour is used by her manager and she does not feel able to confront him. This noted it was clear from other incidents that Jessica actively argued with management when they physically hit or punched her:

> Unbelievable. I sit there, like, 'What do you think you're doing?' 'Oh, I'm really sorry. I didn't mean it.' Like, 'What do you mean you didn't mean it? You just punched me with a piece of paper. Doesn't mean that it was for fun or it wasn't hurting me, but why would you do that? (Jessica)

Jessica did not perceive verbal abuse (disguised as humour) as being as offensive as physical abuse. This suggests that similarly to Lucy, Jessica did not react effectively or identify her own problems with the use of humour seen.

In terms of how participants used humour themselves, Holly and Tom both offered incidents where humour was evident. Holly joked with her colleagues about clients who were not responding or were annoying them in order to ease their own frustrations at work. Tom jokingly suggested to a customer that phone charger use required payment of 'a fiver an hour'. Neither of these incidents showed appropriate use of humour and the participants confirmed they were treating them as humorous to relieve stress and pressure felt during work.

Summary

(1) To appreciate fields of study linked to humour use in the workplace.

Superiority, relief and incongruity theory were all outlined as key fields of knowledge on the use of humour. These offer a framework from which to consider the use of humour and application between people. Within these, the superiority theory is seen as negative since it seeks to scorn or mock someone from an authoritarian position. Relief and incongruity humour theory identify how humour can make awkward situations humorous instead of difficult, and how bizarre occurrences can create humour as they are seen as out of the ordinary.

(2) To identity how humour is perceived in tourism, events and hospitality.

Humour use has been recently presented by Pabel and Pearce from hospitality contexts. Written and verbal communication uses humour in attractive customers or starting conversations with customers. Showing a light-hearted and less formal position can lead to increased loyalty with a company and a familiar atmosphere to enjoy leisure experiences. However, there are problems in humour use in that it can lead to misunderstanding, offending people and conflict. Authors on humour in tourism, events and hospitality attend to traditional humour theory (discussed in this chapter), but add to this in offering an understanding of it within leisure experiences. In particular, tourist experiences often create humorous conversation owing to misunderstandings or difference of opinions on usual leisure requirements.

(3) To evaluate the use of humour in service encounters and identify if this is appropriate and professional in every context.

All of the examples given in this chapter show how humour, teasing and ridicule are used in service encounters in tourism, events and hospitality industries. This was witnessed and narrated by all participants. It is an emerging theme from the literature since, although it relates to some of the other theories in legal protection and communication, it was not seen in the literature as being important for service encounters. Current tourism and hospitality research in this area uses the philosophical definitions of humour (superiority, relief and incongruity) to identify how humour is manifest in these business contexts. There is some evidence that humour can relieve and support staff well-being, but this is still scarce in terms of supporting service encounter delivery. Using humour in the narrated accounts offered in this chapter highlights a more problematic element to working in the sector, as the humour was not fully understood or liked by the participants. Jessica especially knew that the comments made towards her were unfair and harmful, but she shrugged them off as if she just had to accept such behaviour. Tom confirms this by noting that you have to 'get used to it.' In terms of looking for a theoretical reason for this, People 1st (2011, 2013) reports that working in the tourism, events and hospitality industry requires long unsociable working shifts and that staff turnover is very high. If staff work long hours, their colleagues become their friends and family, as they have little time to socialise with people outside of working hours. The long hours also mean that staff suffer more stress and fatigue, meaning that their emotions are also affected (discussed in Chapter 3). None of the participants tackled this if they felt uncomfortable with the humour used. Lucy clearly did not like the manager being made fun of and she seemed to accept the teasing name given to her colleague from management. Ultimately, this humour, as seen from the narrations, is presented as harassment, bullying and emotional stress. None of the participants perceived it in that way even after completing the stimulated recall. They simply accepted it as a part of working in the industry. This chapter, therefore, supports previous scholars in tourism, events and hospitality by identifying a gap in current research into this topic area. It adds to this debate by identifying that staff in these contexts may feel insulted, belittled and de-motivated by the humour used and that further research and training is required to enable staff to effectively respond to humorous incidents.

Annotated bibliography

Ball, S. and Johnson, K. (2001) Humour in commercial hospitality settings. In: *In Search of Hospitality: Theoretical Perspectives and Debates* (pp. 198–216).

This is the most widely cited early publication on humour use for the tourism, events and hospitality service sectors. Both authors are from the north of England and their chapter offers a detailed discussion on potential issues and benefits of humour use in hospitality. Linking humour to caring, noting staff well-being and drawing examples of unintentional humour are all research topics still relatively underdeveloped in this field. The authors acknowledge that humour use should be appraised as a skill for staff in hospitality and that linguistic methods can be applied in service encounters to use humour to increase customer satisfaction. Caveats are maintained in the appropriate use of humour in these contexts and that it can lead to insult or humiliation if used incorrectly. A large part of this chapter underlines the organisation culture of a business and how humour can form part of its essence to entice new customers. This suggests that companies should use humour in their strategy and goals in order to appear more appealing to diverse customer groups. Their review of Peterborough columns is particularly amusing for those who have not come across these publications.

Question: If a company embraces a humorous organisational culture, how are new entrants (staff) meant to relate or conform to this? Is this as simplistic as looking and sounding right or is humour use a more problematic skill?

Frew, E. (2006) The humour tourist: A conceptualisation. *Journal of Business Research* 59 (5), 643–646.

Interestingly, from reading Pearce and Pabel's (2015) book, I learnt that Elspeth Frew is also a stand up comedian. This author therefore not only researches and writes about humour, but she is also well versed in creating comical performances. This perspective piece addresses the formal and informal use of humour in tourism contexts. The specific focus is on formal humour offered at comedy festivals and therefore touches upon an events management operation also (although not specifically acknowledged). The conclusions note how tourists choose to attend comedy events and their satisfaction is directly linked to understanding and appreciating humour as part of an audience. The psychological benefits of this are noted, but this has importance for contemporary tourists as well-being and self-development are known to be a driving factor for new tourism experiences.

Question: Have you attended a comedy festival? What happens if the audience does not understand the joke? Do audience members laugh regardless of the joke and do they laugh at the social cues for laughter at specific points? How much does this rely on co-creation?

Pearce, P. and Pabel, A. (2015) *Tourism and Humour*. Bristol: Channel View Publications.

Currently the only book on humour use in tourism, this is an excellent account of humour theory and practice for tourism contexts. The authors are based in Queensland, Australia, but they refer to a range of studies and international contexts in which humour can be seen in tourism. The chapters review sociological, philosophical and psychological tenets of humour use, due to the definitions from esteemed philosophers. Their suggestions for further studies documented in the conclusion identify how spontaneous humour is still relatively unknown and yet this is seemingly a core part of creating satisfactory service for tourism customers.

Question: As emotional, aesthetic and sexualised labour are known forms of staff performance, how is humour labour (noted in figure 6.2) also a performed component of service encounters?

Pabel, A. and Pearce, P.L. (2018) Selecting humour in tourism settings – A guide for tourism operators. *Tourism Management Perspectives* 25, 64–70.

This paper, based on Pabel's PhD research, offers a new framework for developing humour in tourism companies. This is interesting as in their 2015 book they conclude that further research is required on spontaneous humour. However, all academics like a good framework! Page 66 of this article offers a seven-point model of how tourism management can plan to deliver humour in tourist experiences. This uses a traditional and circular plan, operate and review strategy to identify how humour can be used for tourists. This framework is present, but not tested with empirical research and it is hoped (by the authors and by myself) that this will be used in industry and tested to ascertain if formal and organised humour is beneficial to tourists. The form of humour suggested in this article does not seem to require co-creation from the customer. Instead, they require management to assess whether the tourism provider and context is able and appropriate to the delivery of humour.

Question: Which tourist experiences would it be appropriate to develop and integrate humorous elements? Which experiences would not be conducive to this form of service encounter or labour?

Sanders, T. (2004) Controllable laughter: Managing sex work through humour. *Sociology* 38 (2), 273–291.

Sanders is based at the University of Leeds and writes from a sociology discipline. The article reports on doctoral research using interviews and observations of over 200 sex workers in the north of England. She states that humour use is a relief strategy for these workers in order to distance themselves from the nature of their work. Sanders notes how humour can be a form of emotional labour used in service to make customers feel more at ease and comfortable in their working situations. This article addresses the staff-to-staff, coded and internal humour used in these working environments to identify how relief humour can support employee well-being. Conclusions identify how sex workers use emotional labour to perform stereotypical roles which their customers will expect.

Question: Sanders notes the internal humour and coded conversations between staff to support their discussion of clients requirements and unusual sexual requests. Is this form of communication present in hospitality businesses when a customer asks for something different or odd? If so where and how is this communication manifest?

Notes

(1) For example, when you change your language when talking to a manager compared to family member. Metalinguistic comments will be offered when a joke or humorous comment is rendered mute to try and rectify the professionalism in the encounter.
(2) For example, see the Faulty Towers Dining Experience: http://www.torquaysuitetheatre.com/.

10 Management of Service Encounters in Tourism, Events and Hospitality Management

Chapter Learning Objectives

(1) To outline the customer and management demands made to staff in service encounters in tourism, events and hospitality.

(2) To demonstrate the skills and knowledge required of staff to manage service encounters in tourism, events and hospitality.

(3) To identify an incident from your own experience and critically analyse this using one of the theories present in this book.

Introduction

This book aims to offer readers an insight into the demands made on staff in service encounters in tourism, events and hospitality roles. Using data from research completed in these industries, this text hinges on storied incidents offered by workers in these industries from which the reader can reflect on and apply theoretical knowledge. This concluding chapter offers a summary of the contributions to knowledge and emerging issues found from an exploration of staff incidents from working in these industries.

Demands Made of Staff

The incidents offered in the chapters of this book identify a range of demands placed on staff by their colleagues, management, suppliers and customers. In Chapter 2, the staff-to-staff element of these has been identified as an addition to knowledge and is raised as a future area of research required in support of staff training and development, which in turn should improve customer satisfaction.

As previous studies concentrate on customer demands, management meeting these demands and management training staff on meeting customer demands, results from participant data add further insight into staff perceptions of customer and management demands. This is an addition to current knowledge on service encounters and is summarised in Table 10.1 for clarification:

Table 10.1 Staff perceptions of customer and management demands

Customer demand	Management demand
(1) Requesting a different dish, drink or menu item	(1) Being asked to use scripted service
(2) Asking for a sexual service	(2) Completing more work due to colleague holidays
(3) Stating the staff's culture and language ability	(3) Human error in pricing leading to staff reprimand without dialogue with staff
(4) Inquiring about the staff's background	(4) Unclear email address making work difficult
(5) Speaking with a different accent making it difficult to communicate	(5) Work in other departments and teams is required to complete a role in a large organisation
(6) Unexpected customer behaviour	(6) Staff not receiving holiday entitlement
(7) Not offering usual tips due to cultural background	(7) Being asked for illness reason in front of colleagues
(8) Wanting to hold numerous venues on hold	(8) Not being paid on time
(9) Not confirming a booking with a contract	(9) Being told to speak in a local accent
(10) Using the phonetic alphabet to communicate clearly	(10) Changes in work expectations without consultation
(11) Customers not wanting to pay their bill	(11) When staff use initiative, management request staff to do their job and not others
(12) Customers needing specific information to pay	(12) Insulting nicknames were given to staff
(13) Managing inebriated customers	(13) Being reprimanded by management in front of customers
	(14) Unfair treatment from management
	(15) Staff training is inconsistent and applied from management needs and not staff requests
	(16) Discrimination and racism of staff and customers

Each of the demands noted in Table 10.1 present new perspectives on customer and management demands made of staff. These present as humorous, interesting, insulting and harmful pressure placed on staff working in tourism, events and hospitality roles. If research focus maintains pace on customer satisfaction and management training of customer satisfaction, retention and satisfaction of staff in these roles will undoubtedly have an adverse effect. Equally, in order for staff to appraise their own reactions and actions completed in service encounters, they also need to be aware of and reflect on potential demands to be made of them.

The theory and incidents offered in each chapter of this book can be used as illustrative, reflective case studies for staff development in tourism, events and hospitality roles. For management, Table 10.2 shows the skills and knowledge required to demonstrate what is expected of staff in order to navigate the roles and demands made of them.

From identification of the demands, skills and knowledge used by staff in customer service encounters it is clear that staff competence in managing these situations needs to be sufficient, reflective and consistently developed. Education and training for roles in these industries, unlike medical or teaching vocational education, does not require staff to complete postgraduate courses in order to become fully employer-ready for their role in the industry. Unlike medical and teaching education, staff in these roles can move directly into tourism, events and hospitality roles with an average of level 4 or below in qualifications (People 1st, 2011).

Baum (2002a) noted that staff training is largely completed on the job rather than in a structured and assessed framework. Bailly and Léné (2012: 88) confirm this and note that businesses pay 'scant attention in training programmes'. This poor attention to staff training

Table 10.2 Staff skills and knowledge used in customer service encounters

Skills	Knowledge
Interpersonal skills: interact with different people, communicate with different people, and manage different people.	Explicit knowledge: phonetic alphabet, legal issues in hospitality, human resource management, components of certain drinks or food, opinions on customer types, nationality, culture and religion, health and safety in the workplace.
Maintaining professionalism: smiling appropriately, remaining calm, responding appropriately.	
Communication: verbal and non-verbal forms. Entrepreneurial skills: using initiative, adapting service to suit a range of guests, adhering to company standards while maintaining customer satisfaction.	Relational tacit knowledge: empathy and understanding customers' needs. Collective tacit knowledge: organisational cultures, customer behaviour, appropriate reaction and behaviour with others.
Society skills: team working, awareness of others, adapting behaviour.	
Acting.	
Positive attitude.	
Numeracy: handling bills.	
Professionalism.	

is mainly due to sector composition. Within the tourism, events and hospitality industries, the majority of businesses are private small and medium-sized businesses, rather than public or large multinational companies (46% employ fewer than five staff and only 1% employ more than 100; People 1st, 2013). This suggests a reason as to why employers require new staff who already possess adequate competencies to deal with their customers; they may not have the resources with which to train them on the job, as there is no nationally available accreditation. If businesses in these industries need staff with adequate competencies and are unable to train their applicants on these within their roles, then it stands to reason that trainers, researchers and educators should provide this further guidance.

Create Your Own Incidents and Diary of Service Encounters

Review the following three excerpts from worker diaries completed in consideration of service encounters. Use these to write your own accounts of incidents of service encounters based on your own experience of working in tourism, events and hospitality roles. Identify how the theory offered in this book can be aligned to these and discuss your own perceptions of there.

Charlotte (notes during a week at work related to intercultural service encounters)

Due to loss of main supplier director was stressed. Staff were trying to ensure customer orders would be met. Discovered this was a Taiwanese company where contracts mean very little.

The Japanese order was queried – stated wrong item but was reassured it was correct. Went through main supplier and customer and financial history.

Sarah (notes on company structure and team duties)

Customer Experience Team: Focus on connecting with people. Contacting customers on social media. Contacting bloggers to promote events.

Reactive Team: Put the event/campaign together. Attend events to assist operations and logistics teams. For example, ran a competition for 80 winners who attended a private screening in a suite at Arsenal Emirates Ground of an away game, with buffet, goody bag and photograph. Staff ran this.

The office is made up of departments in which a campaign passes through from start to finish.

Emma (critical reflections on communication forms in service encounters)

Working with staff who are Czech and have little spoken English ability. Difficulties in trying to communicate with them is due to a different native language. I have attempted communication using more body language, facial displays and hand gestures but even this is often dismissed by them. Therefore, when I am working with one of them alone, for example today it becomes awkward and feel as though we are ignoring each other. I have learnt some words in Czech so try to use these as much as possible. Due to difficult communication I sometimes felt anxious to work alongside them.

The three examples of student worker diary incidents offered above serve as an example of how you can consider service encounter stories in written form. Using diaries to record incidents where you faced unusual demands will enable you to reflect on your own reactions and consider alternative positions and behaviour to respond in similar situations in the future.

Summary

(1) To outline the customer and management demands made to staff in service encounters in tourism, events and hospitality.

Twenty-nine demands were outlined from participant data offered in this study. These were outlined as demands perceived by staff completing service encounters with management, suppliers and customers. Some of these demands are usual within all working environments (discrimination and racism are not unique to tourism, events and hospitality). However, as staff are required to perform and act within their roles, these demands lead to increased stress and pressure felt by staff. If research remains focused on customer satisfaction and management training staff on customer satisfaction, retention and satisfaction of the staff in these roles will undoubtedly be adversely affected.

(2) To demonstrate the skills and knowledge required of staff to manage service encounters in tourism, events and hospitality.

Table 10.2 of skills and knowledge used by staff narrating incidents from employment outlines the typical competencies needed in these contexts. Being highly skilled and knowledgeable were traits of all participants noted in this book. The distinguishing factors noted were that they had all reflected on their experiences of service encounters and that they had used back of house relationships with colleagues and management in order to understand and consider any unusual demands made. In circumstances where the demands were seen as unacceptable to the staff, they referred to their management for support. As such, this book advocates for staff to complete critical reflection on the experience of service encounters in order to appraise and develop improved ability in managing these.

(3) To identify an incident from your own experience and critically analyse this using one of the theories present in this book.

The final section offers three examples of written diary excerpts from staff working in tourism, events and hospitality. Use content from these as a guide for you to create your own critical incident diary. With this, you can then reflect individually, or as a group of staff, to consider alternative positions and reactions to the service encounter.

Conclusion

The most recent books on customer service encounters have been written by surprenant and solomon (1987) and Czepiel *et al.* (1985). At that time, the focus was on marketing relations needed in service. This was due to the vast expansion and new economic reliance on services businesses in Western economies. Prior to this, focus had been maintained on products, manufacturing and traditional service of consumer goods. Consuming service is difficult due to the intangible nature of the 'product', in that it is given and taken by individuals who have individual expectations and perceptions. The texts relating to customer service encounters since this point have moved on to consider intercultural, communication, soft skills and co-creation in the encounters. However, these all maintain focus and over-reliance on the customer and a management perspective. Since these publications by Surprenant *et al.* (1987) and Czepiel *et al.* (1985), there has been no book focusing on contemporary issues in service encounters and the original texts focused on a range of industries, with some note of tourism, events and hospitality contexts. This book is the first to consider service encounters from a staff perspective in tourism, events and hospitality.

The incidents in this book link to the ones identified by Czepiel *et al.* (1985), but instead of applying these to management in identifying how they can assist with this, this book is aimed at the workers and students in these industries. This book has therefore offered new perspectives, models and stories from staff in tourism, events and hospitality.

The study presented here offers an insight into staff perspectives of these encounters, and thus identifies new models and links to emergent works of literature (such as co-creation and use of humour). It is acknowledged in this text that there is an over-reliance on service quality theory when considering service encounters. This over-reliance is problematic due to the omission of staff or employees in these theories and models. Therefore, new models on customer service encounters are offered to identify how staff interpret the demands made by customers and their responses in line with these. Further, theory on intercultural aspects of service encounters is also deemed insufficient as these fail to acknowledge the transnational flows of customers and staff present in tourism, hospitality and events, and that not only may the customers be foreign, but staff may not be from the local area either. As noted in the introduction, my own background has led me to have a small culture position to differences between people (Holliday, 2011). As such I see culture as emergent and defined by experience and identity. I am influenced here not simply by my own background in international peace organisations, but my work experience in managing and operating within tourism, events and hospitality industries.[1]

Recommendations Offered

Many of the recommendations offered from the publications discussed in this book are to management on how to train and manage staff for customer service in tourism, events and hospitality. Management are still addressed here, but noted as facilitators to staff development, rather than staff wardens to inspect and frame their creation of the encounters:

(1) Ask staff to reflect on and discuss completion of service encounters: how did they feel, what is seen as usual or unusual, and what additional support do they need?
(2) Staff reactions and coping mechanisms need to be understood by colleagues and management: are these beneficial or leading to further issues?
(3) Consider staff identity and experience when conducting training for service encounters: did they interpret and react owing to their training and education, or because of their experience and family contexts? How do these elements inform their reactions in service encounters?
(4) Nurture the self-awareness, self-reflection, confidence and identity of staff. These are integral to the unique service delivered and should be further enhanced to enable the empowerment and well-being of staff.
(5) As technology use increases in the delivery of services for tourism, events and hospitality, ensure staff are consulted on its use and trained on how to support customer interaction and service failures.

The skills for completing service encounters are significant and staff should not simply be trained on these, but supported to gain more experience and reflect on their abilities. It was noted that through completing the methodology for the study, participants enjoyed time to reflect and offer an honest account of their positions, emotions and perspectives on service encounters.

Suggestions for Future Research

This book combines sociology, philosophy, psychology, management, leadership and education theories to explore and expand current knowledge on service encounters in tourism, events and hospitality. It is acknowledged that this is limited due to the use of only English language sources and bound in the time in which it was published. The following identifies suggestions for future research in support:

- Staff perspectives in different contexts. All narratives used in this book are in English-speaking contexts and European working environments. Even though culture is noted as individual and emergent, it is acknowledged that further research into staff perceptions in other countries and contexts will aid further understanding of these positions.
- Age and position perspectives on service encounters. The narratives offered in this book are all from staff under the age of 30 years. It would be interesting to understand staff perceptions of those who have worked in the industries for over 10 years and investigate if they have more critical or cynical, even, opinions on service encounters and customer service. Cross comparison on staff roles and their perspectives would also be prudent. It has been noted that front-line staff are often the focus for service encounters, but this text outlines a new dynamic here (staff-to-staff). This, therefore, opens up the possibility for researchers to identify how back of house staff-to-staff service encounters are perceived and created.
- Customer culture, gender, aesthetics and disability are all considered in current publications. Further research should focus on each of these to identify staff perspectives on them and seek to understand if they are seen to alter the service delivery.
- Fair wages and decent work have not been linked in this book, but could be investigated further to understand if these affect staff ability to perform service encounters.
- Family business dynamics are a strand of knowledge within tourism, events and hospitality (e.g. see the research of Richard Telling). Consideration of staff perspectives on creating service encounters in these businesses would add a further dimension to the model offered.
- There is an emergent stream of literature on humour use in tourism. This requires further research in order to establish if this is a form of labour (similar to emotional, aesthetic and sexualised labour) and how this is performed, understood and perceived in service encounters.

In addition to the suggestions above, it is hoped that the new models offered in Chapters 2 and 10 will be applied and analysed in context. Within these suggestions, this book aims to support the staff perspective in order to offer new positions on service delivery in tourism, events and hospitality. This will lead to championing the complex professional roles completed by staff in these sectors while acknowledging the transnational flows of people operating in these exciting and vibrant industries.

Note

(1) See my LinkedIn profile for full details: https://www.linkedin.com/in/mirifirth/.

References

Alexander, M., Lynch, P. and Murray, R. (2009) Reassessing the core of hospitality management education: The continuing importance of training restaurants. *The Journal of Hospitality Leisure Sport and Tourism* 8 (1), 55–84, available at http://www. heacademy.ac.uk/assets/hlst/documents/johlste/vol8no1/AP0203Format55to69.pdf (accessed March 30, 2014).

Arasaratnam, L.A. and Doerfel, M.L. (2005) Intercultural communication competence: Identifying key components from multicultural perspectives. *International Journal of Intercultural Relations* 29 (2), 137–163, available at http://linkinghub.elsevier.com/ retrieve/pii/S014717670500074X.

Åstedt-Kurki, P., Isola, A., Tammentie, T., Kervinen, U. (2001) Importance of humour to client-nurse relationships and clients' well-being. *International Nurse Practice* 7 (2), 119–25.

Australia https://www.fairwork.gov.au/leave/sick-and-carers-leave/unpaid-carers-leave.

Bailly, F. and Léné, A. (2012) The personification of the service labour process and the rise of soft skills: A French case study. *Employee Relations* 35 (1), 79–97.

Ball, S. and Johnson, K. (2001) Humour in commercial hospitality settings. In C. Lashley and A. Morrison (eds) *In Search of Hospitality: Theoretical Perspectives and Debates* (pp. 198–216). Abingdon: Routledge.

Barker, S. and Härtel, C.E.J. (2004) Intercultural service encounters: An exploratory study of customer experiences. *Cross Cultural Management An International Journal* 11 (1), 3–14.

Barron, P. and Dasli, M. (2010) Towards an understanding of integration amongst hospitality and tourism students using Bennett's developmental model of intercultural sensitivity. *Journal of Hospitality, Leisure, Sport and Tourism Education* 9 (2), 77–88.

Baum, T. (1989) Managing hotels in Ireland: research and development for change. *International Journal of Hospitality Management* 8 (2), 131–144. Available at: http:// linkinghub.elsevier.com/retrieve/pii/027843198990073X.

Baum, T. (1996) Unskilled work and the hospitality industry: Myth or reality? *International Journal of Hospitality Management* 15 (3), 207–209, available at http://scholar.google.com/scholar?hl=en&btnG=Search&q=intitle:Unskilled+ work+and+the+hospitality+industry:+myth+or+reality+?#0.

Baum, T. (2006) *Human Resource Management for Tourism, Hospitality and Leisure Industries: An international perspective*. London: Thomson.

Baum, T. (2006) Reflections on the nature of skills in the experience economy: Challenging traditional skills models in hospitality. *Journal of Hospitality and Tourism Management* 13 (2), 124–135. https://doi.org/10.1375/jhtm.13.2.124.

Baum, T. (2007) Human resources in tourism: Still waiting for change. *Tourism Management* 28 (6), 1383–1399, available at http://dx.doi.org/10.1016/j.tourman. 2007.04.005 (Accessed October 6, 2011).

Baum, T. (2002a) Skills and training for the hospitality sector: A review of issues. *Journal of Vocational Education & Training* 54 (3), 343–364.

Baum, T. (2002b) The social construction of skills: A hospitality sector perspective. *European Journal of Vocational Education and Training* 54 (3), 74–88.

Baum, T. *et al.* (2016) Tourism workforce research: A review, taxonomy and agenda. *Annals of Tourism Research* 60, 1–22, available at http://dx.doi.org/10.1016/j. annals.2016.04.003.

Baum, T. and Nickson, D. (1998) Teaching human resource management in hospitality and tourism: A critique. *International Journal of Contemporary Hospitality Management* 10 (2), 75–79, available at http://www.emeraldinsight.com/10.1108/ 09596119810207228.

Bell, J. (2009) *Doing your research project: A guide for first-time researchers in Education, Health and Social Science.* UK: Open University Press.

Bennett, M. (1986) A Developmental Approach to Training for Intercultural Sensitivity. *International Journal of Intercultural Relations* 10 (2), 179–196.

Bennett, J. (2017) Shaftesbury modern texts: An Essay on the Freedom of Wit and Humour – a letter to a friend, available online athttps://www.earlymoderntexts.com/ assets/pdfs/shaftesbury1709a_1.pdf.

BERA (2004) *Revised Ethical Guidelines for Educational Research.* London: British Educational Research Association.

Bitner, J., Booms, B.H. and Tetreault, M.S. (1990) Service Encounter: Diagnosing Favorable and Unfavorable Incidents. *American Marketing Association* 54 (1), 71–84.

Binkhorst, E. (2005) *The Co-Creation Tourism Experience.* Sitges: Whitepaper Co-creations.

Binkhorst, E. and Den Dekker, T. (2009) Agenda for co-creation tourism experience research. *Journal of Hospitality Marketing & Management* 18 (2–3), 311–327.

Bold, C. (2012) *Using Narrative in Research.* New Delhi: SAGE.

Bowen, D.E. (2016) Human Resource Management Review The changing role of employees in service theory and practice: An interdisciplinary view. *Human Resource Management Review* 26 (1), 4–13, available at http://dx.doi.org/10.1016/ j.hrmr.2015.09.002.

Bratton, J. and Watson, S. (2018) Talent management, emotional labour and the role of line managers in the Scottish hospitality industry. *Worldwide Hospitality and Tourism Themes* 10 (1), 57–68.

Briggs, A., Coleman, M. and Morrison, M. (2010) *Research Methods in Educational Leadership* (3rd edn). London: Sage Publications.

BSA (2002) *Statement of Ethical Practice.* Durham: British Sociological Association.

Burns, P.M. (1997) Hard-skills, Soft-skills: Undervaluing Hospitality's 'Service with a Smile'. *Hospitality* 3, 239–248.

Butterfield, L.D. *et al.* (2005) Fifty years of the critical incident technique: 1954–2004 and beyond. *Qualitative Research* 5 (4), 475–497.

Byram, M. (1997) *Teaching and assessing intercultural communicative competence.* Multilingual Matters, available at http://books.google.com/books?id=0vfq8JJWhTsC.

Canada https://www.canada.ca/en/employment-social-development/services/labour-standards/ reports/sick-leave.html.

Chan, J. (2011) Enhancing the employability of and level of soft skills within tourism and hospitality graduates in Malaysia: The Issues and challenges. *Journal of Tourism* 12 (1), 1–16.

Chathoth, P., Altinay, L., Harrington, R.J., Okumus, F. and Chan, E.S.W. (2013) Co-production versus co-creation: A process based continuum in the hotel service context. *International Journal of Hospitality Management* 32 (1), 11–20.

Chon, K. and Maier, T. (2009) *Welcome to Hospitality: An Introduction* (3rd ed). New York, America: Cengage Learning.

Clandinin, D.J. (2007) *Handbook of Narrative Inquiry Mapping a Methodology.* London: Sage Publications.

Clarke, L. and Winch, C. (2007) *Vocational Education – International approaches, developments and systems.* Abingdon, UK: Routledge.

Clyne, M. (1994) *Inter-cultural communication at work.* Cambridge, UK: Cambridge University Press.

Cohen, L., Manion, L. and Morrison, K. (2009) *Research Methods in Education* (6th ed.) Oxon, England: Routledge.

Connelly, F.M. and Clandinin, D.J. (1990) Stories of Experience and Narrative Inquiry. *Educational Researcher* 19 (5), 2–14.

Coye, R.W. (2004) Managing customer expectations in the service encounter. *International Journal of Service Industry Management* 15 (1), 54–71.

Czepiel, J.A., Solomon, M.R., Surprenant, C.F. and Gutman, E.G. (1985) Service encounters: An overview. In J.A. Czepiel, M.R. Solomon and C.F. Surprenant (eds) *The Service Encounter: Managing Employee/Customer Interaction in Service Businesses* (pp. 3–15). Lexington, MA: Lexington Books.

Deardorff, D. (2006) Identification and Assessment of Intercultural Competence as a Student Outcome of Internationalization. *Journal of Studies in International Education* 10 (3), 241–266, available at http://jsi.sagepub.com/cgi/doi/10.1177/1028315306287002.

Deery, M. & Jago, L.K. (2002) The core and the periphery: An examination of the flexible workforce model in the hotel industry. *International Journal of Hospitality Management* 21 (4), 339–351.

Deery, M. and Jago, L. (2015) Revisiting talent management, work-life balance and retention strategies. *International Journal of Contemporary Hospitality Management* 27 (3), 453–472.

Duncan, T., Scott, D.G. and Baum, T. (2013) The mobilities of hospitality work: An exploration of issues and debates. *Annals of Tourism Research* 41, 1–19.

Egbert, J. and Sanden, S. (2013) *Foundations of Education Research: Understanding Theoretical Components*. Abingdon: Routledge.

ESRC (2012) *ESRC Framework for Research Ethics (FRE) 2010 Updated September 2012.* Swindon: Economic and Social Research Council.

Fantini, A. (2001) Excploring intercultural competence: A costruct proposal. In *National Council of Less Commonly Taught Languages*. Arlington, USA.

Firth, M. (2011) Resource Guide for Citizenship Education in Hospitality, Leisure, Sport, Tourism and Events Management. *Hospitality, Leisure, Sport and Tourism Network*, p. 14.

Firth, M. (2018) Skills and Knowledge for Service Encounters in the Leisure Industry: Implications for UK Higher Education, available at https://www.research.manchester.ac.uk/portal/en/theses/skills-and-knowledge-for-service-encounters-in-the-leisure-industry-implications-for-uk-higher-education(983f6ae1-131b-408a-b400-d5043892d1f9).html.

Firth, M. (2019) *Employability and Skills handbook for Tourism, Hospitality and Events Students* (1st ed.) Routledge/Taylor & Francis, Abingdon UK.

Fisk, R., Brown, S. and Bitner, M. (1993) Tracking the Evolution of the Services Marketing Literature. *Journal of Retailing* 69 (1), 61–103.

Flanagan, J. (1954) The Critical Incident Technique. *Psychological bulletin* 51 (4), 327–358, available at http://www.ncbi.nlm.nih.gov/pubmed/19586159.

Freud, S. (1905) *Jokes and their Relation to the Unconscious*. Redditch: Read Books Ltd.

Frew, E. (2006) The humour tourist: A conceptualisation. *Journal of Business Research* 59 (5), 643–646.

Geertz, C. (1973) The *Interpretation of Cultures: Selected Essays*. New York: Basic Books.

Germany https://uk.practicallaw.thomsonreuters.com/3-503-3433?transitionType=Default&contextData=(sc.Default)&firstPage=true&comp=pluk&bhcp=1

Giousmpasoglou, C., My, T. and Hoang, H. (2017) Emotional Labour in Luxury Hospitality. In *Visitor Economy: Strategies and Innovcations, Bounremouth, UK*, 4–6.

Grissemann, U.S. & Stokburger-Sauer, N.E. (2012) Customer co-creation of travel services: The role of company support and customer satisfaction with the co-creation performance. *Tourism Management* 33 (6), 1483–1492.

Grove, S.J. and Fisk, R.P. (1997) The impact of other customers on service experiences: A critical incident examination of 'getting along'. *Journal of Retailing* 73 (1), 63–85.

Gummesson, E. (1991) Kvalitetsstyrning i Tjänste- och serviceverksamheter, (Quality Control in Service Businesses), CTF Högskolan i Karlstad.

Gummesson, E. (1991) Marketing orientation revisited: The crucial role of the part time marketer. *European Journal of Marketing* 25 (2), 60–75.

Hall, E. (1959) *The Silent Language*. Doubleday, ed. New York, America.

Hall, R. and Van den Broek, D. (2012) Aestheticising retail workers: Orientations of aesthetic labour in australian fashion retail. *Economic and Industrial Democracy* 33 (1), 85–102.

Harkison, T. (2017) Acccommodating co-creation in a hotel experience. *Hospitality Insights* 1 (1), p. 3.

Harkison, T. (2018) The use of co-creation within the luxury accommodation experience – myth or reality? *International Journal of Hospitality Management* 71 (April 2017), 11–18, available at https://doi.org/10.1016/j.ijhm.2017.11.006.

Harkison, T., Hemmington, N. and Hyde, K.F. (2018) Creating the luxury accommodation experience: Case studies from New Zealand. *International Journal of Contemporary Hospitality Management* 30 (3), 1724–1740.

Hassanien, A. *et al*. (2010) *Hospitality Business Development*. England: Butterworth Heinemann.

Henry, I. (1993) *The Politics of Leisure Policy*. London: Macmillan Press Ltd.

Hobbes, T. (1651) *Leviathan*. Project Gutenberg EBook of Leviathan. Available from: https://www.gutenberg.org/files/3207/3207-h/3207-h.htm.

Hochschild, A. (2012) *The Managed Heart: Commercialization of human feeling with a new afterword* (3rd ed). London, England: University of California Press.

Hofstede, G. (1980) *Culture's Consequences: International Differences in Work-Related Values*. Beverly Hills, CA: Sage.

Hofstede, G. (1995) The business of international business is culture. In T. Jackson (ed.) *Cross-Cultural Management* (pp. 150–165). Oxford: Butterworth-Heinemann.

Hofstede, G. (2006) Dimensionalizing Cultures: The Hofstede Model in Context W.J. Lonner *et al*. (eds). *Online Readings in Psychology and Culture* 2 (1), p. 8.

Hofstede, G., Hofstede, G.. and Minkov, M. (2010) *Culture and Organisations*. McGraw-Hill, (ed). USA: McGraw-Hill.

Holliday, A. (2011) *Intercultural Communication and Ideology*. London, England: Sage Publications.

Hong Kong https://www.labour.gov.hk/eng/public/wcp/ConciseGuide/EO_guide_full.pdf.

HSE (2010) Managing sickness absence and return to work in small businesses, two pages, published by the Health and Safety Executive, UK.

ILO. (2010) Developments and challenges in the hospitality and tourism sector- Issues paper.

INCA. (2004) Inter-cultural Awareness. *Assessors Manual*, available at http://www.incaproject.org/en_downloads/21_INCA_Assessor_Manual_eng_final.pdf.

Jackson, D. (2010) An international profile of industry-relevant competencies and skill gaps in modern graduates. *The International Journal of Management Education* 8 (3), 29–58, available at http://www.heacademy.ac.uk/assets/bmaf/documents/publications/IJME/Vol8no3/3IJME288.pdf (accessed April 1, 2013).

Jackson, D. (2012) Testing a model of undergraduate competence in employability skills and its implications for stakeholders. *Journal of Education and Work* (April 2013), 1–23, available at http://www.tandfonline.com/doi/abs/10.1080/13639080.2012.718750 (accessed March 5, 2013).

Kant, I. (1790) *Critique of Judgement*. North Chelmsford, MA: Courier Corporation.

Katovich M.A. (1993) Humor in baseball: Functions and dysfunctions. *Journal of American Culture* 16 (2), 7–1.

Kenesie, Z. and Stier, Z. (2017) Managing communication and cultural barriers in intercultural service encounters: Strategies from both sides of the counter. *Journal of Vacation Marketing* 23 (4), 307–321.

Kim, Y.Y. (2008) Intercultural personhood: Globalization and a way of being. *International Journal of Intercultural Relations* 32 (4), 359–368, available at http://linkinghub.elsevier.com/retrieve/pii/S0147176708000278.

King, N. and Horrocks, C. (2010) *Interviews in Qualitative Research*. London, England: Sage Publications.

King, P.M. and Baxter Magolda, M.B. (2005) A Developmental Model of Intercultural Maturity L.A. Samovar & R.E. Porter, (eds). *Journal of College Student Development* 46 (6), 571–592, available at http://muse.jhu.edu/journals/journal_of_college_student_development/v046/46.6king.html.

Knemeyer, A.M. and Naylor, R.W. (2011) Using Behavioral Experiments to Expand Our Horizons and Deepen Our Understanding of Logistics and Supply Chain Decision Making. *Journal of Business Logistics* 32 (4), 296–302, available at http://doi.wiley.com/10.1111/j.0000-0000.2011.01025.x.

Kuiper, N.A., Martin, R.A. and Olinger, L.J. (1993) Coping humour, stress, and cognitive appraisals. *Canadian Journal of Behavioural Science/Revue canadienne des sciences du comportement* 25 (1), 81–96.

Laing, J. (2018) Festival and event tourism research: Current and future perspectives. *Tourism Management Perspectives* 25 (November 2017), 165–168, available at https://doi.org/10.1016/j.tmp.2017.11.024.

Langmead, K. and Land, C. (2019) Responsible Management Chapter 5 Can Management ever be responsible? Alternative organizing and the three irresponsibilities of Management. In: O. Laasch, D. Jamali, E. Freeman and R. Suddaby, (eds)., *The research handbook on responsible management. Cheltenham: Edward Elgar. (Forthcoming)*, 1–20.

Lashley, C. (2000) In search of hospitality: Towards a theoretical framework. *International Journal of Hospitality Management* 19 (1), 3–15.

Lashley, C. (2009) Marketing hospitality and tourism experiences. In Oh, H. (2009) *Handbook of Hospitality Marketing Management, Routledge, 576 pages*. p. 29.

Lashley, C. and Morrison, A. (2007) *In Search of Hospitality; Theoretical Perspectives and Debates* (2nd ed). Abingdon, UK: Routledge.

Lashley, C., Morrison, A. and Randall, S. (2004) More than a service encounter? Insights into the emotions of hospitality through special meal occasions. In *CAUTHE Conference 2004, Brisbane Australia*, available at https://search.informit.com.au/documentSummary;dn=200294050259402;res=IELBUS.

Leitch, S. (2006) *Prosperity for all in the global economy – world class skills*, available at http://www.official-documents.gov.uk/document/other/0118404792/0118404792.pdf.

Lessor, R. (1984) Social movements, the occupational arena and changes in career consciousness: the case of women flight attendants. *Journal of Occupational Behaviour* 5 (1), 37–51.

Lin, C.F. and Fu, C.S. (2017) Advancing laddering and critical incident technique to reveal restaurant niches. *Service Industries Journal* 37 (13–14), 801–818, available at https://doi.org/10.1080/02642069.2017.1351551.

Lovelock, C., and Young, R. (1979) 'Look to Consumers to Increase Productivity,' Harvard Business Review 57 (May–June), 168–78.

Lovelock, C.H. and Young, R.F. (1979) Look to consumers to increase productivity. *Harvard Business Review* 57 (Summer), 9–20.

Lucas, R. (2004) *Employment Relations in the Hospitality and Tourism Industry*. London: Taylor & Francis.

Lyle, J. (2003) Stimulated recall: A report on its use in naturalistic research. *British Educational Research Journal* 29 (6), 861–878.

MacLeod, N. (2006) The Placeless Festival: Identity and PLace in the Post-Modern Festival. In *Festivals, Tourism and Social Change: Remaking Worlds*. Clevedon, UK: Library of Congress Cataloging in Publication Data.

Marinakou, E. (2019) Talent Management and Retention in Events companies: Evidence from four countries. *Event Management2*.

Mathisen, L. (2019) Storytelling: a way for winter adventure guides to manage emotional labour. *Scandinavian Journal of Hospitality and Tourism* 19 (1), 66–81.

Mattila, A. and Enz, C. (2002) The Role of Emotions in Service Encounters. *Journal of Service Research* 4 (March 2014), 268–277.

May, R. (1953) *Man's Search for Himself*. New York: Random House.

McCollough, M.A., Berry, L.L. and Yadav, M.S. (2000) An Empirical Investigation of Customer Satisfaction after Service Failure and Recovery. *Journal of Service Research* 3 (2), 121–137, available at http://jsr.sagepub.com/cgi/doi/10.1177/109467050032002 (Accessed November 7, 2013).

Medina-Lopez-Portillo, A. (2004) Intercultural Learning Assessment: The Link between Program Duration and the Development of Intercultural Sensitivity. *Frontiers* 10 (1979), 179–200.

Miles, M. and Huberman, A. (1994) *Qualitative Data Analysis: An Expanded Sourcebook*. London: Sage.

Minaham, S. (2007) *The Aesthetic Turn in Management*. Taylor & Francis.

Mooney, S. and Ryan, I. (2009) A woman's place in hotel management: Upstairs or downstairs? *Gender in Management* 24 (3), 195–210.

Moore, R., Moore, M.L. and Capella, M. (2005) The impact of customer-to-customer interactions in a high personal contact service setting. *Journal of Services Marketing* 19 (7), 482–491.

Morrison, A. and O'Mahony, B. (2003) The liberation of hospitality management education. *International Journal of Contemporary Hospitality Management* 15 (1), 38–44, available at http://www.emeraldinsight.com/doi/abs/10.1108/09596110310458972 (Accessed May 26, 2015).

Navarro, S., Andreu, L. and Cervera, A. (2014) Value co-creation among hotels and disabled customers: An exploratory study. *Journal of Business Research* 67 (5), 813–818, available at http://dx.doi.org/10.1016/j.jbusres.2013.11.050.

Navarro, S., Garzón, D. and Roig-Tierno, N. (2015) Co-creation in hotel-disable customer interactions. *Journal of Business Research* 68 (7), 1630–1634, available at http://dx.doi.org/10.1016/j.jbusres.2015.02.007.

Navarro, S., Llinares, C. and Garzon, D. (2016) Exploring the relationship between co-creation and satisfaction using QCA. *Journal of Business Research* 69 (4), 1336–1339, available at http://dx.doi.org/10.1016/j.jbusres.2015.10.103.

Neal-Smith, S. and Cockburn, T. (2009) Cultural sexism in the UK airline industry. *Gender in Management* 24 (1), 32–45.

Nickson, D. (2007) *Human Resource Management for the Hospitality and Tourism Industries*. Oxford, UK: Butterworth Heinemann.

Nickson, D., Warhurst, C. and Dutton, E. (2007) The Importance of attitude and appearance in the service encounter in retail and hospitality. *Managing Service Quality* 15 (2), 195–208.

Nyquist, J. *et al.* (1985) Identifying Communication Difficulties in the Service Encounters: A Critical Incidents Approach. In Czepiel, J, Solomon, M and Surprenant, C. (1985) *The Service Encounter*, MA: Lexington Books, 195–212.

Nyquist, J. and Booms, B. (1987) Measuring Services Value from the Consumer Perspective. In Surprenant, C. (1987) Add Value to Your Service, Chicago, *American Marketing Association*, 13–16.

Oppermann, M. (1999) Sex tourism. *Annals of Tourism Research* 26 (2), 251–266.

O'Sullivan, K. (1994) *Understanding Ways: Communicating Between Cultures*. Sydney, AUS: Hale and Iremonger.

ONS (2017) Sickness absence in the Labour Market, 2016, accessed at https://www.ons.gov.uk/employmentandlabourmarket/peopleinwork/labourproductivity/articles/sicknessabsenceinthelabourmarket/2016#which-groups-have-the-highest-sickness-absence-rates, accessed on 17th May 2018.

ONS (2018a) Office for National Statistics: Employment by occupation, accessed at https://www.ons.gov.uk/employmentandlabourmarket/peopleinwork/employmentandemployeetypes/datasets/employmentbyoccupationemp04, accessed on 17th May 2018.

ONS (2018b) Office for National Statistics: Labour Market Economic Commentary: April 2018, accessed at https://www.ons.gov.uk/employmentandlabourmarket/people inwork/employmentandemployeetypes/articles/labourmarketeconomiccommentary/april2018, accessed on 17th May 2018.

Pabel, A. and Pearce, P.L. (2016) Tourists' responses to humour. *Annals of Tourism Research* 57, 190–205.

Pabel, A. and Pearce, P.L. (2018) Selecting humour in tourism settings – A guide for tourism operators. *Tourism Management Perspectives* 25, 64–70.

Pabel, A. *et al.* (2019) Crack a smile: the causes and consequences of emotional labour dysregulation in Australian reef tourism. *Current Issues in Tourism* 0 (0), 1–15, available at https://doi.org/10.1080/13683500.2019.1629579.

Parasuraman, A., Berry, L.L. and Zeithaml, V.A. (1991) Perceived service quality as a customer-based performance measure: An empirical examination of organizational barriers using an extended service quality model. *Human Resource* ... 30 (3), 335–364, available at http://onlinelibrary.wiley.com/doi/10.1002/hrm.3930300304/abstract.

Pearce, P. and Pabel, A. (2013) Humour, tourism and positive psychology. In S. Filep and P. Pearce (eds) *Tourist Experience and Fulfilment: Insights from Positive Psychology* (pp. 17–36). Abingdon: Routledge.

Pearce, P. and Pabel, A. (2015) *Tourism and Humour*. Bristol: Channel View Publications.

People 1st. (2011a) Hotels UK Industry Profile.

People 1st. (2011b) State of the Nation Report 2011, Uxbridge.

People 1st. (2013) *State of the Nation Report 2013*, Available at: http://www.people1st.co.uk/webfiles/Research/State Of The Nation/2013/SOTN_2013_final.pdf.

Pettinger, L. (2017) Brand Culture and Branded Workers: Service Work and Aesthetic Labour in Fashion Retail Brand Culture and Branded Workers: Service Work and Aesthetic Labour in Fashion Retail. *Consumption Markets & Culture* 7 (2), 165–184.

Pettinger, L. (2008) Developing aesthetic labour: the importance of consumption. *International Journal of Work Organisation and Emotion* 2 (4), 327–343.

Pettinger, L. (2005) Gendered work meets gendered goods: Selling and service in clothing retail. *Gender, Work and Organization* 12 (5), 460–478.

Piller, I. (2011) *Intercultural Communication: A critical introduction*. Edinburgh: Edinburgh University.

Pine, J. and Gilmore, J. (1999) *The Experience Economy: Work is Theatre & Every Business a Stage* (1st edn). Boston, MA: Harvard Business School Press.

Plester, B. (2009) Healthy humour: Using humour to cope at work. *New Zealand Journal of Social Sciences Online* 4, 89–102.

Reimann, M., Lunemann, U.F. and Chase, R.B. (2008) Uncertainty Avoidance as a Moderator of the Relationship between Perceived Service Quality and Customer Satisfaction. *Journal of Service Research* 11 (1), 63–73, available at http://jsr.sagepub.com/cgi/doi/10.1177/1094670508319093 (Accessed October 31, 2013).

Ren, X. (2017) Exploiting women's aesthetic labour to fly high in the Chinese airline Industry. *Gender in Management* 32 (6), 386–403.

Richardson, S. (2009) Undergraduates' perceptions of tourism and hospitality as a career choice. *International Journal of Hospitality Management* 28 (3), 382–388.

Richardson, S. (2010) Generation Y's perceptions and attitudes towards a career in tourism and hospitality. *Journal of Human Resources in Hospitality and Tourism* 9 (2), 179–199.

Rihova, I., Buhalis, D., Moital, M. and Gouthro, M. (2015) Conceptualising customer-to-customer value co-creation. *International Journal of Tourism Research* 17 (4), 356–363.

Robinson, R.N.S. *et al.* (2014) Thinking job embeddedness not turnover: Towards a better understanding of frontline hotel worker retention. *International Journal of Hospitality Management* 36, 101–109, available at http://dx.doi.org/10.1016/j.ijhm.2013.08.008.

Robinson, R.N.S. and Barron, P.E. (2007) Developing a framework for understanding the impact of deskilling and standardisation on the turnover and attrition of chefs. *International Journal of Hospitality Management* 26 (4), 913–926.

Ryan, C. and Kinder, R. (1996) Sex, tourism and sex tourism: Fulfilling similar needs? *Tourism Management* 17 (7), 507–518.

Ryoo, H.-K. (2005) Achieving friendly interactions: a study of service encounters between Korean shopkeepers and African-American customers. *Discourse & Society* 16 (1), 79–105, available at http://das.sagepub.com/cgi/doi/10.1177/0957926505048231 (Accessed October 31, 2013).

Saito, H. *et al.* (2015) The staff break room as an oasis: Emotional labour, restorative environments and employee wellbeing in the hospitality industry. In *CAUTHE 2015 Rising Tides and Sea Changes: Adaptation and Innovation in Tourism and Hospitality*, available at https://search.informit.com.au/documentSummary;dn=225705311266308;res=IELBUS.

Samovar, L.A. and Porter, R.R. (1982) *Intercultural Communication*: A Reader (3rd ed), USA, Wadsworth.

Samovar, L. *et al.* (2013) *Communication Between Cultures*. 8th ed. Wadsworth Cengage Learning.

Scollon, R., Scollon, S. and Jones, R. (2012) *Intercultural Communication: A discourse approach* (3rd ed). Oxon, England: John Wiley & Sons Ltd. 1996.

Scott, D. and Usher, R. (eds) (1996) *Understanding Educational Research*. London: Routledge.

Seymour, D. (2000) Emotional labour: a comparison between fast food and traditional service work. *International Journal of Hospitality Management* 19 (2), 159–171.

Sharma, P., Tam, J.L.M. and Kim, N. (2009) Demystifying Intercultural Service Encounters: Toward a Comprehensive Conceptual Framework. *Journal of Service Research* 12 (2), 227–242.

Sharma, P., Tam, J.L.M. and Kim, N. (2012) Intercultural service encounters (ICSE): An extended framework and empirical validation. *Journal of Services Marketing* 26 (7), 521–534.

Simon, H. (1951) A Formal Theory of the Employment Relationship, *Econometrica*, 19 (3), 293–305.

Smith, J. and Warburton, F. (2012) *Cambridge IGCSE Travel and Tourism*. Cambridge, UK: Cambridge University Press.

Solnet, D., Kralj, A. and Baum, T. (2015) 360 Degrees of Pressure: The Changing Role of the HR Professional in the Hospitality Industry. *Journal of Hospitality and Tourism Research* 39 (2), 271–292.

Solomon, M.R. *et al.* (1985) A Role Theory Perspective on Dyadic Interactions: The Service Encounter. *Journal of Marketing* 49 (1), 99–111.

Sparks, B. and Callan, V.J. (1992) Communication convergence and the service encounter: the value of. *International Journal of Hospitality Management* 11 (3), 213–224.

Sparks, G.G. and Greene, J.O. (1992) On the validity of nonverbal indicators as measures of physiological arousal: A response to Burgoon, Kelley, Newton, and Keeley-Dyreson. *Human Communication Research* 18 (3), 445–471.

Spiess, L. and Waring, P. (2005) Emotional and aesthetic labour: Cost minimization and the labour process in the Asia Pacific airline industry. *Employee Relations* 27 (2), 193–207.

Strauss, B. and Mang, P. (1999) Culture Shocks' in Inter-cultural service encounters. *Journal of Services Marketing* 13 (4/5), 329–46.

Stinchcombe, A.L. (1990) Work institutions and the sociology of everyday life. In K. Erikson, S.P. Vallas (eds) *The Nature of Work: Sonological Perspectives*. New Haven, CT: Yale University Press.

Sundaram, D.S. and Webster, C. (2000) The role of nonverbal communication in service encounters. *Journal of Services Marketing* 14 (5), 378–391, available at http://www.emeraldinsight.com/10.1108/08876040010341008.

Surprenant, C.F. *et al.* (1987) Predictability and Personalization in the Service Encounter. *Journal of Marketing* 51 (2), 86–96.

Tam, J., Sharma, P. and Kim, N. (2014) Examining the role of attribution and intercultural competence in intercultural service encounters. *Journal of Services Marketing* 28 (2), 159–170.

Taras, V., Rowney, J. and Steel, P. (2009) Half a Century of Measuring Culture: Approaches, Challenges, Limitations, and Suggestions Based on the Analysis of 121 Instruments for Quantifying Culture. *Journal of International Management* 15 (4), 357–373, available at https://libres.uncg.edu/ir/uncg/f/V_Taras_Half_2009.pdf.

TEF (2017) Teaching Excellence Framework, UK Government Report https://assets.publishing.service.gov.uk/government/uploads/system/uploads/attachment_data/file/658490/Teaching_Excellence_and_Student_Outcomes_Framework_Specification.pdf. Accessed on 5th May 2019.

Telling, R. (2017) A typology of next generation employment preferences in family businesses. (Doctoral thesis). Supervised by Martin, E., & Goulding, P. http://doi.org/10.7190/shu-thesis-00107.

The Dearing Report. (1997) *Higher Education in the learning society*, available at http://www.educationengland.org.uk/documents/dearing1997/dearing1997.html.

Torkildsen, G. (2005) *Leisure and Recreation Management* (1st ed). Routledge.

Tsai, C. (2019) The Role of Self-Confidence in the Criteria of Aesthetic Labour Recruitment. *International Journal of Tourusim Management in the Digital Age* 3 (1), p. 22.

UK Gov (2018a) Employment Contracts, accessed at https://www.gov.uk/employment-contracts-and-conditions, accessed on 17th May 2018.

UK Gov (2018b) Contract types and employer responsibilities, accessed at https://www.gov.uk/contract-types-and-employer-responsibilities, accessed on 17th May 2018.

UK Gov (2018c) Taking Sick Leaver, accessed at https://www.gov.uk/taking-sick-leave, accessed on 17th May 2018.

UK Gov (2018d) Workplace Bullying and Harassment, accessed at https://www.gov.uk/workplace-bullying-and-harassment, accessed on 18 July 2018.

USA https://www.dol.gov/general/topic/benefits-leave/fmla.

University of Manchester. (2014) Policy on the ethical involvement of humans in research v5, p. 8.

Van Der Wagen. (2014) *Human Resource Management for the Event Industry*.

Walker, J. (1995) Service encounter satisfaction: Constructualized. *Journal of Services Marketing* 9 (1), 5–14.

Wallace, M. and Wray, A. (2011) *Critical Reading and Writing for Postgraduates* (2nd ed). London, England: Sage Publications.

Walsh, G. *et al.* (2019) Effects of service employees' negative personality traits on emotional labour and job satisfaction: Evidence from two countries. *Management Decision*.

Warden, C.A. *et al.* (2003) Service failures away from home: benefits in intercultural service encounters. *International Journal of Service Industry Management* 14 (4), 436–456, available at http://www.emeraldinsight.com/10.1108/09564230310489268.

Warhurst, C. and Nickson, D. (2007) Employee experience of aesthetic labour in retail and hospitality. *Work, Employment & Society* 21 (1), 103–120, available at http://wes.sagepub.com/cgi/doi/10.1177/0950017007073622 (Accessed November 6, 2012).

Warhurst, C. and Nickson, D. (2009) 'Who's Got the Look?' Emotional, Aesthetic and Sexualized Labour in Interactive Services. *Gender, Work & Organization* 16 (3), 385–404, available at http://doi.wiley.com/10.1111/j.1468-0432.2009.00450.x.

Weiermair, K. (2000) Tourists' perceptions towards and satisfaction with service quality in the cross-cultural service encounter: implications for hospitality and tourism management. *Managing Service Quality* 10 (6), 397–409.

Westwood, A. (2002) *Is New Work Good Work?* London: The Work Foundation.

Wijesinghe, G. (2009) A display of candy in an open jar: Portraying sexualised labour in the hospitality industry using expressive phenomenology as methodology. *Tourism and Hospitality Planning and Development* 6 (2), 133–43.

Williamson, D. and Chen, T. (2018) Linguistic labour: International hospitality employees' use of non-English native language in service encounters. *Hospitality Insights* 2 (2), 7–8.

Witz, A., Warhurst, C. and Nickson, D. (2003) The Labour of Aesthetics and the Aesthetics of Organization. *Organization* 10 (1), 33–54, available at http://org. sagepub.com/cgi/doi/10.1177/1350508403010001375 (Accessed August 8, 2011).

WTO and ILO. (2014) *Measuring Employment in the Tourism Industries – Guide with Best Practices*.

WTTC. (2017) *Tourism Economic Impact 2017: World*. Available at: https://www.wttc.org/-/media/files/reports/economic-impact-research/regions-2017/world2017.pdf.

Wu, C. and Liang, R. (2009) Effect of experiential value on customer satisfaction with service encounters in luxury-hotel restaurants. *International Journal of Hospitality Management2* 28, 586–593.

Wu, C.H.J. (2007) The impact of customer-to-customer interaction and customer homogeneity on customer satisfaction in tourism service-The service encounter prospective. *Tourism Management* 28 (6), 1518–1528.

Yang, C., Cheng, L. and Lin, C.J. (2015) Total Quality Management & Business Excellence A typology of customer variability and employee variability in service industries. *Total Quality Management and Business Excellence* 26 (8), 825–839, available at http://dx.doi.org/10.1080/14783363.2014.895522.

Yeoman, I. and Mars, M. (2012) Robots, men and sex tourism. *Futures* 44 (4), 365–371.

Yim, F., Cheung, C. and Baum, T. (2018) Gender and Emotion in Tourism: Do Men and Women Tour Leaders Differ in Their Performance of Emotional Labor? *Journal of China Tourism Research* 14 (4), 405–427, available at https://doi.org/10.1080/193881 60.2018.1515683.

Yorke, M. (2006) Employability Employability in higher education: What it is – what it is not. *Higher Education Academy*.

Photo references

Photo sources all from unsplash.com specific photographers are acknowledged below:

Cover photo by Joshua Rodriguez

Chapter 1 service encounters Taylor Davidson

Chapter 2 staff to staff @rawpixel

Chapter 3 soft skills Lan Pham

Chapter 4 Emotional Labour Brooke Cagle

Chapter 5 Aesthetic and Sexualised Labour HYPERLINK "https://unsplash.com/@buliamti?utm_source=unsplash&utm_medium=referral&utm_content=creditCopyText" Steven Cleghorn

Chapter 6 intercultural sensitivity Philipe Cavalcante

Chapter 7 co-creation and co-production Jatniel Tunon

Chapter 8 legal frameworks Jeremy Stenuit

Chapter 9 Tourists laughing – Omar Lopez

Best Western Photo – https://www.pinterest.co.uk/pin/688206386783783567/?lp=true

Dogs welcome photo – https://www.pinterest.co.uk/citynites/funny-hotel-signs/?lp=true

Motel sign – HYPERLINK "http://www.twoeggz.com/int/4910653.html" www.twoeggz.com/int/4910653.html

Chapter 10 Japanese Restaurant – Alva Pratt

Index